CAMBRIDGE STUDIES IN RUSSIAN LITERATURE

Nikolay Novikov

CAMBRIDGE STUDIES IN RUSSIAN LITERATURE

General editor HENRY GIFFORD

In the same series

Novy Mir:
A case study in the politics of literature 1952–1958
EDITH ROGOVIN FRANKEL

The Enigma of Gogol:
An examination of the writings of N. V. Gogol and their place in the Russian literary tradition
RICHARD PEACE

Three Russian writers and the irrational:
Zamyatin, Pil'nyak, Bulgakov
T. R. N. EDWARDS

Word and music in the novels of Andrey Bely
ADA STEINBERG

The Russian revolutionary novel:
Turgenev to Pasternak
RICHARD FREEBORN

Poets of Modern Russia
PETER FRANCE

Andrey Bely:
A critical study of the novels
J. D. ELSWORTH

Nikolay Novikov

ENLIGHTENER OF RUSSIA

W. GARETH JONES

Senior Lecturer in Russian
University College of North Wales, Bangor

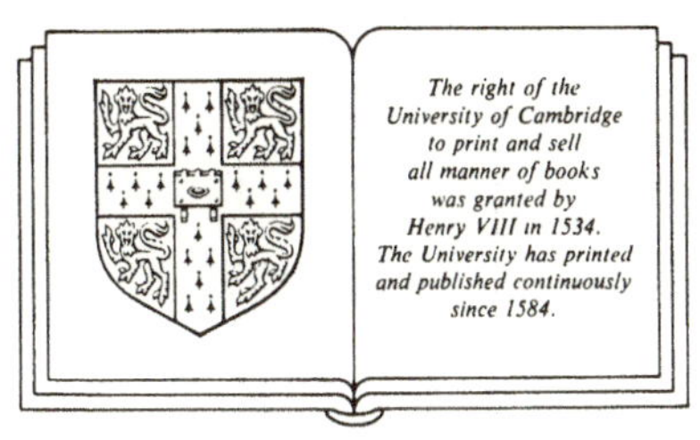
The right of the
University of Cambridge
to print and sell
all manner of books
was granted by
Henry VIII in 1534.
The University has printed
and published continuously
since 1584.

CAMBRIDGE UNIVERSITY PRESS

CAMBRIDGE

LONDON NEW YORK NEW ROCHELLE

MELBOURNE SYDNEY

CAMBRIDGE UNIVERSITY PRESS
Cambridge, New York, Melbourne, Madrid, Cape Town, Singapore, São Paulo, Delhi

Cambridge University Press
The Edinburgh Building, Cambridge CB2 8RU, UK

Published in the United States of America by Cambridge University Press, New York

www.cambridge.org
Information on this title: www.cambridge.org/9780521111447

First published 1984
This digitally printed version 2009

A catalogue record for this publication is available from the British Library

Library of Congress Catalogue Card Number: 83-19040

ISBN 978-0-521-25822-7 hardback
ISBN 978-0-521-11144-7 paperback

For Mavis, Meurig and Llywelyn

Contents

Acknowledgements

It is many years ago that Dame Elizabeth Hill first introduced me to Nikolay Novikov, and ever since I have had cause to be grateful to her for the hours spent in the company of this fascinating man. A number of Russian colleagues have freely given their time to listen to what must have seemed to them idiosyncratic views on Novikov, and I thank them for their patience and encouragement. I am indebted for constructive criticisms and support to those who have read the book at its various stages; the late Dr Barry Hollingsworth, Dr Isabel de Madariaga, Dr Kenneth Craven and Professor Henry Gifford. I wish to acknowledge my gratitude to the editorial board of the *Slavonic and East European Review* for permission to use findings first published in that journal. In particular I would like to record my thanks to all the members of the Study Group on Eighteenth Century Russia whose friendly learned society under the inspiration of Professor Anthony Cross has contributed so much to this work.

W.G.J.

Foreword

Did Nikolay Novikov foster the Enlightenment or support the anti-Enlightenment in Russia? That question has had no unanimous answer.[1] He was an enlightener, it is claimed, because he criticised his society and upheld the basic truths of the Enlightenment: tolerance, the conviction that an improvement of social organisation would ameliorate human life, that an enlightened group – a natural aristocracy of the intelligent – should develop an influential public opinion. However, it is objected that in his enthusiasm for the past, for religion and especially for historical and ecclesiastic ritual, he seemed to react against progressive ideas. Particularly reactionary was his orthodox Christian view that man was burdened with original sin, and his conviction as a committed freemason that man must seek to perfect his own corrupt state, that social salvation was attained primarily by personal regeneration.

In all these judgements, Novikov is measured by the standards and behaviour of the French *philosophes*. It is a deceptive measure in his case. His background was very different from that which in France had thrown up a distinct Enlightenment party. In mid-century Russia there was no strong bourgeoisie struggling for economic and political freedom. Among the articulate intellectuals there were no major grievances against the structure of the state. Social grievances were to be largely disarmed by the emancipation of the nobles. The church in Russia formed no oppressive power centre. The lack of a suitable ground meant that the ideal, French form of the Enlightenment could not be transplanted into Russia. As Pushkin wrote in *Eugene Onegin*:

> With us enlightenment did not take
> And after it, there was left o'er
> Affectation – nothing more.[2]

The impression is also given that Novikov was a contemporary of the French *philosophes*. Yet by 1769 when Novikov began to write and organise writing in Russia, most of the great works of the Age of Enlightenment had already appeared and made their influence felt. What the next two decades did was to diffuse the radical ideas of the *philosophes* of the previous generation. And this working of the ideas of the Enlightenment into the consciousness of Europeans was as essential a part of the Enlightenment as the composition of the seminal works had been.

It is as a director of this process that we would claim Nikolay Novikov to be 'Enlightener of Russia'. Journalist, historian, educator, printer, philanthropist, agricultural improver – the variety of interests might have spread the energy and enthusiasm of one man, however naturally gifted, far too thinly in a generally uncaring society. Yet in each field, Novikov became a dominant personality and left a distinct mark on subsequent Russian culture. What above all prevented the dissipation of his endeavours was his constant aim, in all his multifarious activities, to advance the enlightenment of his country. And what makes him more recognisable as a man of the final, diffusing stage of the European Enlightenment was his love of craft and commerce, united in the business of printing, which he shared with contemporaries in other lands, such as Denis Diderot and Benjamin Franklin.

Pushkin, while denying Russia the ideal Enlightenment, was well able in another context to give a vivid description of the society that had sustained Novikov's activities. This was a portrayal of men anathematised towards the close of the 1780s as followers of the mystic Saint-Martin or 'martinists' – a label which they themselves, as freemasons, vehemently rejected.

> At that time there existed in Russia men known as *martinists*. We have come across some old men who belonged to that semi-political, semi-religious society. A strange mixture of mystical piety and philosophic free thinking, selfless love for enlightenment and practical philanthropy distinguished them from the generation to which they belonged. Men who profited from malicious libel attempted to present the martinists as plotters and ascribed criminal political views to them. The empress, who had long regarded the strivings of the French *philosophes* as matches between skilful wrestlers and had encouraged them with her regal applause, viewed their triumph with alarm and turned her suspicious attention on the Russian martinists whom she considered preachers of anarchy and followers of the *encyclopédistes.*[3]

Eventually a whole period of Russian cultural history, the ten years from 1779–89, was to be declared by Klyuchevsky as

'Novikov's decade'.[4] Yet, despite this claim, Nikolay Novikov has never been firmly established, as were his successors Karamzin and Pushkin, as representative of a distinct literary 'age'. As a result of the 'malicious rumours' to which Pushkin referred, Novikov disappeared into the prison limbo of the Schlüsselburg Fortress for the last four years of Catherine's reign, to emerge not wholly rehabilitated, so that even for his immediate posterity he remained a shadowy and dubious figure. Significantly, Pushkin in discussing the 'martinists' did not single out Novikov as their leader, nor remind his readers that Novikov alone suffered personally for their activities. It is ironic that most of what we know of Novikov's life comes from his depositions in reply to questions put to him by Sheshkovsky, Catherine's most trusted prosecutor, at Novikov's final interrogation which ended with his imprisonment;[5] and that our knowledge of the private attitudes of the Moscow freemasons is determined by their letters, assiduously collected by police authorities as evidence against them.[6] The state evidence has survived: but with Novikov condemned to a 'civic death' papers associated with him seem to have been consciously destroyed by his contemporaries out of prudence.

The private Novikov speaks to us directly in two portraits: one by his staunch friend Levitsky and the second, painted after Novikov's fall from favour, by Levitsky's pupil Borovikovsky. Levitsky, whose sitters included Catherine II and Diderot, portrayed Novikov at the height of his powers, full face and confident, with large eyes slightly hooded by heavy lids but ready to spark with humour, a prominent nose and full lips puckered in self-satisfaction. The challenge of the face is matched by the energy of his powerful half-open hand which seems ready to reach out from the restraining left corner of the frame. Borovikovsky had moved away from the general statements of official eighteenth-century portraiture to the personal concerns of sentimentalism and it was a more frail, fallible Novikov that emerged from his brush: the same eyes, slightly dimmed and strained, are now averted from us, the powerful nose only reinforces the cleft of worry on the brow and a certain sourness has crept into the tauter set of the mouth. The good humour remains in this private Novikov, but we fail to catch the gaze of a man now more circumspect in his approach to strangers.

1

Noble beginnings (1744–69)

If you ask me 'who is he?' then I . . . will not tell you. 'The name is not the man', Russians used to say in olden days.

Karamzin

A family home

The surname of Novikov is a common one in present-day Russia,[1] and most of its bearers would probably assume that it came from *novyy*, the Russian for 'new'. But, as so often with popular etymology, they would be wrong in thinking of it as a Russian equivalent of Newman. It is derived from *novik*, a term used in Muscovy to describe a young nobleman who had recently entered service at court, an apprentice courtier or pageboy, a 'new man' of a particular sort.[2] Doubtless one of Nikolay Novikov's forbears had been given the name as a son of a *novik*, although it is not known when this happened, for the most distant-known ancestor in his family tree, Merkuley Mikhaylovich, already had the family name of Novikov at the beginning of the sixteenth century.[3]

By the name that he bore, therefore, Nikolay Ivanovich Novikov was conscious of himself as a nobleman, born into a class of the Russian nation which accounted for some 1 per cent of the population. Within this sliver of Russia even, Nikolay Novikov had a special position. Even if Russians knew the genealogy of their clan which ensured their noble status, unlike the nobility of Western Europe they rarely had roots in an ancestral home. Chaadayev, who gave voice to the Russian nobility's sense of alienation at the beginning of the nineteenth century, stressed the rootlessness of the Russians as one of the reasons for their social unease:

the carelessness of a life without experience and conjecture, one which is unrelated to anything more than the ephemeral existence of the individual detached from the species and which adheres neither to honour nor to the advancement of any community of ideas or interests whatever – not even to the family inheritances and to this fund of prescriptions and perspectives which regulate both public and private life in an order of things founded upon the recollection of the past and the probable outcome of the future.[4]

In an illuminating aside, Marc Raeff has compared with the American experience the ease with which Russians could adjust to existence in any region throughout European Russia, but on a superficial level: 'the American, too, is at home everywhere in the United States and yet rooted almost nowhere'.[5]

Novikov, however, had his roots. Although his family had estates scattered over Russia – in Meshchersk, Suzdal′, Dmitrov and Beloozero – from the time when the Novikovs had moved to the Moscow region over two centuries previously their family home had been at the village of Avdot′ino, some forty miles to the east of Moscow. Here Nikolay Novikov was born on 27 April 1744,[6] and here he died at four o'clock in the morning of 31 July 1818. It was not only the name that he bore, but the place which he recognised as home, where he spent his childhood and youth, the best years of his maturity and the last years of his life, which would have given Novikov a sense of belonging in a generally rootless society. Having an ancestral home in the Russian heartland around Moscow set one apart within the shifting, ill-defined ranks of the eighteenth-century Russian nobility; it is not surprising that in the debates in the Legislative Commission of 1767 on the status of the nobility it was, on the whole, the deputies representing the old-established noble families of central Russia, particularly those with family estates around Moscow, who pressed for a closed caste to be established, and for the paramount importance of heredity and birthright to be recognised.[7]

This conservative argument had been pleaded with the greatest clarity in the Commission by Prince Mikhaylo Shcherbatov, and on a sentimental journey to Avdot′ino in 1858, Longinov, an antiquarian who was one of the first to rekindle a serious interest in Novikov, noted that one passed the settlements of Prince Shcherbatov on the country track which led him twelve rutted miles off the high road from Bronnitsy to Kolomna.[8] Two miles beyond the Shcherbatov property, three churches grouped together in a dale where the river Severka ran to join the river Moscow made a picturesque sight. Three sprawling villages – the Russian village does not have the neat coherence of the English hamlet – were given their sense of identity by these churches and, in one of them, the Church of the Tikhvin Mother of God, lay Novikov's tomb at the foot of the icon of the Saviour to the left of the altar, while to its right was the icon of the Madonna in its rich silver setting which gave the alternative, official name of Tikhvinskoye to the village commonly known as Avdot'ino. There the church still stands. Longinov noted the richness of the church silver donated by Novikov, dwelt in particular on the 1791 folio bible with its heavy, jewel-studded silver casing and regretted that the frescoes, executed to Novikov's designs, had been painted over in 1843. The stone church, some 200 yards from the Novikov house, although renovated by his sons and consecrated in its new form on 25 June 1776, had been built by Novikov's father, Ivan Vasil'yevich Novikov, in the reign of Empress Elizabeth.

Ivan Vasil'yevich was one of the many bearers of old Muscovite noble names who identified themselves closely with the reforms of Peter the Great. To the status derived from birthright and lineage was added the demonstration of eminence in arduous service to the Tsar and state. Ivan Vasil'yevich had served in Peter's navy and attained the rank of captain before retiring temporarily in Anna Ivanovna's reign only to re-enter state service, this time as *voyevoda*, or governor, of the town of Alatyr', where he married Anna Ivanovna Pavlova.[9] There he remained for ten years before returning to his estate at Avdot'ino as a retired state counsellor, the lowest of the four senior ranks of the Civil Service. He had five children: three boys, Andrey, Nikolay and Aleksey, and two girls whose names are not known. Nikolay Ivanovich was the middle son, Andrey being seven years his senior and Aleksey four years younger.

The young Nikolay's childhood was remarkable in one respect; his impressionable years would have passed in the presence of his father, and one who, moreover, was endowed with the full authority of a naval officer and high government official. Although the Russian family was still predominantly patriarchal, paradoxically the father would be usually, for reasons of state service, an absentee from home. The sons of the nobility, as memoirs show, would grow up in permissive anarchy, punctuated by the sharp spells of strict discipline from returning fathers.[10] The confident energy which distinguished Novikov in later life might have owed much to the stability of his relationship with a father settled in an ancestral home.

However, lineage itself and a father's devoted service to the state were not sufficient to endow Ivan Vasil'yevich's sons with the qualities necessary for success in Russian society. Schooling for nobles had been made mandatory by Peter the Great and, despite resistance from backwoodsmen which continued well into Catherine's reign, institutional education became a routine stage in the young nobleman's life.[11] It retained its utilitarian Petrine purpose of giving a rudimentary grounding to those destined to serve in a modernised army and bureaucracy but, increasingly, schooling was seen as a means of imparting a veneer of sophistication which would be an outward badge of nobility. Lacking a legal definition of their noble status, the Russian gentry looked to the schools for social justification: the inner unease of the class was masked by an outward display of a sophisticated life style learnt at school.

The Moscow University gymnasium

Novikov was ten years old when on 12 January 1755 the ukase was signed in St Petersburg establishing Moscow University, a project elaborated by Mikhail Lomonosov, poet and scientist, a towering figure in Russian intellectual and academic life, and supported by Ivan Shuvalov, the Empress Elizabeth's favourite. More important, a gymnasium was to be established to prepare candidates for the university since, as Lomonosov explained to Shuvalov, without a preparatory gymnasium the University would be 'ploughed land without seeds'.[12] In the event, two separate but parallel gymnasia were established – one for nobles and one for non-nobles – and in each there were four streams, called 'schools'; a Russian school, a Latin school, a school of basic science and a school of modern languages, French and German. Science and languages were for boys destined eventually for military service if they were nobles, and for commerce and industry if they were not; the young Nikolay, after completing the obligatory year in the Russian class, accordingly moved to the French class.[13]

The building converted by Shuvalov into Moscow University was an old government building which before the 1737 fire of Moscow had housed the Main Apothecary and Medical Chancellory, and later served as administrative chambers. It stood at the

Voskresenskiy gates to Kitay-town, the old merchant quarter of Moscow, on the site of the present Historical Museum. Its main façade, three storeys high with classical columns, faced the Kremlin. As well as classrooms it housed the means by which Novikov would make his future impact on Russian culture, a University Press. However imposing this building, it was insufficient to cope adequately with the initial enrolment, and so in the October of the University's first year, a property owned by the Repnin family was purchased, a little further down the hill in Mokhovaya Street where Moscow University still stands today.[14]

It was three of Lomonosov's pupils and protégés from St Petersburg who were appointed to head the teaching staff at Moscow: Barsov, Yaremsky and Nikolay Nikitich Popovsky, who became the first rector of the new University in his mid-twenties. Popovsky was later to be treated as one of the paragons of Russian intellectual life by Novikov in his *St Petersburg Academic News* of 1777. He was renowned for his translations, via the French, of Locke's *On Education* and Alexander Pope's *Essay on Man* (Russians were eager to point to the suitability of the name 'Popovsky' for their 'Russian Pope') which was published by the fledgling Moscow University Press in 1757 at the same time as Lomonosov's works. It was Popovsky who on 26 April 1755 gave the inaugural address which launched Europe's newest University; and classes began, not as yet in the University itself, but in the preparatory gymnasia.[15]

It is difficult to judge the quality of the formal education dispensed in the new gymnasia. Denis Fonvizin, one of the first pupils, looked back in his memoirs with smiling disdain on his schooling, which suffered from the laziness of the pupils and the drunkenness of the teachers. Novikov's own teacher in charge of the French class, Nikolay Bilon, was once retrieved from a debtors' prison only on the exercise by the University of the right of its jurisdiction over its members. Shuvalov himself soon became aware that all was not well at the University and, as one of the two visitors, suggested that the matriculation certificates should note the extent of the pupil's knowledge and not merely note, 'studied diligently'. 'It is possible', explained Shuvalov caustically, 'to be diligent, yet through lack of understanding, know nothing.'[16] In theory, the pedagogical programme was heavy, with classes from 7.0 a.m. to 11.0 a.m. and then, following dinner, from 2.0 p.m. to 6.0 p.m., the only respite being two short periods of annual holidays – from 18 December to

6 January and 10 June to 1 July. However, in practice this timetable was ignored by many of the pupils and their teachers estimated that, thanks to the round of family celebrations, church festivals and country holidays, the majority of the schoolboys did not attend classes for more than thirty or forty days in the year.

The location of Moscow University had proved to be a mixed blessing. Its rationale, as the ukase establishing it had indicated, was to save the Muscovite nobility the expense of maintaining domestic foreign tutors who were often ill qualified to teach. However, while rescuing the young gentlemen from foreign mountebanks by sending them to a well-run day school, it was unable to isolate them from their own families. The Novikovs had a house on the outskirts of Moscow, near the Serpukhov gate in the parish of Catherine the Martyr, where a number of Moscow's principal families had houses. The adjoining property was Brigadier Glebov's large park which was a favourite resort for fashionable Muscovites. The accessibility of his family and the nearness of the home estate of Avdot′ino perhaps account for the sorry end to the young Novikov's school career. Only the bald facts about it are known: in his second year he was awarded a prize, as the 12 May 1758 issue of the *Moscow News* announced, but on 28 April 1760, the same official gazette listed Nikolay Novikov's name as one of those expelled 'for laziness and absence from classes'. The University disciplinary committee expressed the reason for expulsion in kinder terms, 'for absence of which nobody was informed'; but, however it was, Novikov appeared in good company. Among those expelled for the same reason was Grigoriy Potemkin, destined to be Catherine the Great's most powerful favourite.

By the age of seventeen, therefore, Novikov's formal education seems to have been desultory. But judging by the reverence shown to him later in Novikov's publications, the influence of Nikolay Popovsky must have been great. Moscow University at its inception created not only a society literate in Russian – for all the gymnasium pupils were obliged to spend their first year in the Russian school and Popovsky as a matter of deliberate new policy gave his philosophy lectures in Russian rather than the customary Latin – but a consciously literary society. During Novikov's time, the Press and Library were run by Mikhail Kheraskov who gathered around him a group of young men distinguished not only by birth but also by literary taste. He himself was a half-brother of Yuriy and Nikolay Trubetskoy and, in 1760, after Popovsky's death, he took over the editorship of a literary journal at the University called *Beneficial Amusement* (Poleznoye uveseleniye) whose pages were filled by the tentative compositions of the Naryshkin brothers, Aleksey and Semen, the Fonvizin brothers, Denis and Pavel, Ippolit Bogdanovich, Aleksey Rzhevsky, Sergey Domashnev and others. Literary accomplishments were considered to be one of the clearest indications of nobility: the same adjective, *chistyy* – pure, or refined – was to be applied by Novikov later both to correct Western-style dress which set the minority of Russians apart from the mass of their fellow countrymen, and the language itself, which was suitably 'refined' only amongst the literary elite. Although leaving the gymnasium without apparently contributing to the journal, Novikov subsequently made a point of noting in his *Essay at an Historical Dictionary of Russian Writers* if a writer's literary interest had been awakened at Moscow University; the benefits of the infectious literary atmosphere were noted too by Denis Fonvizin who, however much he might criticise the University's formal education, admitted that he had 'received there a taste for literary science'.[17] Little is known directly of Novikov's friendships at this time, but many of his future literary collaborators were fellow pupils in the gymnasium's first, enthusiastic years which produced so many literary figures who filled the pages of his *Historical Dictionary*. Nor did Novikov ever lose touch with his Alma Mater, having his first business dealings with the university bookseller Christian-Ludvig Vever in 1766, becoming one of the first members of the University learned society, the Free Russian Assembly, in 1771 at the invitation of its secretary Professor Anton Barsov and finally returning, as if to his spiritual home, to take charge of the University Press in 1779, to renew social links and eventually a relationship through marriage with Kheraskov and the Trubetskoy brothers.

All this seems a strange sequel to Novikov's expulsion from the gymnasium but, presumably, with the formal classes counting for so little, he could have continued to benefit from the extra-curricular camaraderie of his contemporaries, for Novikov remained at home for a further two years until 1762 when he moved to St Petersburg to begin his military service.

Army service and early literary pursuits

As was the custom with the Russian nobility, Nikolay Novikov's name had been sent to an army regiment during his childhood. Peter I had demanded in the interests of his meritocracy that all men, irrespective of rank, should serve through the ranks and be commissioned on merit: the wealthier nobility, however, had circumvented this provision by enlisting their sons as children, thus allowing them to be promoted automatically through the lower ranks so that they would be ready for their commission on actually joining at their majority. In 1762 Peter III planned a new war against Denmark in the interests of his native Holstein and the College of War ordered all young noblemen attached to regiments to join the colours. Novikov's regiment was the Izmaylovsky, the third senior Guards regiment after the Preobrazhensky and Semenovsky, formed by the Empress Anna Ivanovna on 17 August 1730 and named after the village of Izmaylovo, the empress's summer residence outside Moscow. In 1732 the newly formed regiment moved to St Petersburg where it built quarters for itself near the Church of the Assumption. Each company occupied a street which was given the number of the company, and these numbers remained when the district was eventually traversed by Izmaylovsky Avenue, to be retained after the Revolution as Red Army streets.

Peter III's harsh Prussian military training, his affront to Russian traditions and particularly to her religion and above all the threat of a distant campaign in the role of Holstein mercenaries brought the Guards regiments – which had developed during the century the habit of making and breaking Russian sovereigns – to the point of revolt. On 28 June 1762, the Izmaylovsky Regiment, founded by one empress, struck in favour of another. Early in the morning, the Orlov brothers, Grigoriy, her lover and Aleksey, brought Catherine from the summer house of Mon Plaisir at Peterhof to the capital and the Izmaylovsky Regiment. That regiment having sworn loyalty to her, Catherine moved on to receive the homage of the Semenovsky and Preobrazhensky Regiments, the Horse Guards and the Artillery.

Novikov would have embarked upon his service career at a singular time. From his military service, followed as a matter of course, the Russian nobleman would confirm a view of life in which rules and regulations had a universal force, in which there was an absolute hierarchical organisation, in which external manifestations of social placing – dress, forms of behaviour, the due processes of the bureaucracy – were of paramount importance. Training in externals seemed able to change men; witness the way in which village serfs were fashioned into European soldiers on the parade ground.[18] However, the intelligent nineteen-year-old was conscripted at a moment when the officer corps, the noble estate in uniform, was in disarray: its certainties, few and superficial as they were, had been shaken by the caprices of Peter III who suddenly had changed the orientation of Russia's military organisation. To judge from his later literary career, the experience of this disarray reinforced Novikov's conservative impulses to maintain the image of the officer–nobleman who alone could regulate the life of the society around him. One thing is certain; Novikov was within the body of the Izmaylovsky Regiment which acted out a return to the old assurances in its coup in favour of a new charismatic empress, who was led by Guards officers to Kazan′ Cathedral where she was declared empress by Archbishop Dmitriy in the presence of the Orthodox hierarchy. At ten o'clock the same evening, in the uniform of the senior Preobrazhensky regiment, she set out to confront her deposed husband Peter III. All the participants of the coup were rewarded by gifts and promotions and Novikov, by virtue of being an Izmaylovsky man, shared in the triumph: he was promoted *unter-ofitser*.

For the first time the paths of Catherine II and Novikov had crossed. It is true that as a member of his regiment he had been irresistibly drawn into the events that had placed her on the throne, yet there can be little doubt that Novikov would also have been ready to give Catherine his personal support. The summer of 1762 was spent on preparations for her coronation at the Cathedral of the Annunciation in Moscow, and on 1 September the first and third battalions of the Izmaylovsky Regiment set out to accompany their new empress on her royal progress to the old capital. The coronation on 22 September was the signal for extensive celebrations culminating in the pre-Lenten season of the following year by a street carnival, 'Minerva Triumphant', produced by Russia's foremost actor Fedor Grigor′yevich Volkov – the 'Garrick of Russia' as he was later called by an English traveller, Coxe – and elucidated by Moscow University's Mikhail Kheraskov. In that spring,

Novikov's father fell ill and died in June. Then in August 1763, after a year's absence, the Russian empress, her court and the Izmaylovsky battalions made their way back to St Petersburg.

The demands of the regiment on its officers' time were not great, and Novikov, while still serving, began to take an active interest in the book trade. His interest in literature, nurtured at Moscow University, was not confined to the study or drawing-room: he was not afraid of the dust of the bookshop, or of staining his fingers with printers' ink. In Russia there was little sense of the *dérogeance* of the West, the feeling that certain activities, particularly trade, were demeaning to the nobility.[19] From Fonvizin's memoirs we learn that students were eager to enter into commercial agreements with their University bookseller, Christian-Ludvig Vever, who promised the young Fonvizin payment in kind, namely foreign books to the value of fifty roubles for a Russian translation of Holberg's fables.[20] It was the same Vever who in 1766 financed Novikov's first ventures in the book trade, to judge from the copy of a promissory note issued in Moscow on 13 February 1766, which read: 'Note for 120 roubles. In three months counting from this year 1766 by this my note, I promise to pay Christian-Ludvig Vever, bookseller of the Imperial Moscow University, or Order, the sum of 120 roubles in current silver. Received from him this sum in full. Issued by *Fourrier* of the Life Guards, Izmaylovsky Regiment, Nikolay Ivan's son, Novikov.'[21] Possibly this could have been an advance payment for books which Novikov intended to supply Vever, for 1766 saw his first attempts at publishing. Meanwhile, during his off-duty hours in St Petersburg he must have moved in literary and book-trading circles, for one of his ventures was a catalogue of books sold by 'the bookseller in Knudson House in Bol'shaya Morskaya Street'.[22] He published too a translation of Fénelon's *Les Aventures d'Aristonoüs* by Mikhail Popov, a courtier of Novikov's age – Popov was born in 1742 – who had also been a student at Moscow University.[23] The young translator, in a prefatory letter to his publisher, while formal and conventional in praising Novikov for his love of virtue and learning, gives us a glimpse of their literary friendship:

> the feeble products of my mind were the cause of our acquaintance, it was they which gained me your affection, and henceforth you favoured me with your friendship. All my feeble compositions and translations have had the good fortune to please you: it was not, perhaps, their elegance that was the

reason but your amiable disposition. However that may be, I have promised to send you all my compositions, both original and translated from other languages.

We can only guess at the cast of the young officer's mind in 1766, but it is safe to say that Novikov could have been far from frivolous. The young publisher's taste in issuing Fénelon was decidedly serious, and high moral pretensions were reflected again in his choice of a work for publication towards the close of the year; *The Spirit of Pythagoras*, a moral work ostensibly discovered among a friend's papers, was printed by the press of the Kadetsky Korpus in an edition of one thousand copies, which was more a reflection, perhaps, of the naive optimism of the earnest tyro publisher than that of the market for moral works in Russia.

Minute-taker at the Legislative Commission

Novikov's first steps in publishing were interrupted in 1767 by the need to return again to Moscow as minute-writer at the Legislative Commission established by Catherine. The choice of Moscow, the ancient capital, rather than the official capital of St Petersburg, was a calculated decision. The French diplomatist Rossignol saw it as a move to make an accommodation with the old nobility by demonstrating her authority in their stronghold:

> The most ancient nobility, living there in great numbers, has little respect for the empress apparently, and expresses itself on this subject quite freely. It despises also the lords who are attached to her, and looks upon them as inferior beings forced to cringe at the will of the sovereign, whereas it considers itself in its aloof position too powerful to be at all apprehensive about its feeling.[24]

By returning to the old capital accompanied by Senate and Holy Synod, Catherine was demonstrating that she was acting in accord with old Russian custom in summoning a commission, for its forerunners were the *zemskiye sobory*, or national advisory assemblies of the higher clergy, boyars and elected representatives of the gentry, merchant and artisan classes summoned by the tsar to help set the nation in order. But Catherine poured the new wine of the Enlightenment into the old vessel through her Instruction to the Commission, the *Nakaz*, a literary pot-pourri of ideas culled from Montesquieu, Beccaria and others, which was to lead Russia onwards into a happy utopia. The *Nakaz* was also designed to create in Europe an image of Catherine as an enlightened ruler determined to modernise her country. With her eighteenth-century *Nakaz* and her seventeenth-century staging of the Commission, Catherine appealed to both progressives and conservatives and kept them in superb political balance. The same sense of political balance was exercised in the weighting of the classes represented at the Commission. By moving into the old, Russian heartland – although prudently escorted by some 40,000 troops – Catherine seemed to be making a concession to the old nobility, as Rossignol felt, and so only one voice was raised, that of Mikhaylo Shcherbatov, to complain that the nobility was to be in a minority at the Commission and that the device of the ballot was to be used to nullify their personal influence. Again the Muscovite staging of the Commission masked Catherine's real aim of checking the power of the principal nobles and attempting to nurture a middle class in Russia. In April 1766 she had written to Mme Geoffrin that a middle class should be developed and that 'this motive will make me resolve and act with assurance, since I count it as an essential duty of my position'.[25] Furthermore, in her *Nakaz* Catherine had included a section on the need to expand the middle classes. In the event, since the nobles did not elect all the deputies to which they were entitled, elected deputies from the towns outweighed noble deputies, and thus the townspeople's own sense of their importance in the state was fostered.

Later in the century William Coxe sensed at first hand the way in which a burgeoning urban middle class might check and balance the powers of the Russian nobility, and drew on a historical comparison with twelfth-century Europe, 'when the feudal system was gradually declining; when the unbounded authority of the land owners over the slaves was beginning to be counterbalanced by the introduction of an intermediate order of merchants . . .'[26] But in Russia, this was a mere beginning, for Coxe confessed his amazement at the backwardness of the Empire.

> I must own I was astonished at the barbarism in which the bulk of the people still continue. I am ready to allow that the principal nobles are perfectly civilised, and as refined in their entertainments, mode of living and social intercourse, as those of other European countries. But there is a wide difference between polishing a nation and polishing a few individuals. The merchants and peasants universally retain their beards, their national

dress, their original manners; and, what is most remarkable, the greatest part of the merchants and burghers of the large towns, even the citizens of Petersburgh and Moscow, resemble, in their external appearance and general mode of living, the inhabitants of the smallest village.[27]

It was clearly difficult to form a third estate, an intermediate order of merchants, from this human material, and Catherine possibly hoped to counterbalance the aristocracy of the principal nobles by an embourgeoisement of the less affluent gentry. There are indications of this policy, as we shall see, in Novikov's later periodicals: his position in the Legislative Commission might have prepared him for these journals.

As well as taking minutes in the general assembly of the Commission, Novikov acted as minute-writer for the seventh of its nineteen sub-committees which was concerned with defining and drafting a constitutional code for 'the middling sort of people'. A signal from Adjutant-General Count Kirill Razumovsky dated 17 August 1767 to Procurator-General Vyazemsky informed him that twenty-two military men from St Petersburg had been commanded to join the secretariat of the Commission, one of them being Novikov.[28] From 24 October 1767 the minutes of the sub-committee 'on the middling sort of people' were in turn signed by him, Fedor Shiskhov, Mikhail Lykov and Petr Soymonov, all of whom were from the Izmaylovsky Regiment. They took down the deliberations of the five deputies appointed to the sub-committee; only one of them was of 'the middling sort' himself, Mikhaylo Stepanov, representing the burghers of the town of Venev in Moscow Province. Defining the middle class was to be predominantly the task of the principal nobles: Count Ernst von Münich of the Chief Customs Chancellory, Prince Ivan Vyazemsky, deputy of the Dmitrov nobles, Prince Mikhaylo Shcherbatov, deputy of the Yaroslavl nobles, and Semen Naryshkin, deputy of the Mikhaylov nobles.

As minute-writer, Novikov served in the apparatus set up to record the proceedings of the general assembly and sub-committees in daily journals. The director of the assembly's journals, A. P. Shuvalov, was responsible to the empress, who showed a keen interest in the written record of the proceedings. One of the tasks given to Bibikov, the Commission's marshal, was to have organised the writing of a monthly report for the *St Petersburg News*, the official gazette, for which Catherine had a model in mind, 'Mr. Marshal!' she wrote to Bibikov, 'I enclose journals of the English

Parliament, in order that you can have them read by the person to whom you will entrust the making of the monthly account of your daily minutes for publication in the *News*. Catherine.'[29] Catherine clearly hoped that the Commission would produce the equivalent of the journals of the House of Commons.[30]

The importance that the empress attached to the keeping of well-written records of the Commission's proceedings meant that a number of highly literate men were needed, and these tended to be young men from the Guards regiments with a predilection for literature, many of them graduates of Moscow University and its gymnasia. The minute-writers naturally formed themselves into a literary coterie. Among them was Mikhail Popov, published by Novikov in the previous year, and Vasiliy Maykov whom he would publish the following year; together with A. Ablesimov they would be significant contributors to Novikov's first journal in 1769. Among the deputies, too, there were numerous literary men, including Shcherbatov and Semen Naryshkin who sat on Novikov's particular sub-committee. An important figure at the Commission with whom Novikov would shortly have personal dealing was G. V. Kozitsky, who had played a leading role in drafting the final version of Catherine's *Nakaz* and was to be her literary secretary in future years.

As well as reinforcing his personal acquaintanceship with other literati of the day, who were thrown together in the Commission which met in the Kremlin's Granovitaya Palace (within a short step of Moscow University), Novikov, like the other young men, must have sharpened his political wits and social observation in such an assembly. Deputies had been gathered from all corners and classes of the Russian Empire, and in the debates, clumsy as they were at times, they groped towards the formation of a rudimentary public opinion in Russia.

Before the onset of the Christmas season, however, the Commission was adjourned in mid-December and left Moscow to be reconvened in St Petersburg at the beginning of February. In the New Year promotions, Quartermaster Nikolay Novikov and Sergeant Fedor Shiskhov of the Izmaylovsky Regiment became fully commissioned officers in the rank of *poruchik*, or lieutenant, and Novikov was transferred to the Sevsky Division's Muromsky Infantry Regiment, although he was meanwhile to remain attached to the Commission.[31] With a war against Turkey imminent, Catherine was obliged to adjourn her Commission indefinitely at the close of 1768; but the war was not used as a pretext to bring all its activities to an abrupt end. The sub-committee 'on the middling sort of people' carried on to complete its work in March.

A new literary summons

At the age of twenty-four, therefore, Novikov had, as an individual, shown an enthusiasm for publishing books of a markedly moral nature. As a social animal, he had been drawn into the centre of Russian political life; there, he was obliged by the chance of his appointment to consider daily the advantages of the 'middling sort of man' whom Catherine wished to foster in her state. He must also have become aware, as a literary man of the world, of the possible benefits to be won from imperial patronage: Novikov's single publication in 1768 was a poem by his fellow minute-writer, Vasiliy Maykov, entitled *Parnassus Triumphant, a prologue on the recovery of Her Imperial Majesty and His Imperial Highness from their smallpox inoculation*.

Young men with a literary bent at that particular time, however, did not have to be over-assiduous in courting patronage: it was soon to be thrust upon them. The empress' delight in literary pursuits had already manifested itself in the Legislative Commission, which had differed from previous Russian commissions in being accompanied by the literary panoply of the *Nakaz* (Instruction).[32] This compilation, it is true, had drawn heavily and openly on Montesquieu's *L'Esprit des lois* and Beccaria's *Crime and Punishment*, but the overt borrowings did not lower the work in the estimation of her contemporaries. For them the work was an extension to the literature of the European Enlightenment which was often a collective and anonymous labour – the *Encylopédie* was to be the best example of this – in which fine phrases as well as ideas were generously exchanged by the *philosophes*. The latter were often more astonished by the prestige freely given by a sovereign to the work of others than by plagiarism. The response of Catherine's age to her *Nakaz* was summed up by Jeremy Bentham:

> It is impossible to gaze without admiration on the spectacle of a woman descending from the triumphal car to devote herself to the civilisation of so many semi-barbarous hordes, and to offer them the noblest teachings of philosophy, sanctioned, so to speak, by the touch of her royal sceptre.

> Superior to the vanity of compiling such a work herself, she borrowed all that was best in the writings of the wise men of her time; but, by adding thereto the weight of her authority, she did more for these men than they had done for her.[33]

Equally important for Catherine, as we have seen, was the literary record of the proceedings of the Commission, and its reporting in the *St Petersburg News*.

The Commission was suspended, but Catherine had no desire to put an end to its accompanying literary activities. She cast around for a means of perpetuating the essential literary side of her moulding of public opinion, of which the *Nakaz* was one example and the records of proceedings another. They were collectively written by men who readily borrowed literary formulae as well as ideas, were closely involved with the art of government and the fashioning of society. What now met Catherine's requirements was the most significant literary discovery of the eighteenth century, the moral–satirical journal modelled on the *Spectator* of Addison and Steele: again it was collective, again it was borrowed, again it had a serious social intent, again it was to be sanctioned by the touch of the 'royal sceptre'.

Accordingly, at the beginning of 1769, *All Sorts* (Vsyakaya Vsyachina) – a surprisingly light-hearted but quite legitimate sequel to the *Nakaz* – was launched on the St Petersburg public. Although its editor was then anonymous, Novikov later in his *Essay at an Historical Dictionary of Russian Writers* presumed that he had been G. V. Kozitsky.[34] The latter, Catherine's literary secretary, would indeed have been a natural choice for executive editor of an imperial journal, for his fluent pen had already collaborated in drafting the *Nakaz* and had helped to translate it into Latin. Knowing that Kozitsky was its editor would have been enough to signal to the public that *All Sorts* was officially inspired. So, when other editors were invited by *All Sorts* to follow its example, there was an immediate response, and seven imitations were soon published with their titles mostly mirroring that of their progenitor: *All Sorts* inspired *This and That*, *Neither This Nor That*, *Medley*, *The Pleasant and Useful*.[35]

Between the imposing political and philosophic anthology of the *Nakaz* and the lightweight, teasing miscellany of *All Sorts*, there was, of course, a marked difference in style. From handsomely bound volumes destined for the libraries of Europe's leading *philosophes* and legislators, there was a descent to a flimsy trifle. Here was a weekly offering of eight small pages of print that fitted the palm of the hand, cheap and disposable enough to be recirculated as hair curlers, a common fate for such periodicals in the eighteenth century.[36] Yet, on closer examination, it is clear that Catherine was not being perversely frivolous in the midst of war, but had made a choice of literary medium that best suited her aims. For Catherine, intent as before on drawing her subjects into cooperation with her, the modest format of the weekly sheet would allow her state presses to print them cheaply for young, would-be editors. Flimsiness and brevity were to the weeklies' advantage.[37] To consumers unschooled in book buying, the few small pages of print made no great demands on their purse or their attention. They could slip into the hands of new readers, weaning them perhaps to sample the bookseller's more solid wares. For the author-cum-publisher they demanded no great outlay of capital or time. Their miscellaneous content meant that he could rely on friends for his literary contributions. And there was always the hope that should the venture last for a year, a book would have grown from the assembled papers and its author would be rewarded with a modest profit and possible patronage.

The type of journal prescribed by Catherine could not have been more suited to Novikov's inclinations; the original *Spectator* made a moral appeal to readers and promoted a distinctly middle-class ethos. In early May 1769, therefore, Novikov published the first number of a journal which responded to the lead of *All Sorts*. Unlike his fellow writers, however, Novikov did not slavishly ape its title. His journal was set apart from its fellows by the distinctive title of the *Drone* (Truten'). Some Soviet scholars hold the rather fanciful view that the reason for the choice of title was based on class, because the *Drone* suggested that the gentry were a class of idlers who consumed the labours of the peasant workers.[38] Rather, the choice of name quietly affirmed Novikov's independence, confidence and, as we shall see, hinted at his understanding of the potentialities of the genre of the *Spectator* type of journal. Ten years previously, in 1759, during Novikov's student days, Sumarokov, the undisputed doyen of Russian writers, had pioneered the Russian independent, private moral journal with his *Busy Bee* (Trudolyubivaya pchela).[39] Echoing this title in the *Drone* was a way for a humble apprentice to pay playful homage to his master;

and this sense of obligation was underscored by the choice of a line from a Sumarokov fable as an epigraph to the journal: 'They work while you consume their labour.' The title, which might also recall Johnson's *Idler*, was meant as well to characterise the anonymous editor of the journal who made a virtue of his lazy nature. The *Drone*'s first issue, with its Idler's avowal that he would do no writing himself, but would merely collect the work of others, suggests that the epigraph has a wholly innocent literary significance: the contributors work, and the Drone will consume their labour. Any suspicion that the exploitation is other than literary does not arise.

The Russian tradition of periodical journalism: the background to the 1769 weeklies

In hoisting the title of the *Drone* to his masthead, Novikov signalled his own link, through Sumarokov, with a tradition of Russian journalism. It was a reminder that Catherine II had not launched the new moral weeklies into a void, but that they drew strength from previous Russian journalism. Ever since satire had appeared in the wake of the Petrine reforms as a weapon in the hands of their supporters, moralists of the eighteenth century were conscious of their debt to the most important of their forerunners, Antiokh Kantemir. Although his works were first published in a French translation in London where Kantemir had spent a number of years as Russian envoy, their first printing in Russian in 1762 had given them a new lease of life. In common with all Russian periodical literature, the new journal owed much to Kantemir's satire with its targets of obscurantism, bigotry, ignorance and pseudo-sophistication.

It was not only previous Russian experience, however, that gave more resonance to the modest little sheets of 1769. They were magnified, out of all proportion to their mean appearance, by a glorious European tradition – that of the periodical paper that imitated Addison and Steele's *Spectator*. European example enveloped Russian tradition in the new satirical journal, as it had in the Legislative Commission. Kantemir may have put Russia's particular satirical butts into the sights of the writers that followed him, yet Russian eighteenth-century satirical journals owed far more to the influence of the English periodicals. By the middle of the century, the latter had become not only the most particular creation of all the literary genres of the European Enlightenment, but their influence had pervaded most Russian periodicals.

Even the official gazettes like the *St Petersburg News* (Sanktpeterburgskiye vedomosti) or the semi-official magazines published by academic institutions such as the Academy of Sciences, the Cadet Corps and Moscow University, all used material culled from the English periodicals. As early as 1731, the first *Spectator* essay had been printed in a supplement to the *St Petersburg News*, and twelve other English essays followed in the next two years.[40] Numerous pieces from such magazines as the *Spectator*, *Tatler*, *Guardian*, *Rambler*, *Universal Magazine* and the *Gentleman's Magazine* found their way into the school journals. Among the contributors to those edited by Kheraskov at Moscow University was Mikhaylo Permsky, who had been sent in 1758 as deacon to the Russian Embassy Church in London and then returned to Moscow in 1760 to teach English at the University.[41] In *Free Hours* (Svobodnyye chasy) (1763) he published his first essays in translation: 'Mr Spectator!' (*Spectator* No. 196) and the 'Journey of a Chervonets', a paraphrase of the *Tatler*'s 'Tale of a Shilling' (*Tatler* No. 249). The school journals, by banding together young writers (like Permsky) and encouraging them to rummage for material in European journals, undoubtedly gave a marked impetus to the development of Russian journalism.

The genre of the miscellany periodical was, therefore, firmly established by the close of the 1760s, and each Russian magazine contained translations from an English *Spectator* type of journal as a mark of its parentage. Catherine's *All Sorts* canonised this hereditary relationship not only by rifling through the *Spectator* for material to paraphrase.[42] Indeed the kinship of her sponsored journal with the well-mannered paragon of the Western European Enlightenment was flaunted: 'There is not a little salt in the English *Spectator*, and *All Sorts* resembles it', commented the latter, 'so why should it not contain something useful for society?'[43] When the *babushka* (Russian grandmother), who the editor of *All Sorts* pretended to be, called for imitators, the prospective 'grandsons' clearly knew what was expected of them. Young writers had flexed their muscles in the school journals, and had also formed conscious literary groupings, particularly around Kheraskov, who had occasion in *Innocent Exercises* (Nevinnoye uprazhneniye) to refer to his 'republic of letters'.[44] It is worth noticing that by summoning this 'republic of letters' to act as minute-takers and reporters in her Legislative Commission Catherine, whether consciously or not, had engineered in Russia that identification of the parliamentary reporter and magazine essayist – one thinks in particular of Samuel Johnson – which existed in London: the situation was reversed in St Petersburg, of course, since the natural political and polemical instinct of the London journalist had to be held in check by a wary Parliament, whereas in Moscow and St Petersburg, Catherine, of necessity, went out of her way to train her young scribblers as political animals.

A variety of material, and the various modes of the magazines from the formal moral essay to the character sketch and the plotted story, had also been rehearsed in Russian in the 1760s. All these were to be used again: Mikhaylo Permsky's version of the *Tatler*'s 'Tale of a Shilling' for example, was echoed by the story of another coin, a *chervonets* in the *Drone*'s tenth issue.[45] Important in considering the relationship between *All Sorts* and the *Drone*, as we shall see, was the brief rehearsal in *Leisure Time Used Beneficially* (Prazdnoye vremya v pol'zu upotreblennoye), the Cadet Corps journal, of the quarrel on the true nature of satire and the invocation of the authority of the *Spectator* in this matter.[46] Novikov was no innocent when he penned the first paper of his *Drone*. The date of his birth, his literary penchant and early schooling and state service, his friendships and discussions in the burgeoning 'republic of letters', the example of other Russian publications, all seemed to have destined him for the task in hand. It was with confidence that the 24-year-old Novikov moved at his sovereign's prompting – he might almost have seen it as in the nature of an official posting – from the minute-taker's table to an editorial chair.

2
A family of satirical weeklies (1769–73)

Measures and not men, is the common cant of affected moderation; a base, counterfeit image . . .

Junius

Did Novikov remain a loyal and obedient servant in that editorial chair, or did he use it as a pulpit to assail the shortcomings of Catherine's government? The empress had hoped to preside over a lively family of moral weeklies for whom the official presses of the Academy of Sciences and the Cadet Corps would provide a hospitable home sanctioned by the government. Yet the appearance of other journals in the wake of *All Sorts* has been seen as a challenge to imperial authority.[1] The present dominant view is that Novikov, somewhat like a radical opportunist, took advantage of the new imperial example to begin a satirical magazine, using it to unmask the unseemly reality of Russian life against Catherine's wishes.[2] There does indeed seem to be ample evidence on the pages of the *Drone* to indicate Novikov's disaffection and his rejection of Catherine's seductive flattery. From its very first pages the *Drone* appears to point in this direction, for the introductory self-portrait of its editor certainly does not project an assiduous civil servant. Great weight has been attached to the portrait, since so little is known about the personality of the young Novikov: his biographers have gratefully drawn on it for details of his attitudes at the time.[3] Here, seemingly, is a young man declaring that he shuns the usual avenues of advancement: careers in the military, bureaucracy and at court are spurned, and the insecure independence of a critical writer preferred. Already in 1769 he appears to have chosen the alienation of the nineteenth-century intelligentsia and is consequently declared to be their forerunner.

A second prominent feature of the *Drone* confirms the initial impression of a rebellious young satirist, seizing the opportunity of challenging authority. It is undeniable that a sharp, sustained polemic developed between *All Sorts* and the *Drone* on the true nature of satire and its permitted bounds. The *Drone* took issue with *All Sorts* over its indulgent approach to human failings. For Novikov a knave was a knave and had to be scourged with satire; *All Sorts*' 'grandmother' preferred to see no knaves but merely the general afflictions of mankind. Again, scholars have been beguiled by an apparent personal ideological confrontation between Catherine II and Novikov. There is a strong temptation to tell of how a valiant young man stood up against the might of the Russian autocrat and won some sort of victory.[4]

The temptation should be resisted. A drama of conflict between sovereign and subject would be a correct reading only if the background to the 1769 weeklies were ignored and the *Drone* were viewed as an organ of opinion in the nineteenth-century mould, with an editor vaunting his personal independence and prepared to engage in spirited polemics. But it would be anachronistic to see the *Drone* in that light. One must recognise that both the self-portrait of the *Drone*'s 'editor' and the 'polemics' were dictated to Novikov by the conventional demands of the European moral weekly. Indeed the *Drone* was conspicuous for the way that it fully conformed to the conventions of the *Spectator* type of journals.

The family likeness of editorial 'personae'

So, literary men in the St Petersburg of 1769 would not have looked for Novikov's true likeness in Mr Drone's self-portrait. They knew that a moral or 'satirical' weekly of the kind exemplified by the *Spectator* would purport to be the work of a fictitious author who would give tone and unity to the periodical paper. This use of an editorial *persona* was indeed the main distinguishing feature of such a journal: it served as a guarantee that the journal would not be an organ of party nor a mouthpiece for the real editor's own views.

The *Drone* in shunning the recognised avenues of advancement was not cocking a snook at authority but paraphrasing the *Spectator*'s own introduction.[5] His fault of laziness made him as well equipped to be a journalist as Mr Spectator's fault of taciturnity; his failing, while preventing him from entering as a practical man into those areas of Russian life open to a young gentleman, enabled him to review the various sections of his own society. Even the choice of the idle Drone as a Russian heir for the English Spectator was not, perhaps, a completely unguided choice on Novikov's part, for Addison had indicated the lazy man as one of his 'Fraternity of Spectators who live in the World without having any thing to do in it; and either by the Affluence of their Fortune, or Laziness of their Dispositions have no other Business with the rest of Mankind but to look upon them'.[6]

Catherine surely would have applauded the young writer who had demonstrated the keenness of his literary culture in creating a fictional editor corresponding to the *babushka*, the benign Russian grandmother, who similarly presided over the fortunes of *All Sorts*. Unlike the other 1769 journals, he had not been misled into copying the title of *All Sorts* and thus underlining the miscellany nature of his creation: the *Drone* alone stressed that its editorial destinies were guided by an editorial *persona*. In so doing, Novikov was serving Catherine's designs punctiliously by conforming to the conventions of the genre.

The bounds of criticism: a family quarrel

For the same reason, the polemics between *All Sorts* and the *Drone* do not necessarily signify a real rift between Catherine and Novikov. Again the latter bowed to convention. The controversy has to be seen against one of the central literary quarrels of the eighteenth century: the skirmishing over that indeterminate line marking off moral correction, or healthy satire, from diseased lampoonery and invective. As long ago as 26 October 1710 Steele in the *Tatler* had suggested the demarcation between what he claimed to be genial and general 'true Satyr', and false satire, peevish and personal.[7] One of the most reprehensible features of false satire was that it 'was aimed at particular persons', the *ad hominem* formula reproduced in *All Sorts* as *satira na litso*. The latter's aim was to prescribe a code of conduct for the editors of the weeklies so that they would continue the *Spectator* traditions of promoting a spirit of tolerance among their readers. It was an attitude admirably suited to the *persona* chosen by *All Sorts* of the 'benign grandmother'.

It is plain that with her *All Sorts* Catherine wished to establish a group of magazines agreed on a common aim; they would be viewed by her as a united manifestation of collective literary activity.[8] But no sombre general line was enforced. Rather, there was an air of playfulness about the venture. To judge from the letters sent by Catherine to her own *All Sorts*, it seemed that she wished to infuse a belligerent spirit of inter-journal rivalry into the group of 1769 weeklies. The playfulness was also apparent in the way that Catherine's participation was formally concealed behind the presiding *babushka*. As the *babushka*'s 'grandchildren and nephews', the editors of the other magazines were indulgently allowed to engage in polemics under the guise of banter and plain speaking within the family. Many made mordant comments on the grandmother's feebleness, smugness and superciliousness; they squirmed under her grandmotherly attempt to bring the other journals under her influence. The family fiction even permitted them to raise questions such as 'Is the grandmother capable of child-bearing? Has she become mentally senile?' Emin began his journal *Hell's Mail* (Adskaya pochta) with an ironic response to the grandmother's wish that the title of his journal be changed: her lineage, he suggested, would add lustre to the unseemly names of the devils whose correspondence he would publish. Ruban's *Neither This Nor That* mocked the *babushka*'s criticisms: 'as far as the grandmother is concerned', wrote a correspondent, 'she may be excused for she has already outlived her years and is very forgetful'. This was followed by a declaration of the independence of the 1769 journals from her tutelage: 'We, *babushka*, although your grandchildren, have neverthless come of age.' The boldness would certainly have been unacceptable if Catherine's proprietorship of *All Sorts* had been openly admitted: but this was not the case. Anonymity was a rule of the literary game, and the other journals bent it to their advantage.

The *Drone* was not, therefore, outstandingly bold in engaging *All Sorts* in controversy: in common with his fellow editors, Novikov seemed to recognise that a modicum of publicity and authority, essential for a new weekly, could be obtained by joining in the fun and drawing the mock-irate fire of the 'official' journal.[9]

The promotion of a third estate outlook

Allegiance to these authorised literary conventions did not stifle Novikov. His Mr Drone was no mere schematic imitation of Mr Spectator; his polemics were no mere empty echo of a stale literary debate. The conventions were positively exploited by Novikov: and they were utilised in a way consonant with Catherine's outlook.

Already Catherine's desire to foster the growth of a third estate in Russia had been signalled to her Legislative Commission, and her wish given physical expression in the sub-committee on 'the middling sort of men' on which Novikov had served. The moral weeklies too in general reflected the values of a high-minded, industrious, honest third estate. In launching her *All Sorts*, the German-born empress no doubt wished, in part, to emulate the German *Spectator* type of journals of the 1740s whose middle-class editors were intent on forging an acceptable image for the bourgeois way of life.

Novikov's use of the convention of the fictitious editor is very significant in this respect. Whereas the Germans in their quest for social authority tended to upgrade their fictitious editors to the rank of nobleman,[10] Novikov, the nobleman of substance, placed his fabrication, Mr Drone, beneath him in the social hierarchy. This was a clear indication of Novikov's acute political sense. The young editor of the *Drone*, we learn, is from a provincial backwater, from a destitute gentry family and therefore will be forced to make his own way in the world although eventually he may receive – on condition that he behaves according to the lights of a conservative uncle – an inheritance of 300 serfs. This was indeed a politic placing of the 'editor'. While remaining a titular nobleman, Mr Drone was put in the lower ranks of the gentry from which a new middle class could emerge. A successor magazine, the *Painter* (Zhivopisets), demoted its 'editor' further to a craftsman–painter, a position that was disturbing to the less sophisticated gentry, to judge from an encounter described in that periodical between an educated nobleman and a vain, empty-headed young noblewoman whose only use for the *Painter* was for curling her hair. He attempted to demonstrate the value of the satirical weekly by comparing his Painter with Gottlieb Wilhelm Rabener – significantly a writer who had himself been forced to spell out the ironies of his satirical writings for the benefit of unsophisticated readers in Germany.[11] The girl was not impressed. 'Is it not base', she asked contemptuously, 'to be a friend and acquaintance of craftsmen and painters! You are not yourself one of Ham's descendants are you?'[12] In his reply the educated nobleman deftly explained the point of the satirical journal's *persona*. But more striking was his need to stress that although the fictitious editor might be from the middling sort, yet his manipulator was indisputably a man of rank. There is a sense of defensiveness here on Novikov's part. It is as if the dubious social rank of the Painter really had disturbed some of the magazine's reading audience, so that he is forced to reveal his nobility. 'My girl', replied the nobleman, 'pardon me, you are of course mistaken in the name of the Painter, which is used only for the title of the book, and the writer himself has a completely different name, and is not only a nobleman but what is more, a learned nobleman, that is, one who writes books.'[13]

Lowly though his fortunes might have been, Mr Drone's blood would not have been cause for any noble reader to feel ill at ease. Through his uncle we have an explanation for the 'insuperable obstacles' mentioned in the first issue which the young man's upbringing had placed in the way of a literary career: the uncle revealed himself as an obscurantist philistine, deeply suspicious of the apparently unprofitable new learning which a young metropolitan *prokuror*, or procurator, had brought with him to his provincial post. There was a hint that Ivanushka's education had been the learning-by-rote of the old Muscovite tradition and, although the reader had to wait until 4 August 1769 and the fifteenth issue of the *Drone*, the suspicion was confirmed by the uncle in another letter. Until the age of twenty, Ivan had pleased his late father – who had been grieved by the effect of secular education in the Cadet Corps on his elder son – by learning at home not the modern, useless sciences but 'the Wrath of God'. His only reading had been the lives of the saints and the Bible; his only achievements, vast feats of memorisation and the ability at the age of sixteen to know the whole calendar of church services by heart. But Ivan had wandered from the paths of righteousness to read secular works, to learn foreign languages in order to read schismatic books and even translate them in order to corrupt those ignorant of foreign tongues.[14]

What is striking about this portrait is that it was a dynamic one. Society was presented with a mentor who had himself undergone a personal cultural revolution. With deliberation Novikov characterised the fictional Drone as a poor young nobleman who had rejected employment in a corrupt bureaucracy; instead he had elected to advance socially by embracing those cultural values which were becoming the tenuous delineations of a new concept of nobility. Already Novikov, through the creation of his Idler, demonstrated the choice that later lay between being a *chinovnik*, a state bureaucrat, or a member of the intelligentsia. Novikov had struck the Russian reader's political nerve. The leap that Ivanushka had made from the ignorant provincial obscurantism of the old Muscovite gentry to the new secular Western culture was one that many of the *Drone*'s readers (the bulk of whom belonged to the higher ranks of society) must have witnessed, or even made themselves; the attraction of the *persona* of 'Mr editor of the *Drone*' was undoubtedly the reader's recognition of the character and – a force always essential to good journalism – a sense of identification.

A cast of related characters

Novikov's acute political sense also manifested itself in his transposition of another *Spectator* character to the Russian context. The first character to stride onto the *Drone*'s stage was Ivanushka's uncle, who appealed to his nephew as a clansman to seek patronage in order to sustain the honour of the clan. The appeal was treated with disdain by the young modern: clan pretensions of this sort were so antiquated by 1769 that the uncle was hardly a difficult target to ridicule.[15] The tone of the satire was mild, amused and patronising; very much the polite satire of the *Spectator* which established its own tone with the smiling portrait of the lovable, if rascally, Sir Roger de Coverley.[16] The uncle could well be a Russian Sir Roger: both were antique survivals into a world that had passed them by, but the uncle and the old Tory country squire, reactionaries both, preserved traits which were potentially dangerous. Behind the patronising amusement of Addison and Steele and also of Novikov, there is a wary unease at a possible recrudescence of the old ways. In this portrait as well, Novikov demonstrated his full understanding of the *Spectator* type of periodicals. The *Spectator*'s bright urbane world is illumined by being set in the shadow of Sir Roger de Coverley's; and the *Drone*'s world in order to be endowed with a sense of reality – Novikov seems to have understood it clearly – had to issue from the dark society of his Muscovite uncle. Once more, Novikov presented his readers with a reincarnation rather than a flaccid imitation; the uncle is less a redrawn Sir Roger than a typical ignorant provincial of the older generation, a Russian compendium of the eighteenth-century satirical targets.

Clans had at least given a distinct framework to human dealings, and in his attack on the 'uncle' Novikov did not wish to attack all kinds of social relationships. The exclusiveness of clanship was certainly abhorrent to him: the appeal of his journal was intended to be broad, and this was stressed in the year-end numbers of 1769 when the *Drone*'s 'readers' were paraded in their variety. By showing their reaction to the personality of the Drone, Novikov demonstrated how he had achieved his amalgam of instructive enlightenment (in his appeal to serious, educated readers), diversion (in his appeal to a giddy-headed fop) and social liveliness (in his appeal to the intelligent woman reader).[17] It was in the breadth of his appeal that the Drone took pride.

Nevertheless, this desire for mass appeal did not prevent the journal from sketching a distinct social grouping of its own: like-minded correspondents were gathered around the person of the Drone, as they had been around Mr Spectator. Both realised that their authority could be augmented by rallying men who shared their disposition. As early as its fifth issue the *Drone* began to receive letters from correspondents such as Pravdulyubov (Truth-lover) and Pryamikov (Straightforward) who acknowledged their 'drone-like' dispositions. 'Letters to the editor', reflecting a variety of styles and outlook, were one of the marked features of all the weeklies. Through them a tone of intimacy was established between the *Drone*'s editor and his correspondents which was consistently maintained through the fifty-three numbers of the journal.

There was no attempt by Novikov to make them members of a club in the manner of the *Spectator*. Clubs of that particular sort were as yet unknown in Russia: although when, shortly, they were established, they would be consciously founded on the English model and the 'English Club' was to be the inevitable choice of name for the most renowned St Petersburg institution. Yet Novikov, as we shall see, was essentially a clubbable man, and the pages of his journal, even in 1769, were able to suggest the club atmosphere of the original *Spectator*. The periodical was enlivened by the appearance, not only of the central *persona*, but by supporting characters who, briefly sketched and undeveloped though they might be, nevertheless corresponded to what has been called the *Spectator*'s *dramatis personae*.[18]

And these, too, were indicative of Novikov's support for Catherine's policies. The empress had put much hope on the office of procurator, an inspector of justices, in her campaigns against bribery, and this was the profession of the first positive companion to the Drone. The young man's character was as clear as his name of Pravdulyubov (Truthlover): he was a stern moralist, with the firm polemical style of an advocate, and also a talent, when necessary, for legalistic qualifications. Catherine's enthusiasm for the middle class was well served by a 60-year-old bourgeois merchant from Tver': Chistoserdov (Pureheart), interested in the laws, commerce and customs of other nations, was one of the reasonable and knowledgeable readers and supporters of the *Drone*, noble in all but rank. Not all the characters, however, were drawn in response to political fashion. A garrulous raconteur, who shared with Novikov the initials N.N., made his presence felt by the number and length of his appearances, bringing the breath of Moscow streets into the journal with the rush of his vernacular, his critical eye and salty proverbs. A fashionable young lady characterised herself:

> A girl of about eighteen, not bad looking, not foolish, not vain, not capricious, who is able to give others and herself their due; a lover of literature who likes to discuss things and does not cause weariness or boredom in conversation with others. She is pleased when men give her her due, but is at once angry if she notices that they wish to flatter her. N.B. I almost, almost forgot to inform you, Mr Editor, that this girl's taste is not bad and that she dresses elegantly in accord with fashion and her person.[19]

With their allegorical names, Truthlover and Pureheart, or their anonymous labels, N.N. and 'young lady writer', these characters are, as might be expected, to a degree abstract, generalised and one-dimensional. In this, Novikov was bound by a well-established tradition of drawing characterising sketches that went back to the French works of Lesage, Prévost and Marivaux.[20] There is no hint in the *Drone* that Novikov might have been able to fuse together in one sketch an evocation of character, such as the controlled moral indignation of Pravdulyubov, a precise social placing as in Chistoserdov's case and N.N.'s concrete locale. Nevertheless, there is sufficient differentiation in the character portrayal to suggest the multifarious aspects of the society with which the *Drone* had dealings. Novikov well understood that the form of his periodical enabled the society which it served to become more conscious of itself and, in particular, more conscious of its variegated make-up. It was a lesson learnt in Catherine's Legislative Commission as men rose in public to propound their differing viewpoints and reveal their differing prejudices: similar men – and women – now made their entry on to the pages of the *Drone.*

The 'dramatis personae' in the polemic

Some of the same *dramatis personae*, endowed with their manifest third estate outlook, articulated the *Drone*'s arguments in the polemic with *All Sorts* on the limits of satire. If the issue of *All Sorts* where Catherine is supposed to have promulgated an aesthetic doctrine binding on all other satirists is examined, one finds no imperial decree. Rather the controversy springs from the conventional social setting of the moral weeklies.

The attitude to criticism is conveyed through a sketch – in the form of a typical 'reader's letter' – of a misanthrope who so annoys a gathering with his peevishness that after his withdrawal the urbane company decide: '(1) never to call weakness a vice; (2) to preserve a love of humanity in all circumstances; (3) not to think that perfect people can ever be found, and therefore (4) to implore God to grant us a spirit of meekness and indulgence'. In a postscript the writer of the letter, 'Afinogen Perochinov' (the surname means Pen-sharpener), added two more points as an afterthought: '(5) that nobody should argue about what he does not understand; and (6) that nobody should think that he alone is capable of reforming the world'.[21]

As early as its fifth issue, the *Drone* seized the opportunity of engaging in debate. The riposte was in similarly oblique terms: Perochinov's 'letter to the editor' was answered by one from Pravdulyubov. The latter's debating tactics employed a procedure used extensively in political controversy in contemporary eighteenth-century England. In his study of the language of politics, J. T. Boulton has shown that whereas conservative publicists like Burke tended to argue from generally accepted positions in order to lull their readers with a series of abstract generalisations, the radical Junius or Tom Paine would cite instead the concrete example, and subject the soothing generalisation to the rough test of reality. Boulton has called the process 'translation'.[22]

Pravdulyubov directed this process of 'translation' at the centre of Perochinov's advice not to refer to human weaknesses as 'vices':

Yea, I know not what weakness means in the opinion of this lady. Nowadays it is usually called a weakness to fall head over heels in love with somebody, that is, with somebody else's wife or daughter. But this imagined weakness leads to disgracing the home we frequent, and setting a husband at odds with his wife, or a father with his children – and would this not be a vice? Whoever gives this more careful thought than I in his leisure will justly call this lawlessness. Love of money is also a weakness; for that reason a weak man may be forgiven for taking bribes and enriching himself with plunder. Drunkenness is also a weakness or rather a habit; nevertheless a drunkard may beat his wife and children until they are half dead and brawl with his true friend.[23]

A somewhat similar debating trick of Pravdulyubov's was to change his opponent's words so as to give a darker shade to their meaning. Where *All Sorts* had used the bookish *sniskhodit'*, a *calque* on the French *condescendre*, to express leniency towards human frailty, Pravdulyubov used the blunt, colloquial and unmistakeably Russian *potakat'*. And a similar effect was obtained by 'translating' sophistry with a home-grown proverb: 'I was not pleased', commented Pravdulyubov, 'by the first rule of the abovementioned lady, that is, never to call weakness a vice, *as if Ioan and Ivan are not ever one.*' It was this device of translation, of course, that underpinned Pravdulyubov's whole argument that 'weakness' was the conservative's own deliberate back-translation of 'vice'.[24]

Already in the sally at the un-Russianness of the word *sniskhodit'*, Pravdulyubov had hinted at the inter-dependence of language and political attitudes. This developed in his second letter into a harping on Madam All Sorts' deficiencies in the Russian language, her failure to express herself competently or understand Russian writings. Does this prove Novikov's extreme belligerence? Was he indeed bold enough to cock a snook – even indirectly – at the empress? The view has been advanced that Novikov's aim was not only to criticise the 'programme' of Catherine's journal, but also to unmask the real person of Catherine lurking behind the assumed name of *All Sorts*' grandmother. Since it was generally known that the German-born Catherine's Russian was broken, runs the argument, then Pravdulyubov's linguistic criticism is a deliberate pointer to her authorship. This argument, however, is something of a *tour de force*, and depends heavily on partial quotation from Pravdulyubov's letter.[25] A more persuasive indication of the personal identification of Novikov with Pravdulyubov's polemic is the fact, indicated by Makogonenko, that the latter's first letter was dated 9 May 1769, which was Novikov's saint's day.[26]

Pravdulyubov seemed to be using the same weapons as contemporary English radicals; but did this make the *Drone* an oppositionist journal and Novikov a radical publicist? To some extent these letters must reflect in Novikov at this time a young man's impatience with his society. Not satisfied with generalities, he had an urge to present his readers with portrayals of the concrete, identifiable ills of Russian society. Yet, much more remarkable than the moral zeal in the inexperienced 25-year-old journalist was the cautious manoeuvring for room to criticise.

A young editor's prudence

If Novikov, by finding space for Pravdulyubov's criticisms, was able to hunt with the outspoken hounds then he also ran with the wary hares. Novikov might playfully suggest through his saint's day date that he had an affinity with Pravdulyubov; but with greater insistence he distanced the latter. Only with reluctance was a second letter from Pravdulyubov published; the editor of the *Drone* deferred to *All Sorts*' injured feelings, pleading that it was a painful sense of justice that obliged him to place Pravdulyubov's 'justification' before an 'intelligent and dispassionate public'.[27] And when the end of the *Drone* was already in sight, Novikov took pains retrospectively to separate the *personae* of Pravdulyubov and the fictitious Drone.[28]

Not only was a safe distance placed between them, but Pravdulyubov was eventually revealed as an establishment figure. In the ninth issue it was confirmed that he was a procurator, an inspector of justices, and so was very much a symbol of Catherine's reformist zeal. Readers should not have been surprised to find that he was a lawyer, for his letters had not merely rejected *All Sorts*' prescriptions out of hand; rather they displayed the skilful advocacy and subtle casuistry of an attorney patiently arguing a case. To be truly philanthropic, he pleaded, one had to call vice a vice, correct it and not defer to it by calling it a weakness.[29] His brief was to convince *All Sorts*, as the official journal, that criticism of vice must be allowed in a moral journal with the aim of improving society.

All Sorts was also being persuaded that it shared with the *Drone* a common enemy. What stood in the way of robust satire was not so much Catherine's personal objection as the reaction of prominent men and important sections of Russian society who took any social criticism as a personal attack on their prerogatives. Pravdulyubov's second letter was flanked by one from Chistoserdov (Pureheart), who was eventually identified as an intelligent burgher.[30] That social placing was important: not only was he the kind of citizen that Catherine, through her Legislative Commission, had hoped to promote; more important, he could understand better than most that it was often unwarranted aristocratic arrogance – something with which Catherine had been forced to contend in the Commission – that caused vice to pass as mere weakness. He specifically warned the *Drone* of the danger that highly placed persons would see themselves in its satire, but begged him:

Write satires against the gentry, burghers, administrators, justices who have sold their consciences and all sinful men; ridicule the bad habits of the inhabitants of town and country; destroy ingrained prejudices and repress weaknesses and vices, but not in the principal nobles, for then more salt will be found in your satires. Few know the use of English salt[31] here, so use Russian salt in your satires; they are accustomed to it. And it will be more pleasant for those who are not fond of eating salty things. I have often heard the following reasoning: in the positive degree, or in the little man, thieving is a crime against the law; in ascending, i.e. the middle degree, or in a middling man, thieving is a vice; but in the highest degree, or man, according to true mathematical calculations, thieving is nothing more than weakness.[32]

Novikov did not merely engage in his controversy with *All Sorts* for the sake of a literary battle: he was attempting to persuade the grandmother to modify her prescriptions sufficiently to allow him the opportunity of dealing with those vices which corroded Russian society. They had a common enemy. It was an attempt by Novikov at the outset of his career to gain a certain freedom of action, it is true; but he desired a latitude sanctioned by authority. He was working in a situation where there were no clear guidelines for journalistic initiative, and there was always the possibility of administrative displeasure. The skill with which caveats were placed in Chistoserdov's rambling, good-humoured letter was a further reflection of this caution. First, the reader was reminded of the *Drone*'s disclaimer in its first issue: 'And although in your preface', wrote Chistoserdov, 'you let it be known that you would not publish your own contributions, but those submitted to you, nevertheless men whose hearts are filled with malice hold you responsible for them.'[33] Later in the letter, therefore, when the

Drone was taxed for merely pretending to print the work of others by a malicious 'little gentleman courtier', the latter was already discredited. Nevertheless, Chistoserdov was probably reporting with some truth the attitude of certain influential circles to the moral weeklies. Caution also made Novikov remind his readers and *All Sorts*, at this point, that it was Catherine's own policy to allow more freedom to the press: Chistoserdov's little gentleman was dissatisfied with this policy.

> It is true that *All Sorts* recently gave him [the Drone] a very good wigging. But that is really nothing. In the old days he would have been sent to labour for the good of the state, describing the customs of some Russian imperial possession, but now they have been given leave to portray and ridicule principal noblemen and are not punished for such satires.[34]

What Novikov wished to suggest was that it was the *Drone*'s detractors who were opposed to the authorities' will, and not he himself. On the contrary, the *Drone* was dutifully following official policy and playing its rightful role in the collective endeavours of the satirical weeklies.[35]

Another defence for Novikov might have been Chistoserdov's reference to 'English salt' and its unpalatability for Russians. *All Sorts* had clearly based itself on the English model of the *Spectator* type of journals which was relatively untrammelled in its satirical attacks. If the *Drone*'s satirical acerbity had made some influential people squirm, then it was only because Novikov had dutifully followed English usage by employing the 'English salt' recommended by his mentor, *All Sorts*. Once again he implied that in reality he was following the latter's prescriptions. Finally, Novikov defended himself from the general wrath of the principal nobles by making Chistoserdov mention at the end of the letter that there were seven aristocrats of his acquaintance who approved of the *Drone*'s satires and enjoyed them. This was partly a riddle for the delight of readers, for the seven paragons were indicated by their initials: but the aside gave all prominent noblemen the possibility of not being offended by Chistoserdov's charges against the vicious ones within their ranks.

A difference in satirical tone

At this point in June, Novikov might well have withdrawn from his controversy with *All Sorts*: his fledgling journal would have won a degree of notoriety, and therefore welcome publicity in taunting the 'official' magazine, yet his politic manoeuvres would have left him in no bad odour with the authorities. But Novikov was not allowed to bow out of the polemics. At the beginning of July, *All Sorts* deliberately rekindled the controversy by publishing a letter allegedly sent to the *Drone* by a character with the telling name of Tikhon Dobrosovetov (Tranquil Goodadvice). Catherine, as has been suggested, may have enjoyed infusing a contentious spirit into the 1769 family of magazines; in the light of this, it is not surprising that it was *All Sorts* that took the lead in reactivating the rivalry, and not the cautious *Drone*. Was it Catherine personally who suggested that her journal should cross swords with undoubtedly the most popular of the moral weeklies? It is impossible to say to what extent the empress was engaged in overseeing her journal; but, to Novikov's contemporaries, the fictitious names of Gerasim Kurilov, Galaktion Kakorekov, Gervasiy Koldovalov under some of the controversial letters were an unmistakeable indication of Georgiy Kozitsky. The self-mocking names of Cockcrow (Kakorekov) and Soothsayer (Koldovalov) suggested that the apparent rivalry between the magazines need not be taken too seriously; certainly the war of words did not prevent Kozitsky from becoming subsequently Novikov's chief friend at court and a rich source of patronage.[36]

Their positions were maintained in the following months: the grandmother remained indulgent, while the young editor of the *Drone* yearned for the scourge. But the general impression is of much literary rib-nudging, leg-pulling and, at worst, mock indignation between understanding fellow editors.

Nevertheless, the underlying difference in position was crucial at the time. The main argument against allowing more latitude in satire was on the grounds of taste; and Addison had put the nub of the matter squarely in *Spectator* No. 451: 'There is nothing so scandalous to a Government and detestable in the Eyes of all good Men, as Defamatory Papers and Pamphlets; but at the same time there is nothing so difficult to tame, as a Satyrical Author.'[37] *All Sorts*, as a reflection of the autocracy, naturally bridled at the criticism of identifiable ills in Russian society from sources insistent on their independence and vaunting themselves as representatives of a coherent readership crystallising around them. Catherine would have judged correctly that behind the wrangling over literary formulae, there lurked political impulses. In his *Tatler* examination of satire, Steele had argued that under a humane government, it was Horace's polite satire alone that could flourish while Juvenal's rage only made sense under a tyrant: 'In the Days of *Augustus* to have talked like *Juvenal* had been Madness, or in those of *Domitian* like *Horace*.'[38] The *Drone*'s itch, therefore, to emulate Juvenal and 'attack Vice as it passes by in Triumph' could be construed as implying that Catherine's Russia was nearer the Rome of Domitian than the city of Augustus.

While *All Sorts* did not – or possibly could not – articulate its unease, it obviously sensed the danger from the *Drone* and characterised it once as a 'buzzing in the ears'.[39] The caution with which Novikov conducted his controversy was also a clear indication of the seriousness of purpose which lay behind his enterprise: he was aware of the nature of his undertaking, and the skilful equivocations were not a sign of the timidity of his resolve, but of his editorial expertise.

3

The *Drone*

1769–70

> Expression is the *Dress* of *Thought*, and still
> Appears more decent, as more suitable.
>
> Pope

From abstractions to reality: a principle of editorial organisation

A recognition of the *Drone*'s affinities with its related journals and its acknowledgement of their common conventions is the first necessity for a full understanding of its purpose. We have seen that the Drone endeavoured to be a loyal grandson to *All Sorts*' *babushka*. However, the editor of the *Drone* was not shackled by the apron strings of convention. The grandson was able to stand firmly on his own feet: the weekly may have been one of a kind, but more striking was its individuality. What were the particular features which gave Novikov's *Drone* a stamp of its own, ensuring its contemporary popularity and permanent place in Russian literary history?

The fundamental strength of the *Drone* was its ability to present abstractions to its readers in concrete, recognisable terms. What, in fact, gave power to the plea for permission to criticise social evils robustly was that it was not mere formal pleading, no empty echo of an ancient literary quarrel. It was set firmly in the context of Novikov's own practice. It is only with hindsight that the polemical articles which made the points for each side can be extracted to make an isolated, coherent debate:[1] to the readers of the day who received each issue at intervals, the controversy was not so clear-cut and tended to merge with other diverting, miscellaneous material. But the *Drone*'s argument was not swamped but rather sustained by its flow of articles: these moved fable into documentary, parody into reality.

This movement is apparent from the beginning. After the introduction of the fictitious editor came a fable, 'The Promoted Elephant'.[2] In it a lion, an enlightened King of the Beasts, rejected an upstart fox with his vices of cunning, flattery and falsehood and promoted instead an honourable if ponderous elephant, since the latter's honest reason was shown by his observance of *pravda*, the Russian word for 'righteousness' in its biblical sense. A document followed immediately in the form of a letter from the Drone's uncle, begging his nephew to profit from the corruption of Russia's administration and pursue a career through contacts with the influential. Thus the moral of 'The Promoted Elephant' was given its place in Novikov's Russia by the uncle's letter; the generalised fox was transmuted into the reactionary, provincial Russian individual. There was another exemplary tale in the following week's issue.[3] It told of two robbers, one a poor man and the other a rich state servant who had copied the ways of 'minor officials and judges without any conscience': the reader was invited to decide which of them was more worthy of the knout. The basis that this tale had in reality was made plain by revealing its author as the young, upright *prokuror* who had so disturbed the uncle: not only was the reader given the moral tale, but he was also presented with the source of the criticism.

But Novikov could not merely keep on repeating this movement of tale to documentary. His was a periodical that depended for its effectiveness on the novelty of its modes. Already in its fourth issue attention was drawn to a 'new sort of composition' – a parody of the news items in the official gazette. Soon the mock 'news' came from farther afield than St Petersburg: datelines from Moscow, Yaroslavl and Kronstadt pretended to show the breadth of the *Drone*'s interest in Russian life, its sympathy with good citizenship and Russian commerce. Parody of out-of-town news prepared the way for what appeared as real news from a country correspondent reporting the unlawful dispossession of a gentry family by ruthless neighbours. Just as the *Drone* had turned its fables into reality, so now it made its amusing 'new kind of composition' prepare the way for 'real' reportage. That Novikov was conscious of this movement from a disengaged, conventional mode to one of social engagement was shown by the opening sentence of a rambling tale about judicial corruption by N.N. in the thirteenth issue. N.N. had previously contributed tales in conventional frames, such as 'Tales of a Shilling' and 'Dreams'. Now he underlined the shift to reality: 'Mr Editor, You are fond of news, and so I am sending you a true tale: here it is.'[4] It was the readers' delight in authenticity too which made the news items so popular, to judge from a venomous reference to them in Chulkov's *This and That.* According to the rival journal, it was their thinly veiled topicality that struck contemporary readers: 'his news items have been woven from insults and abuse against those near to him, and were he to be believed, then it would be necessary to evoke total revulsion from all'.[5]

Chulkov recognised that the *Drone* dealt with recognisable people as well as real events, and from the autumn of 1769 onwards it was portraiture – however crude and primitive it might seem – rather than any examination of abstract ideas that was to be the mainstay of Novikov's journal. Again Novikov demonstrated his grip on the organising of his material by establishing a firm bridge from the popular 'news items' to the subsequent varieties of portraiture. In the mock 'News' (Vedomosti) of 11 August, an extensive account was given of the habits of one Stozmey (Centisnake) whose name probably referred to Svistunov, a man of the theatre, whose unfortunate surname meant 'hisser'. The following week Stozmey reappeared as one in a series of 'Portraits', short designations supplied by a lady correspondent: 'Stozmey is plain of face, clumsy of body, not rich in intelligence, but rich in heartfelt spite against all around him.'[6] Later we shall see what that plain face and clumsy body signified; but firstly we need to recognise the importance attached by Novikov to the human face itself. His 'portraiture' was clearly in harmony with the general appeal of a journal animated by his fictional *dramatis personae*. Also Novikov's journal had anticipated the tendency of the nineteenth-century Russian novel to set its fictional characters among real, historical figures, for his portraits elbowed their way out of a throng of identifiable contemporaries.

Mere repetition of direct portraits was avoided. Novikov again showed his awareness of his readership's needs and his own talent for imaginative organisation by continuously attempting to retain interest before it flagged with a series of variations on the theme of portraiture. A doctor's prescriptions – a mode used in Sumarokov's *Busy Bee* – was an immediate variation: a man's diagnostic portrait was followed by a cure.[7] Thus Nedoum (Lackmind) suffered from the fever of stressing his breeding and had to be inoculated with reason and philanthropy. October saw a new twist to the doctor's prescriptions; a reader named Zabotin (Concerned) described the diseases of his neighbours and asked the editor for remedies to suit them. November introduced a new variation on pen-portraits: sketches were given of representative types who were then mocked by 'Laughing Democritus'. At the end of the month two women, Prelesta (Charming) and Nelepa (Stupid), were contrasted. This piece was in keeping with similar exercises in the *Spectator* which, as part of its educative intent, portrayed, as good examples, women becoming to their society by their beauty, reason and humility. Contrasted with these were cautionary examples of the shrill, mannered ignorance of such as Nelepa. It was indicative of the way that Novikov in his journal followed his precursor in making a direct appeal to women readers. It had been this aim, possibly, which had prompted him to choose a young lady (called Uzhest′ kak mila – My, how gorgeous! – in the fashionable slang of the day) as his 'correspondent' to introduce the original 'Portraits': and in January 1770 her portraits returned to the pages of the *Drone.* Once more there was a variation; this time the Drone was asked to add a caption to her sketches and this he did.

Another young lady who contributed portraits to the issue of 23 March also explained why the pen-portraiture enjoyed such vogue and was, consequently, the *Drone*'s most common journalistic mode. 'Your Portraits please me most of all', she wrote, 'you cannot imagine how some of them are like my acquaintances; I have read them in their presence so that they were mad . . . and how I laughed . . .'[8] The 'Pictures' contributed by her, however, are yet another variation on the portrait theme. These were of Hogarthian splendour and certainly disprove the often repeated claim that administrative displeasure had weakened the satirical attack of the last numbers of the *Drone.* The first one gives their flavour:

> This picture depicts a man of low birth who has had the opportunity of worming his way into a family of illustrious name. On the right hand side are seen all the sinecures accumulated by him thanks to the kindness of his relatives. On the left is a store almost full of trunks, cupboards and sacks of money; he has filled it by all sorts of forbidden methods, such as stealing and expropriating the wealth of others, taking it into his keep and not returning it, and most was acquired by extortion. Here as well are depicted several widows, orphans and helpless people; they beseech him with tear-stained eyes and outstretched hands, and it seems that they all wish to say: 'Have mercy, show justice!' But he, with a calm countenance, always tells them, 'Tomorrow.' Above his store is an inscription: 'This wealth, despite my little intelligence, God gave to me.' The artist who

painted this picture did not forget to depict in the distance broken scales of justice, hurled to the ground, and also truth cast down.[9]

At the very end of the journal's life a correspondent, recalling the past glories of the *Drone*, was perhaps typical of the readers in recognising that it had been precisely the variety and novelty of its modes that had made the journal so popular, and in particular the variations on portraiture:

In your *Drone* of last year a large number of the compositions were very good and were given their just due, for example: the news items, portraits, prescriptions, your Democritus, some items of verse, also the many prose letters containing so much wit and salt, so much good taste, healthy common sense and purity of Russian.[10]

The same correspondent, with conscious irony, also put his finger on the reasons for the popularity of these compositions as well as recalling the controversy with *All Sorts*: 'There is no need, and God preserve me from saying that in them you aimed at persons known to you.'

A dramatisation of social ideas

In his satirical attacks, of course, Novikov was no radical; he took up his stance squarely on the humane commonplaces of his day. The *Drone*'s innovation – and this powered its satire – was to embody, clothe and animate common ideas, such as those conveyed to the Legislative Commission, and present them with a human face. Novikov's understanding of the genre, his projection of the Drone and other characters, went some way to achieve this; but as we have seen, he also brought abstractions down to a recognisable world by skilful arrangement of his material. The periodical was firmly shaped so that despite the apparent diversity of the miscellaneous material, everything was interlinked by two overriding impulses. One was to act out abstract social ideas on the living stage of Russian society; the second was to promote an image of the social paragon, the 'true noble man' who was partly intimated in the positive characters of, for example, Pravdulyubov, Chistoserdov and the editorial *persona* of the Drone himself, but was more persuasively suggested as the reverse image of the host of rogues and scoundrels satirised.

As an illustration of the acting out of social ideas, let us take the social question which has attracted most attention from commentators on the *Drone* – that of serfdom. There is no denying the journal's central concern with the position of the Russian peasantry. Yet the problem was never presented as an abstract one of social theory, amenable to a solution by any form of social engineering. Serfs were made to appear by Novikov as part of a drama which would point a moral, but did not pretend to present a programme of amelioration. Thus 'Passers-by', a poem attributed to Ablesimov which appeared late in July, portrayed in a charming cameo the real gulf between the Russian peasantry and the Westernised merchants, administrators and gentry by describing an encounter between three peasants with their rustic horns and rough voices, and a genteel assembly for water music playing with orchestral instruments. The peasants, although struck with wonder at the display of sophistication, have the wit to understand that it is their serf labour which creates this luxury, and the question is asked:

> And the labour, may we ask, is whose?[11]

It has been claimed that here, in this line, for the first time in Russian poetry 'the thought is expressed of the people's labour as the source of the wealth and culture of the gentry'.[12] But this thought would not have been wholly new for contemporary readers: a more forceful exposition of the same idea was given in Lukin's preface to the *Haberdasher*, where reference is made to the blood of innocent serfs dripping from the gilded carriages of the rich.[13] The awareness of serf labour as the creator of wealth was merely one of the points which gave focus to the Russian thinking man's view of his society. Another was the awareness of the gulf between the peasants 'out-and-out simpletons' and the Westernised citizens who, as well as forming the audience for the water music, were an important part of the *Drone*'s readership.

> People strolled in groups along the bank,
> Various classes of French and Germans,
> Merchants, administrators and, in short, all manner of men
> In carriages and on foot.[14]

Above all, the peasantry existed in Russian society, and in the pages of the *Drone*, not in their own right, but for the benefit of the main actor, the truly noble man. The extent of the latter's true nobility was partly measurable by the extent of the sympathy he showed to his dependent serfs. True nobility for Novikov involved a great sense of *noblesse oblige*. It was for this reason that a correspondent, Pravdin (Trueman), in October explained that it was because he had noticed the *Drone*'s sympathy for the peasantry that he was enclosing a copy of a report from a bailiff to his master and the latter's instructions – a document often quoted by commentators to argue the case for Novikov's populism.[15] Once more, there was the movement – and Pravdin's letter stressed this – away from the generalised concern for serfs dehumanised by their profligate masters, a concern expressed by Sumarokov in his *Busy Bee* and by many more Russian authors, to the real-life example. There was a 'translation' of the *philosophe* idea into a radical instance. A fortnight previously there had been a playful abstraction: Mr Bezrassud (Reasonless) who believed that peasants were not real Russians and so oppressed them, was given a doctor's note which prescribed gazing at the bones of gentlemen and peasants until he discovered the difference between them.[16] Now came the reality. The bailiff's report told of the forced collection of rent from peasants, their merciless corporal punishment on non-payment and the rapacity of neighbouring landowners; it was remarkable for its authentic ring, which led Dobrolyubov to ask whether the document was a genuine example of this type of report and not merely a skilful parody. Indeed the 'copy' published by Novikov is remarkably near in tone to a real report of this sort.[17]

The hero of the drama – the model citizen

As for the other aim of promoting the social paragon, facets of him are revealed throughout the *Drone*. He is best summed up in the last of the original 'portraits' drawn by the lady correspondent on 18 August.

> *Vot-kto* (There's-a-man!) is a reasonable and virtuous gentleman. He does good to all to whom he is able. He thinks that reason is given to him in order to give service to his state; an illustrious rank in order to protect the oppressed; wealth in order to aid the poor; and that he has been born a man in order to be useful to all his kind. All this he fulfils. *Blagodarny* (Grateful) in depicting him, wrote the following: '*Vot-kto*, an ornament of the illustrious boyars and a friend of mankind'.[18]

This paragon would have been the ideal citizen that Catherine might have hoped that delegates to her Legislative Commission would have recognised and nurtured. In portraying him in these terms Novikov, as editor, would have been to some extent continuing his function as erstwhile official minute-taker.

Qualities were added, however, which Novikov clearly considered of considerable importance, but which Catherine might have considered as wayward traits in the make-up of her ideal citizen. For Novikov, the latter would have fine – even strictly defined – literary tastes and a due regard for the proprieties of the Russian language. Even V. P. Petrov, although promoted by Catherine – with little conviction perhaps – as a quasi-poet laureate to succeed Lomonosov, was pilloried for his literary failings.[19] He stood alongside Svistunov, scorned primarily because he dared to criticise the dramas of famous Russian writers and wished to reform stage technique.[20] However, the main sustained attack in number after number of the *Drone* was against V. I. Lukin (1737–94), who had introduced the new French *drame bourgeois* to Russia with his adaptations from French dramatists such as Destouches, Campistron, Boissy, Regnard and Prévost, and had attempted to give a reasoned case for elaborating a new aesthetic to replace neoclassicism and create a truly Russian national theatre, thus introducing to Russia the new thinking on the theatre stemming from Diderot's *Discours sur la poésie dramatique* of 1758.

It is puzzling to see the *Drone*, so conscious of itself as a mirror of the surrounding Russian realities, swiftly pass to scurrilous attacks on Lukin, a man who had advocated precisely this for the theatre. It suggests that there was great confusion in Novikov's mind about the new aesthetic issues of the day. But if Novikov was confused by, and perhaps impatient of, dramatic theory, he was clear about practice. The only justification for Novikov's treatment of Lukin was that his rejection served to retain Sumarokov as the sole, untouchable master of Russian literary manners. In so far as the reader was made to see that the main vice of men such as Lukin, Petrov and Svistunov was their unwarranted criticism of 'the writer of Russian tragedies', then the attack on them may more charitably be viewed as a spirited defence of Sumarokov.

Sumarokov was constantly praised by the *Drone*, and the influence of his own journal the *Busy Bee* pervaded Novikov's. A number of modes originally used in the *Busy Bee* were dutifully imitated: thus the first consciously 'literary' work in the *Drone*, 'The Promoted Elephant', echoed the fables which were a common feature of the *Busy Bee* from its May 1759 issue onwards. Sumarokov's introduction of a satirical dictionary in the April number of his monthly, 'An Essay at a German Dictionary Arranged in Russian Alphabetical Order', a translation of Rabener's 'Versuch eines deutschen Wörterbuchs', was imitated in Novikov's fifth paper under the heading, 'Articles from a Russian Dictionary'. The doctor attending to the ailments of petty writers had been anticipated in the *Busy Bee* by a doctor who had to find a cure for a poet's disease of writing thunderous odes. That dialogue between doctor and poet had been an attack on Lomonosov: the *Busy Bee*, as well as giving an example of a mode to be widely used by Novikov, also determined the place that a delineation of literary taste would take in Novikov's journal.

Despite his appeal to the literate urban merchants and state servants, Novikov presented as their real-life paragon Sumarokov, the neo-classicist nobleman, and rejected, on their behalf, the commoner Lukin with his urge to enlighten his fellow Russians with the new anti-classicist literary theories of bourgeois Europe. Just as Novikov did not elaborate or hold any dogmatic, progressive aesthetic principles, so he had no thoroughgoing class or political prejudices. The aim of the *Drone* was not to launch an attack on all established authority and march in the vanguard of a rising third estate: its desire was, and the *Drone* had indicated it well enough in its preface, to provide a shifting society with a self-image, to give it a sense of corporate identity for the good of the whole society. Its basis was an intuitive eclecticism, tempered by a cautious conservatism.

It is plain from the nature of his sallies at Lukin, Svistunov and Petrov that the young Novikov moved in St Petersburg literary circles conscious of their exclusivity and delighting in literary allusions. But behind the effervescence, high spirits and occasional impudence of the *Drone* lay the conservative literary taste of the serious translator of Fénelon. It was accompanied by a scholarly temper, to judge from a piece, in accord with his general outlook, which was published in the 23 February 1770 issue and which revealed Novikov's close acquaintanceship with men of academic interests. An extract from a twelfth-century Chinese writer, Chen-Tse, gave instructions for statesmanship which were to a remarkable extent in accord with the eighteenth-century view of enlightened despotism; virtue and reason, the welfare of subjects, the wise choice of trusted noble lieutenants and the training of enlightened administrators – these were the hallmarks of wise government. The translation was probably by A. L. Leont'yev (173?–86), a Chinese expert who had impressed William Coxe during his visit to Russia and had led the latter to declare that St Petersburg might rival Paris as the main channel of Chinese culture into Europe.[21]

The scholarly cast of Novikov's mind was also suggested by lines written on the death of F. A. Emin, who had been the editor of *Hell's Mail*, one of the 1769 group of satirical journals.[22] However, he was not remembered for that. He was lauded as an historian following in the footsteps of Nestor, Lomonosov, Tatishchev and Khilkov, presumed at that time to be the author of the *Kernel of Russian History*. History would be of topical interest, for 1768 had seen the beginning of the posthumous publication of V. N. Tatishchev's *Russian History* which, presented to the Academy of Sciences as long ago as 1739, was still the only distinctly modern, critical history; and the *Kernel of Russian History* was published at the beginning of 1770. Here was the first intimation of a serious, academic interest in Russian history which was soon to dominate Novikov's activities and determine his outlook.

Closure

That hint of things to come was one of the last buzzes of the *Drone*. Although Emin had died only on 18 April, the lines on his death appeared in the issue of 20 April; but the reason was not Novikov's publishing skill. Rather it was the reverse. At the end of the previous November, a 'reader's letter' had complained of a four-week break in the appearance of the weekly. The editorial response was evasive, and it is only possible to guess at reasons for the interruption in the sequence of publication; interference from the authorities, technical problems or a disturbance in Novikov's personal affairs. The numbering of the papers and their dating was not broken, however, although presumably the issues from now on appeared with considerable delay. All the January numbers were published simultaneously at the end of the month but the final numbers dated 20 and 27 April 1770 were only announced in the 6 July issue of the *St Petersburg News*.[23] The young editor seemed to have had difficulty in bringing out his periodical but at least he had the satisfaction of closing it after a nominal full year's run, from 1 May 1769 to 27 April 1770 of 'exactly 52 papers' as he stressed in his fifty-third and concluding number.

One positive reason for Novikov to bring his journal to a close could have been the lag in publication which must have tried the patience of his public, ill-defined as it was and unpractised in the habit of reading periodicals. A two-month lag on a weekly periodical could hardly be made up, and a fresh start must have seemed politic. Another reason was the sharp decline in the circulation of the weekly which depended on subscribers for its existence. The *Drone* itself was explicit on this point. Thus in its issue of 13 April 1770 there was a direct reference, even though in the form of a 'reader's letter', to this fall: 'Your bookseller has told me that the circulation of this year's papers is not a tenth even of what it used to be.'[24] In fact, it is estimated that the average number of copies printed in 1770 was 750 against a mean figure of 1,240 in 1769 and, as the profitability of the weekly declined in proportion, Novikov would not have been encouraged to continue beyond the year's run.[25] There were literary reasons, as well as organisational and economic ones. The *Drone*, as we have seen, did not exist in a vacuum, but was one of the journals making up what Catherine saw as a new, collective literary endeavour to continue the collective work of her Legislative Commission: the literary polemics of the former had been a substitute, perhaps, for the induced debates of the latter. So prominent a feature of the journals was the literary skirmishing that a would-be young editor who wrote to the *Drone* for advice on 13 April 1770 was prompted to ask if it was obligatory for him to quarrel with someone in a journal. The *Drone*'s reply was cryptically enigmatic: 'there are also quarrels'.[26] When *All Sorts* ended its life at the end of April, the *Drone* remained bereft of its fellows, and although Novikov did stress in his 'Last Farewell' with some pride that it had outlasted the others, yet it was unthinkable that he could forge on alone, '. . . the Drone, with great grief at the demise of its contemporaries is also dying. It should be noted, that the 1769 generation of weekly papers is broken with it.'[27] By their very genius, the *Spectator* type of moral journals could not hope to have a long run. At their core was the portrayal of the exemplary man, a fixed witness and mentor of society, not shifting from a firm moral standpoint: the picture is, of necessity, static. Even the original Mr Spectator did not develop much as a character through the 635 numbers penned by Addison and Steele. The static nature of the central character inevitably led to a certain tedium being inherent in the genre which could not be wholly redeemed by the effervescence of the supporting *dramatis personae*. Novikov had attempted to circumvent this by ringing the changes on his methods of portraiture, but this continuous quest for novelty was, in itself, a sign that the energy of the journal was running down, and in his first venture Novikov must have had cause to congratulate himself on completing a full year's run.[28]

The 'Tattler': an attempted sequel

Novikov had not yet abandoned periodical journalism. While announcing the passing of the *Drone*, the same number of the *St Petersburg News* advertised the first issue of a new monthly magazine entitled *Pustomelya*, the word then commonly used to translate Steele's *Tatler*.[29] Permission for the new 'anonymous' magazine had been obtained by one Andrey Fok whose request – in Novikov's handwriting – had been deposited with the Chancellory of the Academy of Sciences on 26 May, and S. I. Volkov was appointed as the Academy's censor.[30] However, the Russian *Tattler* (*Pustomelya* is translated as *Tattler* in modern spelling to distinguish it from the original *Tatler*) was undoubtedly Novikov's creation and the shadowy go-between Fok has never been identified: perhaps it is more than coincidental that the name Fok could be Novikov (transliterated at the time as Navikof or Novikoff) read backwards. It is surely too improbable to see the authorities being so gullible as to allow him to use the subterfuge of an agent to circumvent any opposition from the authorities to his publishing activities. 'Fok' may have been part of the elaborate joke about the hidden identity of the editor of the new periodical – a stratagem to capture the flagging attention of readers weary of the recently defunct periodicals. However, the attempt to rally a new readership failed: only two issues of the *Drone*'s successor appeared.

Yet the *Tattler*, brief though its span was, revealed that Novikov had learnt valuable lessons from his year of journalism. By publishing a monthly which would appear elastically 'by the fifteenth of every month', he clearly wished to avoid the troubles which had beset him in attempting to meet the more demanding schedule of the weekly. He also aimed to move away from the type of periodical which was over-dependent on a static editorial *persona*. The latter was still there: but the character was blurred, elusive, with an avowed weakness for wandering off the point.[31] The garrulous N.N. who had proved – judging from the number of his appearances – to be a great success in the *Drone* was present in the make-up of the Tattler. The authority of the fictitious editor was also decreased by the division of the journal into three distinct parts. The *Tattler* began with a projection of the Tattler himself, but a second division indicated the shift from the *Spectator* genre: both issues had a section of original literary work. And lest this was thought too heavy a diet, the fare was sweetened by closing with a miscellany of short, amusing pieces which made no high demand on the reader's intellect: mock news items, theatrical gossip, satirical riddles and epigrams.

The kinship between the two journals was heavily underlined in the first number by a continuation of the *Drone*'s literary blackballing of Lukin, Petrov and Chulkov. Parodies of the latter's old fashioned conundrums, appearing in his *Haberdasher of Parnassus*,[32] produced sharp sketches of the types satirised in the *Drone*: the social climber who flattered illustrious nobles, the bribe-taking judge, the philanderer, the youth of low rank who hoped for advancement by attracting the attention of rich ladies. The venom of the attack on the corrupt judge certainly did not suggest that Novikov feared annoying the authorities by continuing his attacks on the Russian judiciary:

> Bribegrabber, the judge, without conscience or honour concludes his cases according to his profits: he interprets decrees as he wishes, puts justice to auction, oppresses the poor and helpless, robs the rich and pleases the illustrious; encourages his subordinates to accept bribes by his example; what does Bribegrabber expect for his laudable labours? Reader, guess.[33]

Equally biting was Denis Fonvizin's poem, 'An Epistle to My Servants, Shumilov, Van'ka and Petrushka', a cruel caricature of the existing social contract.[34]

A more conventional exemplary moral tale had occupied most of the first *Tattler*. Its hero would have been recognised instantly by readers of the *Drone*. Goodheart was a young nobleman who could trace his line back to the time of Ivan the Terrible and had received a modern education from his father, Goodtemper. He had learnt the three key languages, French, English and German, acquired a true understanding of things from logic and physics, studied mathematics, history and geography for their practical value, as well as Christian doctrine and true divinity. Shunning the licentiousness of his age, he shyly revealed his honourable passion to Gentlecountenance on his return from St Petersburg where he had formed an attachment for the theatre which purveyed moral precepts. Finally, the bliss of the young paragon in love was broken with the recall of Goodheart to the colours, a topical touch as we shall see. There was little hesitation on their part: Goodheart's civic duty takes precedence over his personal affairs and away he goes, leaving a tearful Gentlecountenance behind.

As before in the *Drone* the fictional exemplar was accompanied by real paragons of Novikov's society. Both numbers of the *Tattler* began with dedications to them, and the second seemed to be deliberately recalling Goodheart when it declared that 'There is no doubt, that goodness of heart is the foundation of all spiritual virtues, and you are endowed with it in the highest degree.'[35] This was addressed to Nikita Demidov (1724–89), grandson of an artisan from Tula who had become the greatest of the Ural iron magnates. The first issue had been dedicated to Nikolay Alekseyevich Ladyzhensky, a close friend of Novikov and a freemason who was presented as a model citizen with his 'good taste, knowledge of literary science and tolerance'. 'But', asked Novikov, 'will you have time to read this trifle?'[36] It was a serious question at the time: Ladyzhensky, in common with many of his contemporaries, was engaged in the Russo-Turkish war and would, as Novikov suggested, have few free minutes to devote to the frivolity of a monthly magazine. There was a suggestion here that public taste might well have been diverted from the satirical periodicals to the stirring realities of military affairs. In two years the circulation of the *St Petersburg News* had doubled from the 600s in 1768 to over 1,300 in 1770, with special supplements on the Russian victories printed in editions of over 2,000.[37] This diversion of public interest might well have been another reason for the fading away of the 1769 group of weeklies, including the *Drone*.

The journals in retrospect

In holding up a looking-glass in which readers could see a distinct self-image, the journals of 1769–70 pandered to a real craving for a code of manners. However extensive his technical knowledge, the

Russian nobleman of the 1760s was acutely aware of himself as rough-hewn and yearned to smooth and polish the exterior of his honest self. This was the picture given by Andrey Bolotov, author of one of the rare memoirs of the century, who recalled 1763 as a special year in his life precisely because it was then that he set himself self-consciously to learn polite behaviour. Bolotov achieved his social confidence and poise by moving in four households where he met with acknowledged social mentors, and he noted:

> Constant intercourse with people is our best mentor and teacher. Somehow or other it is given to us all to assimilate things naturally, without any forcing, from every kind of cohabitation and social life; so, all the more did everything good which I saw and heard in those houses manage to remain with me when I made an effort, and I did not omit to note in my mind trifles of all sorts.[38]

Curiously, Bolotov used for 'trifles of all sorts' the expression *vsyakaya vsyachina*, the exact title of *All Sorts*. Everyday life with people was no doubt the best way of learning the knack of social behaviour, but a reading of the satirical magazines would also be a means of learning vicariously about society and trifles of all sorts: trifles are often the rigid determiners of social classification, and this was underlined by *All Sorts* in its title.

It was among this nobility, anxious and self-conscious about its outward social behaviour, but not necessarily unintelligent, that a readership for the journals had to be formed. At this time no natural audience for Russian *belles-lettres* existed: one of the tasks for the journals had been to gather together and shape the beginnings of a Russian reading public. And, as we have seen, Novikov felt that their readership was not only ill-defined, but fickle. Yet with a readership for Russian literature slowly coalescing, it was a crucial time for that literature. The attitudes struck and the positions taken then would tend to remain fixed in minds as eager, fresh and receptive in their reading as those of men like Bolotov in assimilating the nuances of behaviour.

If one looks back across the sweep of Russian literature to these tentative beginnings, it is possible to glimpse some of the distinctive features of that literature which was to develop vigorously in the following century. It was Novikov who, in many ways, gave these developments their initial momentum.

When Plekhanov suggested to Stepnyak-Kravchinsky towards

the end of the 1880s that they should collaborate in writing a history of 'The Government and Literature in Russia' which would have been a particularly Russian theme, it was not surprising that he suggested that his history should begin with Novikov.[39] The literature with which the young Novikov was involved was – if Catherine is taken to be synonymous with her autocratic government – very much government-inspired and government-directed. The direction too was clear: the government hoped that literature would assist in purifying the society subject to it, and would help to form an ideal citizen.

This fashioning of society entailed a criticism of it, and Novikov's portrayal of the negative aspects of Russian society has readily been seen as preparing the way for the 'realism' of nineteenth-century literature with its critical portrayal of society. Just as the *Spectator* and its imitators prepared their English readers for the English social novels by training them in the elementary analysis of social behaviour and the recognition of characters in literary portraits, so did their Russian counterparts. But the latter's more critical, satirical approach left its mark on subsequent literature.

In Novikov's journals, as we have seen, the satire of the negative character was not an end in itself, but constantly suggested to the reader the reverse image, the social paragon or 'truly noble nobleman'. The urge of the nineteenth- and twentieth-century Russian realists to criticise the dark sides of their society also seems to have an obverse side: the search for the elusive positive hero. Although Novikov's caste sense of *noblesse oblige* was sloughed off, the truly noble man reappeared in a series of moral mutations. And it is interesting to note that in Dostoyevsky's Prince Myshkin, the 'positively good man', the Russian word used for 'good' is *prekrasny*, a word from aesthetics signifying 'fine' or 'handsome' which seems to stress the author's deliberate image-making. The positively good man is also, thanks to the ambiguity of the Russian, a positively fine image of a man.[40]

The enigmatic reply of the *Drone*, 'There are also quarrels', in answer to the tyro writer who wished to know if literary polemics were obligatory, has also reverberated throughout the history of Russian literature. And, on the whole, literary polemics which added spice to the 1769 journals have been a creative force in Russian literature impelling writers to take up their pens in debate, one with the other, and adding zest to the literary life of critics and readers.

Just as polemics have helped to rouse Russian writers, so Western examples have sometimes acted as a powerful catalyst of Russian thought and attitudes. Once again, in retrospect, one can see how Novikov's experience was one more early example of this; how his keen awareness of the possibilities of the genre of the *Spectator* type of journals helped him to channel his attitudes into a positive form. From this early grasping of a literary form, coolly and objectively exploited from a distance, sprang a keen response to form itself, a Russian sense of 'formalism' which was to torture Tolstoy in particular, and eventually lead to the often violent responses to 'formalism' in our century.

That Western catalyst, moreover, in its action has tended to increase the Russian writer's sense of the importance to him of his own language. It was this, perhaps, that accounted for the rejection of Lukin for mishandling Russian and the stress on linguistic purity as a delineating mark of the right-thinking Russian. To turn to Dostoyevsky again, the stupid Lebezyatnikov of *Crime and Punishment* was demonstrated to be outside the pale of enlightened Russians by being presented as someone who was not entirely capable of handling his own language correctly, although Russian was the only language that he knew.[41] And the persistence of this yearning for linguistic purity by the Russian intelligentsia has been underlined in Solzhenitsyn's *First Circle* through his grotesque portrayal of Sologdin with his 'Language of Maximum Clarity'.[42] By stressing literary good taste as well as linguistic purity as the hallmarks of his social paragons, Novikov seemed to have prepared the way for the Russian intelligentsia to become, and to remain to this day, an intensely *literary* intelligentsia.

When Novikov in the *Drone* belittled his own literary trifling, which he considered as insignificant alongside the work of Sumarokov, he could not possibly have realised the effect of his efforts. They were, however, among those works which, although lacking any great intrinsic merit, nevertheless contain vital yeasts which can work in a literary culture. Some of Novikov's nervous impulses in his periodical papers seem to have grown into the strong sinews of Russian literature.

4

Imperial patronage (1770–3)

The greatest modern Criticks have laid it down as a Rule, That an heroick Poem should be founded upon some important Precept of Morality, adapted to the Constitution of the Country in which the Poet writes.

The Spectator

A new posting: the College of Foreign Affairs

With the end of the *Tattler*, the trifling had, for the meantime, to stop; Novikov re-entered state service as a translator in the College of Foreign Affairs. This did not mean, however, that he had abandoned literary life, for in November 1770 he applied to the Academy of Sciences for permission to print a translation of Voltaire's *Sur la guerre des Russes contre les Turcs* which appeared in the following year.[1] Although the translation was anonymous, it is possible that Novikov himself was the translator. That he did translate from the French at this time seems to be proven by a recently discovered document noting the receipt for publication in 1772 of his abridged translation of *Variétés d'un philosophe provincial, par mr. Ch... le jeun.*[2] While dispelling the legend of his ignorance of foreign languages, this choice of an anti-Voltairean work for translation also corrects the view of Novikov as a constant, resolute supporter of the radical Enlightenment. But his work in the College of Foreign Affairs was no doubt only nominally that of translator. During the next two years he was to set about collecting the material which was eventually published as his *Ancient Russian Library* and *Essay at an Historical Dictionary of Russian Writers*. Since these labours must have taken up the whole of his time, his posting must have been an arrangement by which Catherine could exploit a young literary man's considerable energies. Coming so soon after the supposed bitter quarrel between *All Sorts* and the *Drone*, Catherine's active encouragement of Novikov in this new venture has to be explained away. It has been suggested that the empress steered Novikov's interests towards ancient historical documents in order to divert him from his magazines with their supposedly radical stand.[3] This view, however, implies that Catherine believed that rummaging in the archives was of no account and merely a suitable means of neutralising an alert mind. But in 1770, it was precisely the writing of Russian history that had captured Catherine's imagination: this was the latest literary enthusiasm that followed the *philosophe* treatise of the *Nakaz* and the satirical journals.

What had excited her interest was the appearance in Paris of an uncomplimentary portrayal of the Russian Empire by the Abbé Chappe d'Auteroche at the time when her propagandist *Nakaz* was making its way into Western Europe. The empress, understandably enraged by this untimely coincidence, attempted to blacken the Abbé's name; but, having failed to find evidence which would show him to be an incompetent astronomer (for he had journeyed to Siberia in order to observe a solar eclipse), she had to content herself with the publishing in Holland of her anonymous *Antidote; ou examen du mauvais livre intitulé Voyage en Siberie fait en 1761*.[4] But this correction was not enough. The outside world had to be shown that Russia had a history. There is a tradition that G.F. Müller was first approached to write a history of Russia, but he declined on account of his age and recommended Prince M.M. Shcherbatov.[5] And so early in 1770 Catherine took a decision which went against the traditions of the Russian state. Until then, state documents, whatever their antiquity, were not accessible to historians; they were regarded as state secrets. But in January 1770 written permission was given for Shcherbatov to be allowed access to the Moscow archives of the College of Foreign Affairs which contained state and church documents dating from the middle of the thirteenth century as well as diplomatic correspondence. Although Shcherbatov's commission was to write a *History of Russia*, it must have been brought home to him that there was a need for the archival material to be published separately, not only as sources for other writers, but as a demonstration of the riches of Russia's historical heritage.

If one cast around for candidates for this task in 1770, then Novikov must have been a natural choice. Not only would Shcherbatov have recalled his personal qualities from his work in the Legislative Commission, but Novikov had subsequently given hints of the academic cast of his mind in his journals and had shown his readiness to respond positively to Catherine's literary initiatives. A decision having been taken to entrust Novikov with the work, it would have been natural for him to be officially attached to the College of Foreign Affairs. Here he enjoyed the full confidence of the authorities. Even such a highly placed personage as Shcherbatov had required an order in writing from the empress to gain entry to the archives. Yet Novikov was readily given access, through Kozitsky, to the empress's private library in the Winter Palace, and ranged far and wide in search of material. Documents came to him from the Moscow archives of the College of Foreign Affairs and the Razryadnyy archives through Shcherbatov and Gerhard Müller; he combed the libraries of the Academy of Sciences, the Patriarchate, the Kremlin Cathedral of the Annunciation, the Kiev Pecherskaya Monastery, as well as the private libraries of people such as P. N. Trubetskoy, S. D. Kantemir, P. S. Potemkin and N. I. Neplyuyev, *Ober-Prokurator* of the Senate.[6] The organising mind, so apparent in the firm imposition of a meaningful structure on miscellaneous pieces in the weeklies, was now put to bringing order into this accumulation of material.

A biographical dictionary of Russian writers

If Europe had to be shown that Russia had a history, then she, and indeed Russia herself, had also to be shown that the Russians had a national literature. One attempt had already been made, it is true, in an article, 'Nachricht von einigen russischen Schriftstellern' which had appeared in the Leipzig journal *Neue Bibliothek der schönen Wissenschaften und freyen Künste* towards the end of 1768. The hitherto unidentified 'Russian traveller' who wrote this account of Russian letters may be seen as countering Chappe d'Auteroche's strictures.[7] But for Novikov the response had been insufficient: he considered the Leipzig account to be unbalanced, unjust, presenting outsiders with a false picture. The *Essay at an Historical Dictionary of Russian Writers* which Novikov now began to prepare was his way of defending his own view of Russian literature from that misrepresentation.[8] In his preface to the *Essay* he was to stress that he had been prompted to undertake the work chiefly as a reaction to the 'Nachricht', although he was also aware that Russia lacked the sort of biographical dictionaries which preserved the memory of writers in Western Europe.[9] The preparation of such a work demonstrating the extent and vigour of Russia's literary culture at this time was not easy, since Novikov had few written sources to draw on apart from the histories of Shcherbatov and Tatishchev. He had reason to sympathise with the anonymous writer of the 'Nachricht' for being defeated by his task, and stressed in the eventual title that his own corrective work could only be an *Essay*. Nevertheless, Novikov, secure in his official post and having easy access to libraries and archives, was well placed to glean literary documents as well as to locate historical ones. But written material was sparse: he had to rely mainly on his own observations, acquaintanceships and on handed-down reminiscences which he called 'literary traditions'.

Given the circumstances, Novikov managed to produce an excellent reference work which is still a useful source of information on the writers of eighteenth-century Russia, for of the *Essay*'s 317 entries about a third were notes on his contemporaries. The scope of the work was extended by the inclusion of a large number of ecclesiastical writers alongside the secular ones, their inclusion doubtless making for a truer reflection of the range of Russian letters. As a dictionary, the work aimed to be primarily a work of reference rather than one of critical pretensions, but nevertheless Novikov was discriminating in the collation of his material. Articles on the established giants of literature – Kantemir, Lomonosov, Trediakovsky, Prokŏpovich – ran to a number of pages and were accompanied by a fairly full biography, while two or three lines were considered sufficient for unpublished authors. Echoes of the critical positions taken by Novikov in his satirical magazines continued to resound in the *Essay*, and indeed it is the prominent position accorded Lukin by the Leipzig article that may have led Novikov to correct its lack of balance. Thus, the opinion expressed by some that Vasiliy Petrov could be a 'second Lomonosov' was gently questioned, while the collaborators of Novikov's journals, young writers who shared his general views and moved in his society – Fonvizin, Maykov, Emin, Popov, Ablesimov – were fulsomely praised. Among the contemporary writers, of course, Sumarokov was pre-eminent; used as a touchstone of literary taste in the journals, he now figured again as one of the key entries. If foreign conquest was the index of Russia's growing international prestige under Catherine, then the analogous index in the field of literature, Novikov suggested in his preface, was the growing number of translations into foreign languages of original works in Russian. Sumarokov, the correspondent of Voltaire, the one contemporary translated Russian writer, deserved his outstanding place in Novikov's pantheon as a man who made literature conceived in Russian a force in lands of long-standing civilisation.

These two years spent in Russia's libraries and archives, working with historians of the calibre of Müller and Shcherbatov, meeting literary men and drawing reminiscences from them, were crucial in Novikov's career. In his late twenties he stood at the centre of Russia's intellectual life in the knowledge that he was there by virtue of imperial favour and patronage. Yet surprisingly, in April 1772 he turned away from the rigours of his researches to compose another satirical weekly, the *Painter* (Zhivopisets). Once more, however, his pen seemed to have been guided under his sovereign's direction.

Catherine's presence in the 'Painter'

One of the striking features of the *Painter* was its affirmation of a close accord between Novikov and Catherine II. From Catherine's appreciation of the value of publicity had grown a particular relationship between sovereign and writer in Russia. No longer was the Russian writer to be caned at court as had Trediakovsky, the butt of the coarse humour of the Empress Anna and her grandees; no longer was he to be ignominiously thrust aside when considered a nuisance as under the Empress Elizabeth. Now the writer was necessary to help in developing the ambiance of the *philosophes* in Catherine's realm. To bring this new role of the literary man to public notice was plainly in Novikov's interest. His compatriots might well fail to realise that his historical researches and profiles of Russian writers succoured state interests. Only the more literary among them – and they were few – could realise that Novikov, by aligning the genre of the *Drone* as faithfully as he could with that of *All Sorts* and the latter's canonised models, demonstrated that he was composing his journal under the panoply of imperial favour. In his new weekly, he was able to show more directly that Catherine's support for publicist writers was committed and personal.

Early in 1772 performances were given at the Imperial Court Theatre of *Oh, Times*! (O vremya!), a play, based on Gellert's *Betschwester*, by an anonymous author: behind the conventional anonymity, however, stood Catherine herself.[10] So with the *Painter*'s first eulogistic paper, dedicated to the 'unknown writer of the comedy Oh, Times!', Catherine was drawn, even if under a transparent incognito, into Novikov's project. The comedy was, perhaps, partly a response to a new public mood. As the war against the Turks had dragged on without the stirring victories of 1770 having led to a triumphant conclusion, the taste of the Russian reading public for the recital of actualities seemed to pall, and the following year only one supplement to the *St Petersburg News* exceeded 2,000 copies. The exception was significant: 2,444 copies were printed of the one announcing the truce.[11] By the beginning of 1772, not only was the war at an end, but its aftermath, the epidemic of plague which had created turmoil in Moscow in 1771, had run its course. It was a time for diverting amusement. Playfully Catherine pretended that *Oh, Times!* had been written during a stay in Yaroslavl where the anonymous 'author' had sought refuge from the plague.

The satirical comedy was an attack on the vulgar, provincial gentry whom the empress recalled with distaste in her memoirs. Her targets are apparent from the first two scenes. Madam Khanzhakhina, who has the telling name of Bigot and mixes punishments with prayers, condemns herself by relating how out of sorts she is since she has been interrupted in the middle of her religious exercises – fifty prostrations before an icon – by a serf seeking permission to marry. Losing count of her genuflections, Khanzhakhina had flown into a rage, and ordered the serf to be flogged before returning to her devotions.[12] Obscurantism, the ignoble treatment of serfs and crass violence are pilloried as vehemently as ever they were in the satirical weeklies of 1769.[13] *Oh, Times*! gave Novikov an opportunity to make a legitimate claim for the latitude which he had sought in the *Drone* to be frank in his criticisms of social evils. Since the author of *Oh, Times!* was assumed anonymous, it could not be considered mere flattery of the empress for Novikov to eulogise the author and state that the latter was worthy of comparison with Molière in the robustness of his satire. Write satire untrammelled by any fears of retribution from the strong, advised Novikov with some irony. In any case such boldness would not suffer while the wise Catherine ruled for the good of Russia and humankind, he wrote, thus redoubling his flattery: not only did he eulogise the 'anonymous author', but praised Catherine for her patronage of him! Surely, therefore, the author need have no qualms about revealing his true identity, mused the editor of the *Painter*. There might well be 'particular reasons', he assured himself, with tongue in cheek.[14]

The Painter intended to have his brush guided by the author of *Oh, Times!* in depicting the contemporary scene in bold satirical strokes: 'If I am to have success in my enterprise and if my papers bring profit and amusement to my readers, they will be obliged for this not to me, but to you, for without your example, I would not have had the courage to attack vices.'[15]

Soon the *Painter* was fortified not only by Catherine's example but by what appeared to be a contribution from her. For, in its seventh issue, there was a reply to the *Painter*'s request in its first number for a piece from the author of *Oh, Times!* A letter was printed from the author of *Oh, Times!* and of *Mrs Vorchalkina's Nameday*; this play too, allegedly 'written in Yaroslavl', had been composed by Catherine herself.[16] Did Catherine send the letter voluntarily to Novikov or did the latter manage to petition her successfully for a contribution? It is not possible to say; however, the letter may have resulted from some informal collaboration between the two in the composing of the plays. Catherine was never averse to editorial help: G. V. Kozitsky, her literary secretary, was employed to polish and expand her jottings and Novikov might also have been drawn from his historical researches to act with Kozitsky as auxiliary playwright.[17] Certainly the themes of Catherine's plays and those of the *Painter* have much in common. The letter might be another example of Novikov's skill at editorial organisation. A fortnight earlier a black account of life in a Russian village neglected by its squire – the celebrated 'Fragment of a Journey' – was alleged to have led to virulent criticism. The *Painter* made no direct reply. But the 'author' of *Mrs Vorchalkina's Nameday* made a suitable response to any such criticism. He himself, he explained, had been criticised for allowing a gentleman, Firlifyushkov, to be thrashed on stage, on the ground that a nobleman should at all times be exempt from corporal punishment. Such critics were magisterially directed to the contrary advice in the 1649 Code of Laws which remained in force and, in a more peremptory tone, the nobility who complained of their treatment were put in their place: they could not be expected to be treated as nobles should they behave ignobly.

If the first issue of the first part of the *Painter* (the journal consisted of two parts, each containing 26 numbers) had implied a new relationship between Catherine and Russian writers, so did the introductory paper to the second part. A fulsome eulogy of Catherine by a Naval Chaplain recently returned from the Mediterranean expedition was followed by an extract from Frederick the Great's *Matinées royales* under the heading 'On Literary Science' (O slovesnikh naukakh) in which Frederick declared how necessary writers were to a sovereign, for 'they distribute honours and without them it is impossible to acquire any lasting glory'.[18] It was a frank and, to modern eyes, a somewhat naive exposition of the art of public relations, an art generally more effective in ratio to the concealment of its existence. But to tax Frederick with cynicism and impudence in his managing of the writers he patronised is to profit too much from distant hindsight.[19]

This piece, placed so prominently at the beginning of the second part of the *Painter*, affirmed the newly found power of writers in becoming necessary partners to enlightened autocrats. It was Frederick who declared that writers are 'men necessary to the sovereign who wishes to reign autocratically and care for his renown'; it was Frederick who, as a writer, found that matters of state left him little time for the craft and so was obliged to keep at court 'brilliant minds, who will take upon themselves the work of explaining my thoughts'. But, for Frederick, one could read Catherine. The preceding eulogy of the empress encouraged readers to substitute Catherine. If Frederick had entertained d'Alembert, Voltaire and Maupertuis, it was public knowledge that Catherine too enjoyed friendly relations with admiring French *philosophes*; had she not invited Beaumarchais, d'Alembert and Diderot to St Petersburg? The following year Diderot and Grimm would in fact be at her court. Her enthusiasm for the European *philosophes* was matched by her enthusiasm in St Petersburg for Russian letters. Frederick's teasing of authors' susceptibilities can be set aside: the essential point for contemporary readers, and in particular contemporary writers, was his avowal of the importance of the writer's role. What was astonishing for contemporaries was to learn of the special welcome given to d'Alembert, who was invited to Frederick's table, as Diderot was later to be given long personal audiences by Catherine. Diderot, writing to his wife, was particularly struck by the sovereign's condescension to the humble person of a writer: 'I swear to you that the empress, this astonishing woman, does all in her power to come down to my level; but it is at moments like these that I find her ten feet tall.'[20] The piece from Frederick's *Matinées royales* showed the special relationship between writer and ruler; more importantly, it also suggested Novikov's consciousness of the nature of that relationship in which he himself was prepared to play a willing part.

For, if Novikov had contrived to suggest the debt of ruler to publicist, he was also fully aware of the writer's part in the contract. The eulogy from the Naval Chaplain was one of many effusions in praise of Catherine who was continually invoked as a most wise sovereign. An example was a letter from Dominic Diodati, sent from Naples in October 1771 to a Russian who had presented him with a copy of Catherine's *Nakaz*.[21] Diodati (1736–1801) was an Italian archaeologist and, according to Berkov, the copy was sent to him by Kozitsky who had translated the *Nakaz* into Latin.[22] The letter, one of the many enthusiastic responses to Catherine's *Nakaz* in Western Europe, recapitulated the spirit of the document and expressed the hope that Russia would continue to strive for a better world. This last appeal has been seen as veiled criticism of the empress for dismissing the Legislative Commission.[23] More important, however, was the reminder in the letter of the desire for humanity and law which would have no room for cruel serf-owners. Diodati's letter prompted the publication in a later issue of Frederick the Great's positive response to the *Nakaz* in a letter to Catherine, and the introduction to it took pride in the fact that a *philosophe*-monarch had joined in the praise that sovereigns had come to expect from poets and orators.

Novikov evidently continued the tradition of Russia's past poets and orators. The second part of the *Painter* was remarkable for the extent of the homage paid to Catherine from the loyal address with which it began to its close with a triumphal 'Ode to Her Majesty Catherine the Great'. That panegyric had been foreshadowed by 'Verses composed for the occasion when the noble girls of the fourth class, educated in the Novodevichiy–Voskresenskiy Convent, after their nine-year stay in that educational home, made their first appearance in society and took a promenade in the garden of Her Imperial Majesty's Summer Palace on the twentieth of May 1773. This being a day of general promenading in the aforesaid garden', and 'Verses to the ladies of the first class educated in the

Novodevichiy Convent, on their presence for the first time in the garden of Her Imperial Majesty's Summer Residence on May the twentieth in this year of 1773'.[24]

To the poet the symbolism of this promenade of the pupils at the Smol'nyy Convent was obvious:

> As their presence has adorned this garden
> So will the whole land of Russia be adorned.

Not only was the elegant institution a significant example of the court-directed enlightenment to Russian patriots, but a persuasive symbol of the style of Catherine's rule to the outside world. Often, and apparently with unfailing effect, its pupils were shown off to important visitors from abroad, such as Denis Diderot[25] and William Coxe.[26] A call at the Couvent des Demoiselles was as likely for the eighteenth-century traveller as a visit to a Pioneers' Palace for a twentieth-century tourist.

Affirming his legitimate role in relation to the sovereign was plainly to Novikov's own personal advantage. It also allowed him to buttress his bold criticisms of Russian society by invoking the presence of the empress. Yet most of Novikov's Russian biographers have persisted in maintaining that his praise of Catherine was a sham.[27] Far from being fully confident of imperial support for his new venture in the spring of 1772, they argue, Novikov was fearful of Catherine's displeasure. All the literary by-play with the 'author of *Oh, Times!*' was merely a wary move to ward off trouble.[28] Much has been made of the Painter's piece of advice to himself not to part company with the fair lady Caution. It has been claimed that here Novikov, seen as an 'oppositionist' writer, showed his apprehension of a possible exercise of imperial authority against the magazine. Yet, surely, if he had intended to pursue a policy of caution, he would not have gaily flaunted that intent. Caution would have been far more effective for Novikov if kept concealed to himself.

Why then did Novikov have to mention caution? From where did the threats to the *Painter* come? Again and again during later issues the magazine made reference to its own caution, drew attention in footnotes to passages warily omitted for fear of giving offence and published warnings from well-disposed correspondents of public anger. The source of these threats, however, was clearly not the government; they came rather from the same disgruntled squireens who had earlier objected to the *Drone* and had taken exception to the beating of Firlifyushkov in Catherine's own *Mrs Vorchkalina's Nameday*. The implication of all this was plain: if Novikov had to be cautious, he had to beware of the same people as Catherine. One must conclude that the display of 'caution' was an ironic pretence.

So often did the *Painter* flaunt its wariness, however, that the reader must have been led to believe that there were in reality many people violently critical of the magazine's tone. Possibly Novikov had heard mutterings about his satire. But there is no evidence anywhere outside the pages of the *Painter* that such displeasure was even voiced. Indeed, those resentful of the government's attempts to change social attitudes were more likely to rest inarticulate in dumb apathy. If they were given a voice to squeal their protests, it was first the *Drone* and then more extensively the *Painter* that gave them that voice. It is a fascinating feature of the *Painter* that it was Novikov himself – and not his opponents – who gave articulation to the backwoodsmen's latent animosity to cultural change. It was the Painter that engraved the face of their obduracy, and made them recognisable.

An ethical 'Painter'

There were literary reasons, of course, for suggesting a vehement critical reaction from political foes. Without them, satire would have tended to hang limply in a void. And, as before, reactionaries were portrayed as being ignorant of literary fashion and therefore blind to the convention of fictional editor. The first reference to Caution was impudently brandished in the face of malicious literary opponents; for the editorial *persona* of the Painter, as his predecessors, set about the old literary adversaries, Lukin and Petrov, recalled the controversy on the nature of satire and rejected the practitioners of the *drame bourgeois*.[29]

Novikov's confidence in official approval was reflected in a change in the nature of the editorial *persona*. Although the *Painter* was manifestly a linear descendant of the *Drone*, the move away from the fictitious presiding editor, already discernible in the *Tattler*, was now even more marked. Little was given about the character of the Painter, apart from the crucial information that he was a non-noble craftsman. Letters would still be dutifully sent to the Painter and he would still be addressed as an authority; he would still pontificate and comment. But this seemed due mainly to the momentum of a traditional genre. Novikov no longer seemed to wish to create a whirligig of contemporary society as in the *Drone*. Characters appeared, it is true, in particular the fops with their colourful slang; but they appeared more as isolated sitters to be satirised rather than creatures in the living fabric of a social commentary. Perhaps the need for the genre, the necessity of creating an anchored self-image for the shifting ranks of Russian society, was not felt to be so pressing by 1772. Confident of imperial support, Novikov must also have felt less need to shield himself behind the editorial *persona*.

In his Painter, it is not with the man that Novikov was concerned, but with his craft. Although the force of the *Drone*'s *persona* might have waned, his picture-making retained its appeal. The subjects of the portraiture remained unchanged: the *Painter* attacked the ignorant fop, Khudovospitannik (Ill-bred) – a bully, Krivosud (Crookedcourt) – a rapacious magistrate, Shchegolikha (Miss Fop), Molokosos (Milksucker) – a spoilt child, Volokita (Dandy), characterised by his fashionable, French-inspired slang.

What sort of art did the Painter employ? Novikov must have had in mind a painter in words who would be the equivalent of engravers of the day, such as Daniel Chodewicki and William Hogarth. The latter's fame had already penetrated to Russia, and an English observer writing in 1785 noted that: 'I am credibly informed that the Empress of Russia has expressed uncommon pleasure in examining such genuine representations of English manners.'[30] Novikov's editor would be what the eighteenth century called 'an ethical Painter'. Certainly a celebrated piece in the *Painter*'s fifth issue could have been a paraphrase of a contemporary engraving.

'A Fragment of a Journey to *** by I*** T***' described a village where the serfs were tyrannised by their owner; it was a curious mixture, in the Hogarth manner, of realistic detail and allegorical stylisation to which was added a dash of sentimentalism. The description of three abandoned infants discovered in a pigsty of a peasant's hut, even if highly coloured, was direct enough:

> The clinging odour from all sorts of filth, the extreme heat and the buzz of an innumerable number of flies drove me away but the wailing of three abandoned infants restrained me. I hastened to render aid to these unhappy creatures. On approaching the cradle roped to poles in which the

abandoned infants were lying without any care, I saw that one had lost his milk teat; I gave it back and he was soothed. The second was found with his face in a pillow of coarsest sack-cloth filled with straw; I turned him over immediately and saw that without swift aid he would have lost his life, for not only had he turned blue, but black, and was in the hands of death; soon he too was soothed. On going to the third I saw that he was unswaddled, a multitude of flies covered his face and body and mercilessly tortured this child; the straw on which he lay also pricked him and he gave forth piercing cries. I gave succour to this one too, drove off all the flies, swaddled him in other clothes, dry, if unclean, which were hanging in the hut, smoothed down the straw which he had kicked up in his struggles; and he too fell silent.[31]

Yet it must be with a sense of shock that a present-day reader finds that these three peasant waifs have been neatly arranged as allegorical figures. The first, explained the narrator, cried out for food, the second for his life to be spared and the third for an end to torture. They were part of a stylised emblematic landscape where the traveller saw POVERTY and SLAVERY in the shape of peasants whose home was called RUINATION (Razorennaya). Weeping profusely and falling into a dead faint, the traveller's reaction was that of a man on a sentimental journey, who began to describe the village of Ruination 'with a great shudder of my sensitive heart' and showed how his sensibility made him a 'good gentleman' by comforting the village children and dispelling the fear they had of his red coat. It was this final picture of the good, humane squire, his heart shuddering with sensibility and distributing pennies and pies to grateful peasant children, that Novikov most probably aimed to leave in his readers' minds. This Hogarthian fragment still breathed the spirit of *noblesse oblige*. It was still the image of the true nobleman, noble in heart and deed, that Novikov wished to hold up. His organising skill was still at work: the series of vignettes in the previous two numbers that depicted the leisured classes unrefined by enlightenment led up to this sharp engraving showing the results of ignorance – bestiality and the ignoble tyrant.

If the 'Fragment of a Journey' is the plainest example of the Painter's caustic portrayal of the dark side of Russian society, then the supposed reaction to it is an excellent illustration of Novikov's care in suggesting the indignant disapproval that his criticism would evoke. But he did more than merely point to the indignation. He produced an analysis of the latent opposition to social criticisms and, by implication, to social reforms. The foundation of this reaction was a sense of corporate solidarity in the nobility which would not allow any suggestion that reprobate nobles could exist: in the eyes of many conservative Russians, nobility was seen as an inborn, inherited essence, and there could not be, therefore, 'good nobles' and 'bad nobles'. For them, 'The Fragment of a Journey', with its demonstration of an ignoble gentleman, would be subversive. This view was countered in the thirteenth issue by a piece entitled 'An English Promenade' (Angliyskaya progulka), during which the editor was addressed by an honest man who was at a loss to understand 'why some think that this paper [i.e. Paper 5] seems to distress the whole corps of nobility'.[32] Novikov, probably recognising the force of this 'ideological' opposition, made the honest promenader argue reasonably on both economic and moral grounds against caste presumptions. With the other strands in the 'opposition', Novikov was less indulgent. One was its inability to appreciate satire and critical writings because of a lack of culture and literary discernment: 'somewhat bitter for the delicate tastes of noble ignoramuses' was Novikov's ironical postscript to the 'Fragment of a Journey'.[33] (We may recall that the *Drone* in similar fashion had referred to the way in which 'English' salt was not to the taste of Russians, English satire being remarkable in the Russians' view for its purgative quality).[34] The other strand was an intolerance, only recently mitigated by the enthroned wisdom of Catherine: another point made by the postscript to the 'Fragment of a Journey' was that the piece would not have seen the light of day 'when our minds and hearts were infected by the French nation', that is, presumably, under the Gallomanic Empress Elizabeth.

The 'English Promenade' not only brought out into the open the resentment of conservative nobles alarmed at the attack on their corporate privilege, but also revealed the unease of those moderate, well-disposed nobles who were troubled because they could not understand the purpose of the fifth paper. Consequently, during his talk with the Painter, his honest friend attempted to establish the purpose of such pieces in preparation for the continuation of the 'Fragment of a Journey'. The main body of the nobility, he explained, had not been besmirched by the portrayal of a squire exploiting his noble privileges in an evil way. Such men existed, and their treatment of their serfs meant a loss to the state in production. To the economic argument was added the human one: in fact, the censuring of inhumanity exalted the virtuous, philanthropic nobles. The aim of the satire, therefore, was to purify the corps of nobility and exalt those who would not be averse to the honest man's discourse, 'the truly noble noblemen' (*dvoryane istinno blagorodnyye*). The social paragon, suggested by the *Drone*, was firmly drawn by the *Painter*.

The sifting of foreign influences

As the issues of the *Painter* appeared, the reader was made aware of the peculiar position of the Russian elite, supported by Western example on the one side, but ever threatened on the other by the swamp of provincial obscurantism. Both these pressures on the truly noble man were explored by Novikov. The 'English Promenade', Diodati's letter from Naples, the references to Frederick the Great, extensive translations from Boileau's satires – all these stressed that the new outlook was guided by Western Europe. But it is apparent in the *Painter* that Novikov – as a result perhaps of the growing national consciousness fostered by his historical researches – did not accept foreign precepts without sifting them carefully. There are signs of a growing discrimination for cultural importations. No longer was it merely a matter of the amused twitting of the taste for French frivolities, although one still finds a 'news item', such as the one informing readers of a French card-sharping school where the training was *gratis* on condition that pupils practised with ready cash.[35] There was a sharper denunciation of the blind passion for things foreign and for foreigners. A recent example had been the enthusiastic welcome given to a troupe of English players on tour in St Petersburg in 1770–3 with performances of comedies by Suzanne Saint-Livre, Coolman, Murphy and Shakespeare's *Othello*, to which a Rake portrayed in the *Painter*'s fourth number had devoted every Sunday. However enthusiastic the indiscriminate response of the Rake with his Frenchified speech, the honest man of the 'English Promenade' was more critical and was pained that Russian actors, comparable with the best English actors and actresses, should be overlooked in favour of 'the stumbling provincial English players'.

The spread of English literary influences had been reflected by *All Sorts* and its imitators: in the case of the *Drone* the precise character of the English model had been clearly understood and exploited by Novikov. Now he reflected the growing awareness by Russians of the advance of English manners at the expense of the French. The postscript to the 'Fragment', for example, would not have been published '... at that time when our minds and hearts were infected by the French nation'; that time, it was stressed, was in the past. The honest promenader was more frank: 'The French have been replaced by the English: now women and men strive with all their might to take something from the English; everything English now appears good, charming and constantly enraptures us.'[36] Here then was the moment when Gallomania began to cede to Anglomania. What pained the honest promenader was the lack of discrimination in both forms of mania. While admitting that the French and English had much good in them, he maintained that 'We called French impudence a noble liberty, and now English coarseness is termed greatness of spirit.'

What good did Novikov see in English influence? His jealousy of the licence allowed to English satirists would be borne out by the honest promenader's noting that in England 'noblemen are criticised as well as commoners', and that the 'Fragment of a Journey' should be appreciated by those with cosmopolitan tastes since it is 'written in the English taste'. It has been argued that the tendency in the 'Promenade' to limit the force of the 'Fragment' shows that 'Novikov linked a certain temperance in political struggles with the idea of "English"'.[37] Quite the reverse: England for Novikov was a land where vehement controversy was possible, where satire had a saltiness which Russians – regrettably, he suggested – found hard to stomach. And this view was underlined by Novikov in his show of suppressing some of the discourse in the 'English Promenade'; some remarks of the promenader were obviously too salty to be served up to the *Painter*'s readers.

One aspect of the interest in English taste was certainly reflected in the 'English Promenade' – the glimmerings of sentimentalism. To have made the 'Fragment of a Journey' fashionable, said the promenader, it should have been given the title, 'A Journey Written in the English Taste': 'Oh, times! Oh, manners! said this gentleman with a sigh' added the *Painter*, indicating with a pathetic flourish that sensibility was involved. This was possibly an early, if veiled, reference in Russian literature to a work that was to exert a peculiar fascination over Russian writers in the future, Lawrence Sterne's *Sentimental Journey*. Even if its first Russian translation did not appear until 1779 the work, published originally in 1768, had been swiftly translated into French and German. It seems very likely that Novikov, moving in literary circles responsive to any contemporary movements in European literature, should have been aware that the 'Fragment of a Journey' could be given the title of 'A Journey Written in the English Taste' – not as a formalist tag, but as an attempt to give a serious characterisation of the piece. One characteristic that the title would draw attention to would be its outspokenness; another would be its sentimental narrator. Sterne was not understood as a wayward, humorous eccentric by his continental admirers, but as a man professing a philosophy of the heart; his appeal would not be through quiet laughter, but through ready tears. If there is the shadow of Sterne in the 'Fragment' (and the use of the word 'Fragment' (Otryvok) may well be a reflection of the characteristic fragmentariness of Sterne's view which seized on the haphazard moments of life) it was not the jovial Englishman, but the continental Sterne, that cast that shadow.

Sensibility at this time could be merely a literary mannerism without any distinct purpose, as in the *Drone*'s 'Farewell to my Readers'.[38] Sensibility's purposes were many, as Pypin rightly indicated when attempting to define the sentimentalism of Karamzin, a future protégé of Novikov: sensibility could lead to lachrymose meditation, pietism or stormy social protest.[39] If we look for a purpose, a content to the 'sentimentalism' of the 'Fragment', then it is surely in that declaration of the 'emotional optimism' which Pypin recognised in Karamzin: the 'Fragment' ended with the picture of a good noble man, comforting poor children, and a serf crying, 'come here lads, this is not our squire, this is a good squire, he gives away money and does not bully!' It was the good heart that had been affronted by the sufferings of the peasant children; but it was also the emotions of the good heart – and here was the optimism – that had prompted the true noble man to remove those sufferings. For the first time perhaps, there was a sign in the journals that Novikov would move in the direction of the emotional optimistic pietism of Russian freemasonry.

In his correspondence with Lavater, Karamzin related the impression made on him by a certain worthy man who had opened his eyes so that he became aware of his own unhappy condition.[40] This worthy man is generally accepted to be Ivan P. Turgenev, who brought Karamzin back in 1784 from Simbirsk to Moscow where he was to spend four years in the Friendly Society, a Novikov-inspired circle. Now could the I*** T*** who had written the 'Fragment' be Ivan Turgenev who was twenty at this time? This was suggested by Nezelenov,[41] but was rejected by Semennikov partly on the grounds that Turgenev was known not as a writer but as a translator.[42] However, claiming Turgenev as primarily a translator in a way strengthens the case for seeing him as the author of this piece imitating 'the English taste'. An added argument for seeing Ivan Turgenev under the initials I. T. is that in his journal Novikov had customarily indicated the authorship of various pieces by the initials of their authors. But no conclusive case can be made out. Ascribing the authorship of the 'Fragment' has been a guessing game for over a century, and is likely to remain so in the absence of any documentary proof. Novikov himself and Alexander Radishchev, the future author of *A Journey from St Petersburg to Moscow*, are the main candidates, but strong persuasive arguments have been put forward to reject both claims.[43] In the absence of any convincing arguments for the authorship of either, then the candidature of Ivan Turgenev should be restored. After all, Turgenev was soon to be one of Novikov's closest friends. Historically too, it makes greater sense to have the young future freemason and philanthropist as the writer of the touching and somewhat naive 'Fragment', with its undertow of that 'emotional optimism' that would animate the Russian freemasons and captivate the young Karamzin.

The Falaley letters

Although Novikov's powers of editorial organisation had been manifest in the *Drone*, no single point in the first magazines had been as dynamic as the 'Fragment of a Journey' which gathered around it so many allusions to the social attitudes and concerns of the day. And Novikov's placing of his material made it plain that he was illustrating Catherine's own attitudes to serfdom and the nobility, and showing how the philanthropic impulses of the first years of her reign had been frustrated by entrenched conservative attitudes.

A second dynamic point around which the miscellaneous pieces of the *Painter* crystallised was the entertaining series of letters to one Falaley Trifonovich, son of an obscurantist provincial nobleman. As with the 'Fragment', the identity of their author has been the subject of considerable dispute. Denis Fonvizin is the most favoured contender, but the claims of M. I. Popov and Novikov himself have also been advanced.[44]

Even the Falaley letters, although they form an independent cycle, are related back initially to the 'Fragment'. The provincial nobleman expressed his anger at certain magazines which his neighbour Bryuzhzhalov (Grumpy) had brought to him:

> What's up with you Falaleyushka, can all the noblemen be out of their minds, what are they looking for – I would not leave the devil with one rib alive. What sort of painter is that who has appeared among you, some infidel German no doubt, for an Orthodox Christian would not have written that. He says that country landowners torture their peasants, and calls them tyrants, and the accursed fellow does not even know that in ancient days tyrants were the unchristened ones and tortured the saints: take a look yourself into the Cheti Minei [these were works of edifying reading containing the lives of the saints] and you'll see our peasants are not saints, so how can we be tyrants?[45]

With this black logic, the obscurantist backwoodsman was ridiculed, as was the Drone's uncle in the earlier magazine. The two indeed have a great deal in common – even in their bigoted reaction to the arrival of the literature of the enlightenment on their estates: the Drone's uncle was deeply affronted by the young procurator's fables which were published in the *Drone*, as was Falaley's father by the publication of the 'Fragment of a Journey'. Just like the uncle, Falaley's father showed his obscurantism by begging his son to remain devoted to the ancestral church calendars, while bewaring of rapacious priests who had despoiled his simple grandfather. A glimpse of the education of young girls was given; Falaley was told that now his sister Varya was fifteen, she had begun to have reading lessons with the village priest in preparation for her impending marriage. Obscurantism was compounded by a zealous xenophobia: Falaley was warned not to have any dealings with the *nemtsy*, the infidel Westernisers, for intercourse with them would inevitably lead to the loss of his soul. The *Kormchaya Kniga* – the code of church and civil laws which had directed the ecclesiastical courts in Muscovy – still held the allegiance of Falaley's father and it spelt out damnation for those who travelled abroad and made acquaintance with foreigners. Yet now, bewailed Trifon, noblemen were free to travel abroad – a direct reference to the concession to the nobles which had formed part of their emancipation in 1762. If

Trifon regretted the passing of the power of the church, he regretted even more the growing strength and spread of secular power and secular laws which seemed to him to make a mockery of the 'so-called emancipation of the Russian nobles in 1762'. New laws had forbidden the profitable unlicensed distilling of vodka, forbidden the annexation of neighbouring land by force, forbidden bribery, forbidden usury. There was a hint that the peasants, as the only source of wealth remaining to the country landowner, suffered as a result, for Trifon complained, 'and there is not much profit in your peasants even if you skin them alive'.

Even biblical authority was cited to justify their destitution and oppression:

> And in holy scripture, it is stated: 'Bear each other's burdens and fulfil Christ's law'; they work for us, and we whip them if they become lazy, so we are equal – and that is why they are peasants: that is their job, to work without rest. Given emancipation, they would not know what to undertake. This is what we have come to, only I shall not countenance it, let him [i.e. the Painter] speak as much nonsense as he wants, but I know how to deal with peasants . . .

and here the *Painter* broke off, explaining in a footnote that he had cut from the letter, 'opinions insulting to humanity'. Since this was written on the eve of the Pugachev rebellion, a peasant revolt springing from a long tradition of such *jacquerie* but also having some of the distinct features of a consciously class revolt, it is tempting to see Novikov reflecting the disaffections of the serfs.

But again in this letter from Trifon to his son, the point of the satire is aimed not at the iniquity of the institution of serfdom, but at the ignoble nobleman whose nobility is annulled by his inhumanity. Where there is oppression under Khudovospitannik (Ill-bred) there is always hope of a happy peasantry under Well-bred; the village of Razorennaya (Ruination) led I. T. on to the happy village of Blagopoluchnaya (Prosperity) with its good nobleman. Here alongside the cruel Trifon lived a truly grand seigneur, a model serf-owner. Readers left an illusory world to meet none other than Catherine's favourite Grigoriy Orlov. Truly noble in his attitude to serfs, he – and Trifon considered his behaviour shameful – exacted money dues of a mere rouble and a half from his serfs, so that 'the peasants are rich and having no cares live a richer life than some noblemen . . .'[46] The institution of serfdom clearly did not concern Novikov: given enlightenment and a good heart, noblemen could follow the example of Orlov and enable their serfs to be happy.

Orlov was further praised in the following issue by 'a certain clergyman in Moscow' who has been identified as Archbishop Ambrose (1742–1818) who in 1771 was Prefect of the Moscow Academy.[47] Extolled for his patriotism, philanthropy and heroism worthy of a 'true Christian' and 'son of the fatherland', his part in succouring Moscow during the epidemic of 1771 was remembered. Of great significance again was the positioning of the letter. It might have appeared from the mocking of Trifon's hypocrisy and obscurantism that the *Painter* was anti-clerical. The letter balanced the picture; while castigating obscurantist excesses, the *Painter* demonstrated that the enlightened church hierarchy firmly approved of this painter of social icons for whom the faces of the 'true Christian' and the enlightened 'son of the fatherland' were identical. This was the first hint of Novikov's sympathy with the reformist-minded church hierarchy, which would become more apparent with the passage of time.

Trifon's advice to his son was to flee the reformist Sodom and Gomorrah, resign from service and return home where his dogs Skosyr' and Naletka were still alive. It is a cruel satirical stroke at the end of the letter, this picture of Falaley's curs, 'Dandy' and 'Swoop', who are treated by the mother with all the affection which the peasants lack. And it is this touch that suggests Fonvizin might well be the author of the piece, ever ready as he was in his plays to introduce a bestiary into which his satirical figures were drawn. Swoop still figured in Trifon's second letter, informing Falaley of the bitch's death in the same breath as the news that his mother was on her deathbed. Both would be missed: but at least the bitch had the advantage that she had left a litter of pups. To replace his wife Trifon now expected a daughter-in-law and he implored Falaley to come home to marry the niece of the local *voyevoda*. This match would guarantee the successful conclusion of all litigation by Trifon's clan and would open the way to the seizing of their neighbours' land 'right up to their threshing floors'. Such a delightful prospect had been enthusiastically discussed by Trifon and Uncle Yermolay under Falaley's favourite oak-tree where, as his father fondly recalled, Falaley as a boy used to hang the dogs which were poor at hare coursing and flog the peasants whose dogs had overtaken his own.

Uncle Yermolay's letter to Falaley, which followed in the next number, described the passing of his mother surrounded by sorcerers rubbing shoulders with the priest. The brutality of provincial life was heavily underlined by the satirical bestiary: 'I have only just received the news of this; your father, they say, is howling like a cow. That's how it always is with us: whichever cow died, it was the good milker. When Sidorovna was alive your father used to beat her like a pig, and now she is dead, he weeps as though it were over his favourite horse.' Uncle Yermolay was insistent on the need for Falaley to return to the country where life would be gayer than in St Petersburg; otherwise he should enter the bureaucracy where material advance was possible for the sons of poor noblemen who had been known to enter state service with no serfs and acquire two or three hundred. Particularly recommended by Uncle Yermolay was the College of Economy which in 1764 took charge of the serfs who had been attached to the Russian monasteries. This clearly offered opportunities for personal enrichment which had possibly become a scandal of the day: Uncle Yermolay cited the case – to be kept secret of course! – of 'our Avdul Yeremeyevich' who 'although he did not spend much time with the monastery serfs' managed to marry off all his daughters with magnificent dowries of '10,000 in cash and a village worth about 5,000' and kept enough for himself. If he had not been relieved of his position, Uncle Yermolay continued, then he would have made another fortune during the recent recruiting levies.

The use of recruiting levies by serf-owners to increase their income had already been exposed in the *Drone*'s 'Landowner's Decree' which showed how peasant wrongdoers were supplied to the authorities as recruits and then an extra tax was imposed on the remaining serfs to recompense the serf-owners for the loss of a 'soul'. It was the body of the serfs, therefore, that bore the cost of recruits to the war.[48] In Uncle Yermolay's letter it was not the fact of this practice that the *Painter* wished to highlight as much as the attitude of these degenerate noblemen to the war: for them it was a way of making money. Profiteering in serfs, rather than honour, was the stuff of war for them, and again in their case the *Painter* reversed the image of the 'son of the fatherland'. 'Don't run after honour, dear; honour! honour! Honour is no good without any food' (*khudaya chest', koli nechto budet yest'*) railed Falaley's father at his son in his attempts to persuade him to retire from service and return to the estate. The father would prefer to see his son fit and well even if he had no St George Medal – the Order of St George the Conqueror was established in Russia in 1769 as a reward for military service – for the Knights of St George were often injured in limbs or head, and not only did the country noblemen find the sight of their disfigured sons distasteful, but there was also difficulty in finding them a suitably profitable bride.

After the publication of these letters to Falaley, his Uncle Yermolay, in a letter sent directly to the *Painter* from the village of Kradenovo (Plunder), threatened an action for libel, his honour as a Titular Councillor – a low position in the Table of Ranks – having been impugned.[49] Yermolay repeated an argument which he had overheard – these 'overhead' criticisms of the *Painter* reflected no doubt the common criticisms of the journal – that in writing his pieces the Painter dishonoured all noblemen and the whole noble estate.

The reverse image of the 'son of the fatherland' was clearly shown in this picture of the provincial noblemen who clung to the comfort of their estates, had no heart for Catherine's foreign wars, yet tyrannised their own serfs and children. Enlightened society had its obverse in the submission to archaic church law and the anarchical rule of the strong, a cynical manipulation of bureaucratic posts, the mere scraps of education and an oppressive and jealous clannishness.

Falaley himself, victim though he had been of a bullying father and over-doting mother, had somehow escaped from this nefarious influence; his shame and indignation at his relatives' letters were proof that, as surely as the *Drone*'s Ivanushka, he had broken loose into a new way of life. Falaley, when sending the letters from his father and uncle to the *Painter*, apparently included a fourth letter from himself in reply: this letter, intended to reveal the qualities of Falaley himself to the world, did not appear in the *Painter*. It would be one of the first of many failures in Russian literature to realise the positive hero. Even if a letter did exist from a real Falaley which paraded the qualities of the true nobleman, one feels that the *Painter* showed Novikov's editorial flair in withholding it; for the blackness of the letters to Falaley needed no gloss. Their darkness, by contrast, highlighted the resplendence of the image of the young – and true – noble man.

The 'Painter' looks to the future

First announced in the *St Petersburg News* on 24 March 1772, the *Painter* produced a full year's harvest of 52 weekly issues. It took a little over a year, however, to gather that harvest, for the periodical, like the *Drone*, seems to have found it difficult to appear with regularity; again the 52 'weekly' issues did not reach their conclusion until the end of June or the beginning of July 1773.[50] Profiting from his previous experience, Novikov did not date the numbers so that any disorganisation of the editorial timetable would not be so apparent. Planned, like its predecessor, to run for a nominal year, the *Painter*, with its completion of 52 issues, gives the lie to the common view that it also came to a sudden end through imperial intervention.

But the *Painter*'s last issues suggest that Novikov, tired of his creation, was already looking ahead to new ventures. Gone is the miscellany of social satire and instead a version of Boileau in Ruban's drab Russian garb of iambic hexameters in riming couplets trudges through as many as seven issues. Even this extensive translation did not wholly unbalance the *Painter*, for Boileau could be spoken of in the same breath as the satirical weeklies and a correspondent of the *Painter* wrote: 'Just as Boileau is honoured in France, and Rabener in Germany, so intelligent people here praise *All Sorts*, the *Drone* and your *Painter*, their descendant.'[51] By bending Boileau's satirical shafts to recognisable Russian targets, Ruban attempted to adapt his version to the spirit of the satirical weekly. The insertion of so much Boileau may have indicated that Novikov was pressed for material and time, but it might also have been an indication that Novikov had anticipated a growing enthusiasm for the French classic. Boileau's satires were to be enthusiastically reworked by Russian poets for the next two generations: his Parisian society was to remain a useful paradigm of Russia's. They were much exploited by the Arzamas circle at the beginning of the nineteenth century and Boileau's influence was marked on Pushkin's first printed work 'To My Poet Friend' (Drugu stikhotvortsu).[52] The *Painter* was an early indicator of the telling use that could be made of the French classic in contemporary society.

Novikov was also no doubt glad of a respite from composing his journal at this point. An announcement which followed the lengthy translations revealed that he had embarked on a new venture: he had organised a Society for the Printing of Books. Possibly Ruban's Boileau had been presented as an excellent illustration of the kind of work such a Society could undertake.

5
In search of the Russian reader (1773–5)

Assurément, c'est au XIXe siècle que le principe de nationalités se proclame, que les nationalismes s'affirment: mais ils se préparent au siècle précédent. Qu'il est profond, qu'il est vigoureux, le sentiment obscur qui a précédé l'idée.

Paul Hazard

The Society for the Translation of Foreign Books

Even by its title Novikov's Society for the Printing of Books clearly admitted an association with the Society for the Translation of Foreign Books, founded and financed by Catherine in 1768 with V. Orlov, A. Shuvalov and G. Kozitsky as its directors. By 1772 the latter society had published over forty titles, including extracts from the *Encyclopédie*, Montesquieu and Voltaire. This accounted for the encouraging 'news' from Millionnaya Street (St Petersburg's main thoroughfare and book-trading centre) in the *Painter*'s sixth number of a 'great change in bookselling': whereas previously there had been complaints that there were few serious books of enlightenment available in Russian, now many of the best foreign works had been translated. Two further 'news items' served as a commentary to this intelligence. Moscow reported an epidemic as deadly as the recent outbreak of plague – the spurning of Russian scholars, artists and artisans in favour of foreigners. 'Yaroslavl', however, thanks to its recent output of comedies 'exactly in our manners' would save the Russian gentry from the plague of Gallomania as surely as isolation in that town had saved Russians from disease.

The juxtaposition of these items was intended to cast Catherine in the role of cultural nationalist. However, the setting up of the Society for the Translation of Foreign Books was not the simple product of her pro-Russian sentiments. It was partly a response to a general awareness of the weakening of the hegemony of French culture. The French were themselves aware that their world was changing at this time: in a letter to Falconet who was at St Petersburg in April 1772, Diderot, while praising Catherine, realised with a certain regret the decline of French influence. 'Ah, Falconet my friend, how things have changed for us! We are selling our paintings and sculptures in the midst of peace; Catherine buys them in the midst of war. The sciences, the arts, taste and wisdom climb to the North, and barbarism with its train comes southwards.'[1] Diderot's own painful journey to St Petersburg was, perhaps, a conscious enactment of this progress.

Within the French-speaking culture too there was a growing awareness of other languages and this is nowhere more clearly shown than in a letter carried by Mercier de la Rivière to Falconet from Diderot and delivered in St Petersburg at the end of September 1767.[2] In it he sketched out a grand project which he believed would appeal to the empress. This was for a kind of 'dictionary', compiled by one man or a group of linguists, and it has been suggested that Diderot had in mind a French equivalent of Samuel Johnson's *Dictionary* which had been compiled between 1747 and 1755.[3] The first compelling reason given by Diderot, who had the case of Russia undoubtedly in mind when producing this project 'corresponding to Catherine's views', was the prime need for a civilised nation to have a perfected language. His view was given trenchant expression: 'You do not doubt that whatever its progress in the sciences and the arts, a nation must remain ignorant and almost barbarous as long as its language is imperfect.' He recognised that such a project would be beneficial to an under-developed people in that it would transfer not only technical knowledge but also the necessary concepts of the civilised world through the enriching of the national language. He explained that:

> Such work would produce two significant results at a stroke; firstly to transmit from one people to another the total sum of knowledge acquired in the course of centuries; secondly to enrich the impoverished language of an uncultivated people with all the expressions, and consequently all the exact and precise notions, be it in the sciences or the mechanical or liberal arts, of a rich and widely spoken language of a cultured people.

While Diderot offered to put himself at the service of Catherine by using his contacts with scholars, men of letters and artists to supplement his own considerable lights in this venture, the significant fact is that his final vision was of a Russian version of his labour. It was the Russian language – perfected and expanded –

that would carry his philosophical endeavours into the Russian Empire. 'While I work in French, others will be busy translating into Russian. When I have finished, I will travel to St Petersburg myself to confer with my septuagint.' (The reference was to the seventy Jewish translators said to have made a Greek version of the Old Testament about 270 BC.) 'Through the medium of Latin which will be our lingua franca we will make the translation as close as possible to the original and will publish it all under the auspices of the sovereign.'

The project was not accepted by Catherine; nevertheless it may be suggested that Diderot's views on the vernacular as a force in the transference of the enlightenment and the establishment of culture were taken to heart by Catherine. In establishing her Society for the Translation of Foreign Books she had created her own septuagint.

The Society for the Printing of Books: its philosophy

Through his own society Novikov associated himself with this septuagint, for its first publications were works already translated by the Society for the Translation of Foreign Books. This initiative was praised in the *Painter* by a certain Lyubomudrov (Wisdom-lover), in whose exchange of letters with the editor Novikov elaborated his views on publishing.[4] Significantly Lyubomudrov wrote from Yaroslavl which, apart from its literary connections, was also a main centre of Russian paper manufacture: the correspondent did indeed put as much stress on the economic benefits of the book trade as on its contributions to popular enlightenment. A flourishing book trade under the aegis of the Society, he argued, would be a splendid example of how to form joint stock companies for Russian merchants who were ignorant of the elementary laws of business. Lyubomudrov's keen interest in the economics of the book trade and his grasp of current economic doctrines were a harbinger too of Novikov's future involvement, not only in the book trade itself, but in the publishing of economic journals. Communication, essential for commerce and the national economy, was also viewed by Lyubomudrov as necessary if the ideas of enlightenment were to extirpate errors and prejudices from the state.

In all this the Painter, pretending to hear of the Society for the first time, fully concurred, but he added an important rider to

Lyubomudrov's arguments: printing books was not enough – means must be found to distribute them throughout the country. Here Novikov was already intimating another interest which he would later develop – the distribution of books by means of a network of allied shops. Such distribution was for the moment unprofitable, since, as the Painter explained, a book as it passed through the hands of middlemen could more than triple in price on its way to the Ukraine from St Petersburg. Novikov wished to spread the book-reading habit and enlightenment to provincial Russia (this might be a third reason for establishing Lyubomudrov's home at Yaroslavl), but, as always, the philanthropic impulse was tempered by sound business sense. Provincial Russia was seen by the *Painter* as a large reservoir of captive book-readers: not for them the freedom of choice which allowed the society of the capital to attend shows, amusements and routs at the expense of reading. Most important of all, the provincial nobles and merchants did not possess the French language, that veneer of enlightenment which would tend to distract them from Russian culture: the education of the metropolis, 'our enlightenment' as the *Painter* ironically called it, did not sell Russian books in Millionnaya Street: 'our enlightenment, or, rather, the blind attachment to French books, does not permit the buying of Russian ones'.[5]

Publishing had been for Novikov partly a means of attacking the rampant Gallomania and buttressing the cultural nationalism which his 'official' work at the College of Foreign Affairs fostered. These considerations were now strengthened by sound commercial logic. There is danger in over-stressing one side or another of Novikov's impulses. One is truer to the complete man in seeing his publisher's philosophy as an intuitive and dynamic amalgam of hard-headed commercialism and national cultural pride, catalysed by an awareness of an enlightened elite.

In its 'reply' to Lyubomudrov, the *Painter* again took great pains to stress that the new Society would be a helpmate to the empress' Society. The question did arise as to why a separate Society should be necessary. Was not the formation of a new Society an implied criticism of the work of the existing one, even taking into account the difference in their expressed aims of 'printing' and 'translating'? The formation of Novikov's Society by a group of private citizens has been seen as of great significance in being a demonstrative act of independence from the autocrat.[6] But Novikov could not have aimed to create an independent social group in any politically conscious way; although it is undeniable that an independent social consciousness was an inevitable by-product of a society dealing in ideas, such as the Society for the Printing of Books. The private nature of the enterprise described by Lyubomudrov was applauded, but the reason is clear: while the empress could engage in the patronage of literature, she could not be expected to meddle in the book trade. This was a job for private individuals. The conclusion of the *Painter*'s reply made this evident:

> Her Imperial Majesty has instituted a Society for the Translation of Foreign Books into Russian and has set aside annually 5,000 roubles to pay translators for their labours. This one act has brought much benefit: those engaged in translation have gained thereby an honourable and sufficient increase in their incomes, and so have been encouraged to apply themselves to learning much more than by a fixed salary: where there is duty, there is obligation, and learning loves freedom and spreads much more where men think more freely. How much benefit has flowed from books translated under the surveillance of this Society? Dispassionate reader who loves the fatherland, this is well known to you. But how much more benefit should one expect from these books when, by means of trade, they will be brought to the noblemen and burghers living in our distant provinces? But it is private individuals and not the sovereign who must think about the expansion of this trade.[7]

Not all Novikov's friends were happy with his commercial instinct and readiness to step into the book trade. Dating Lyubomudrov's letter 28 February 1773 might well have been a private joke on Novikov's part, for 28 February 1773 was the date of a letter he had received from his friend N. N. Bantysh-Kamensky, an official in the Moscow Archive of the College of Foreign Affairs, in response to the news that Novikov was establishing his Society.[8] 'You are taking on yourself, dear friend', wrote Bantysh-Kamensky, 'a heavy task, you are born for greater and better tasks than these concerns you are embarking on; leave the merchants alone, you supply them with good books . . . '[9] That Novikov's mind at this time was turning to the idea of establishing a network of booksellers in provincial Russia, and that his weekly was being used as a sounding-board for this idea, was confirmed by the *Painter*'s reply in a fortnight's time, in issue No. 20, to a letter from Major-General Yevdokim Alekseyevich Shcherbinin (172?–84), governor of the Slobodsko–Ukrainian province (later Kharkov province) in which the latter outlined his scheme for establishing a press attached to the Kharkov educational institutions. Slobodsko–Ukrainia was a frontier province, not yet fully assimilated into the Empire. The province, military in constitution, was peculiar in that it retained many local privileges and charters, its Cossack regiments being organised into districts and Cossack elders appointed as assistants to the Great Russian Governor.[10] Shcherbinin was important as exercising through his person the imperial presence in the region, unwilling to allow the Cossack chieftains to take part in the elections to the Legislative Commission and supervising those elections closely.[11] He was, therefore, an exemplary figure. If he, a fine example of the *Painter*'s true noble man, were prepared to establish a press on the half-tamed new frontier of the Russian Empire – an act which would be in full concordance with his career – then how much easier it should be to establish a network of presses and book-distributors in the more cultivated part of the Empire!

Again Novikov laid stress on the economic advantages of book-publishing to a country, this time indicating a Western European influence on his publishing philosophy. 'Allow me to explain briefly my thoughts on the benefits flowing from a press in the following words of one of the famous, learned writers of Europe; he says that a press, really, is a sort of manufacture within the state which brings it honour and profit.' Although no source was quoted, certainly this idea of the book trade as an industry helping the economy of the state was well established in the eighteenth century. The common view was that expressed by Diderot in his *Lettre sur le commerce de la librairie*, where he drew attention to the industrial nature of the book trade, 'un échange d'argent contre du papier manufacturé', and argued, on the example of Bayle's *Dictionnaire*, that a work published out of France was to the detriment of the French economy.[12]

In his general approbation of Shcherbinin's intention and the lead given to other educational establishments, Novikov also took care to stress the need to establish a censorship. Here again he drew on the French example: religion, manners and government were the three subjects which should be liable to censorship. 'The general peace of the state and the security of each citizen in particular demand that there should be a prohibition on the publishing of books, filled with refutations of divine law, opposed to the autocracy and fatherland, capable of harming the hearts and minds of young people or changing innocence to wrongdoing.'[13]

In his views on censorship, no less than in his ideas on the cultural and economic advantages of publishing, Novikov was heavily in debt to the current philosophy of the trade in France.[14] Sure in his publisher's philosophy, Novikov explained how the censorship should be farmed out: religious topics to the church, matters of government to the governor himself and manners and morals to the directors of the educational establishments. His acceptance of the reigning view on censorship was, perhaps, regrettable: in retrospect, in view of the eventual repression of Novikov's work and destruction as a man, it is even tragic. What this passage confirms, however, is that Novikov did not drift into his venture with his Typographical Company in the following decade; already in 1773 he demonstrated that he had absorbed the existing European philosophy of publishing and bookselling. The knowledge of his growing expertise in this field had presumably prompted the young retired lieutenant to proffer his advice confidently to the major-general, Governor Shcherbinin.

The Society's members

Although it had been hinted that publishing could be an object lesson to merchants in the workings of joint stock companies, the Printing Society did not develop into one. Partly this was due to Novikov's dominant role. For too long, ever since his production of Mikhail Popov's translations in 1766, he had been an individual publisher. And his journals must be viewed to some extent as a personal attempt to gain the necessary patronage and capital to support larger-scale ventures. Even while composing his journals, he continued, as we have seen, to publish books.

At last, at the beginning of 1773, the journal of the Academy of Sciences duly recorded a decision 'on the printing for Lieutenant Novikov and his society of various books' which carried on their title page, 'with the support of the Society for the Printing of Books'. Novikov was not wholly alone in his venture. If he was its main instigator, an important financial partner was P. K. Khlebnikov, a lover of books who would later help Novikov with his *Morning Light*.[15] Another moving spirit was K. V. Müller, a bookseller who occasionally, as the Academy of Sciences' journals showed, received books printed 'on their society's account' instead of Novikov.[16] Müller, whose bookbindery was in Millionnaya

Street, had been the main agent for the *Painter*, as the third issue of the journal had announced. This seems to have been their first joint enterprise, since both the *Drone* and the *Tattler* had been handled by Wege, whose bookbindery was also in Millionnaya.[17] Novikov must have been satisfied enough with his new trading partner to invite him to be the main selling agent for the new Society's publications, and the two men's commercial alliance was to continue when Novikov later moved to Moscow and centred his activities there.

Since the Academy's journals mention these two only, it was no doubt Novikov and Müller who looked after the practical publishing side of the enterprise, the printing of the books and their distribution. However, the motto engraved on the Society's publications, *Soglasiyem i trudami* (By Concord and Labours), suggested that the purely literary side of the Society's activities depended on the 'allied labours' of those authors and translators whose books were published by the Society. Some of them were no doubt 'those people striving for the most important things' that Bantysh-Kamensky promised to find as supporters for the Society in Moscow.[18] The Society gathered men known to have been close to Novikov and to have had a strong interest in publishing: M. V. Popov, whose work was the first to be published by Novikov; I. A. Dmitrevsky, who was later to play a part in the typographical company established by Ivan Krylov in 1791; Aleksandr Radishchev who, in his *Journey from St Petersburg to Moscow*, was to review the problems of a free press and recall the time when the state was afraid of giving private persons the right to establish printing presses; Mikhail Kheraskov whose St Petersburg house had become a literary salon; I. G. Dolinsky, a graduate of Moscow University and later vice-president of the College of Trade; I. A. Teyl's, who was later recommended by Novikov as a candidate for a masonic lodge in St Petersburg.[19] Indeed some masonic inspiration for the Society was suggested by the device that accompanied the motto *Soglasiyem i trudami* on the title pages of its productions: the empress's monogram shed rays of light on a pyramid topped by two hands clasped in a handshake.[20] However, personal friendship with Novikov and a love of books were reasons enough to make these men supporters of the Society. It would be wrong to assume that they formed a cohesive literary grouping under the banner of the Society in the spirit of the later masonic brotherhoods or the tightly-knit circles at the turn of the century. Nevertheless, the Society must be seen as a stage in the gathering of individual strivings into a collective endeavour.

The Society's achievement: success or failure?

How successful was the Society? Its first publications were *Beverley, a bourgeois tragedy*, translated from Saurin's French version of Moore's *The Gamester* by I. A. Dmitrevsky, and an anonymous *Notes on Ventriloquists* (Vypiski o chrevoveshchatelyakh ili chrevobasnikakh) translated by M. V. Popov: both had had their translations published by Novikov previously. During the first year of its existence the Society managed to produce a dozen books. Most of them were small – under 200 pages in octavo or duodecimo – and the only large-scale multi-volume project was a translation from the Latin of a work by Antonio de Guevara (1480–1545), counsellor and historian to Emperor Charles V and Bishop of Acquitaine; the Russian title read *The Golden Hours of Sovereigns in the style of the Life of the famous Emperor and Most Wise Philosopher Marcus Aurelius*. However, this publication was not completed until the next decade: the Society for the Printing of Books managed to produce only the first two volumes in 1773 and 1774, and the third and fourth were not published until 1780 by Novikov at the University Press in Moscow.

A second multi-volume project had even less success. This was a description of China by Jean Baptiste du Halde (1674–1743) in a translation by I. A. Teyl's. Novikov, whose general aims for the Society had been proclaimed with such faith and enthusiasm in the *Painter*, no doubt saw this work as an example of the serious enlightenment which books could disseminate in Russia. The advertisement for the eight-volume *Geographical, historical, chronological, political and physical description of the Chinese Empire and Chinese Tartary accompanied by various diagrams and engraved figures* in the *St Petersburg News* bore witness to Novikov's hopes.

> The whole world of learning cannot find sufficient praise for this famous work, perfect of its kind, and the Society is convinced that this history in the Russian language will not be any the less worthy of the goodwill of the lovers of literary science, especially since for the first time in our native language there is being published the history of a state with which Russia,

being a neighbour, carries on great trade and is in constant intercourse. Our readers will find in this book a full description of the political, geographical and historical condition of the Chinese Empire.[21]

Once more, voice was given to the conviction that books could assist in developing trade and the national economy. But the hopes were tempered with some obvious commercial qualms about the appeal of a prestige work to be sold at the high price of 2 roubles 50 kopecks a volume, more than twice the price of any other work published by the Society and more than a whole year's subscription to the *Painter*. The Society's advertisement explained:

But since the printing of this History, so profitable to our compatriots, demands much support, the Society has considered it necessary to open a subscription to it, having no doubts that all lovers of literary science, not so much for their own as for the general good, will promote this enterprise. The greater the number of subscribers, the sooner this History will be published.

Concessions were then offered: those subscribing to the eight volumes would be able to buy each volume at a concessionary price of two roubles, while subscribers to the first volume would also receive certain discounts.

The commercial prudence proved to be well founded. Patriotic lovers of literature, solicitous for the good of their fatherland, were not yet prepared to put down their money for a highly priced multi-volume work of serious scholarship. No doubt the metropolitan book-buying public for this type of work could be excused their apathy on the grounds that they could read the work, with perhaps more facility, in the original French. But more disappointing for Novikov must have been the response of the merchant classes in the provinces who lacked any knowledge of French and were considered, as we have seen from the *Painter*, a fruitful and untapped reserve of book-buyers. Not a single subscriber was found in the provinces. Meanwhile, in the metropolis only twenty full subscribers presented themselves, and since Catherine herself ordered six copies for the court, the order amounted to twenty-five full sets. There were twenty-four subscribers to the first volume alone, and since P. K. Khlebnikov (a patron of Novikov and a foremost member of the Society) ordered two copies of the first volume as well as the full set, the total amounted to twenty-five copies. Altogether, therefore, there were fifty copies of the first volume on order to subscribers. What is particularly striking about the subscriptions is that the Society's support came chiefly from the court itself; for, apart from Catherine's own order, many of the others, as Semennikov pointed out, came from courtiers who followed the lead of the empress.[22] Although the lack of a serious book-buying clientele could have placed Novikov in serious financial embarrassment at this stage of his career, at least he could rely on the patronage of the empress.

The declaration that the Printing Society intended to add loyal support to the activities of the Translating Society was carried out in practice. The Society's third publication was the third and fourth volumes of Swift's *Gulliver's Travels*, translated from the French by Yerofey Korzhavin – like Novikov, a translator at the College of Foreign Affairs – and it completed the work embarked upon by the official Society which had published the first two volumes the previous year. That Novikov and K. V. Müller saw book distribution, as well as printing, to be an essential activity of their Society is also proved by their buying of the first two volumes of *Gulliver's Travels* from the Academy of Sciences Press at cost price.[23] Also acquired from the Academy Press on the same terms were the following works originally translated under the auspices of the Society for the Translation of Foreign Books: all remaining copies of a prose translation from a French version of Tasso's *Gerusalemme Liberata* by Mikhailo Popov; all the 300 copies of Henry Fielding's *Amelia* translated 'from the English by Madame Riccoboni and from the French into Russian by the Collegiate translator, Petr von Berg'; and 100 of the 600 copies of *The World Seen in its Aspects: or the Grandeur and Variety of the Fundamental Purposes revealed in nature and in characters, explained by physical and moral illustrations, adorned by language worthy of these subjects: for the improvement of every condition of men, particularly young orators, poets, painters and other artists*, translated from the German by Ivan Khmel'nitsky.

No doubt in the eyes of Novikov the riskiness of his commercial venture was amply compensated by official favour. His relations with the empress were conducted through the intermediary Kozitsky who, still fulfilling his function as Catherine's literary secretary, was the main organiser of her Translation Society. The most revealing example of Catherine's favouring of the Printing Society was her presentation to it of all the 1,200 copies of the second edition of Marmontel's *Bélisaire* published by 'Her Imperial Majesty's Cabinet'. It was not only the munificence of the gift that highlighted Catherine's approval of the Society's activities; it was also a pointedly personal demonstration of favour, since the empress herself had inspired the translation of the work as a pastime during a royal progress along the Volga in 1767 and had herself worked on the collective task of translation with a team consisting of I. P. Yelagin, Z. G. Chernyshev, S. M. Kuzmin, Grigoriy Orlov, D. V. Volkov, A. V. Naryshkin, A. I. Bibikov, V. G. Orlov and Kozitsky, its organising secretary. A resolution in one of the Academy's journals (1773, No. 729, 16 October) records this presentation 'in execution of her most high Imperial Majesty's personal command issued through Collegiate Counsellor Kozitsky' and notes that the sum of 395 roubles 50 kopecks due to the Academy for the printing had been obtained from the Imperial Cabinet. The Society, for its part, presented Catherine with all its publications. Thus on 30 October 1773 Novikov, through Kozitsky,[24] presented to Catherine 'in the name of our Society' the first part of Bishop Guevara's *Golden Hours* which, like many other books published by Novikov at this time, was dedicated to the heir to the Russian throne, Grand Duke Paul, 'whose wisdom and virtues are known to the whole world'.

Despite imperial encouragement, however, the Society was not a notable success, for evidently a buying public for serious works in Russian was not yet in existence. Only a dozen works were published in 1773, and a mere six the following year. The multi-volume projects were not completed: *Golden Hours*, which should have run to six volumes, was discontinued after the second in 1774 and the *Description of China* by du Halde, which should have appeared in two volumes annually, ceased after the first volume in 1774. (A second volume, it is true, was published by Novikov in 1777, but in his personal capacity and not as an agent of the Society.) A further indication of the Society's comparative failure was that a number of works sent by it to the Academy Press were either not printed or were only printed in some three or four years' time after the dissolution of the Society. Among these works were P. Yekimov's translation of Homer, Popov's translation from the French of John Bell's *Travels from St. Petersburgh in Russia to various parts of Asia*, M. Il'insky's translation of Suetonius' *Lives*, Alexander Radishchev's translation of *Officers' Exercises* and Knyazhnin's translations of three of Corneille's tragedies, *Le Cid*, *La Mort de Pompée* and *Cinna* which should have formed the first part of a complete edition of Corneille's tragedies. These three were translated by Knyazhnin for the Society for the Translation of Foreign Books and the Society for the Printing of Books was charged with their publication. Printed by the Academy Press by October 1775, they were then bought by Novikov, who only put them on sale in 1779.

The unwillingness of the Academy's press to print the Society's work was understandable. Finding it difficult to sell its early publications, the Society had insufficient income to pay the press. Therefore, for example, as far as Suetonius' *Lives* and Bell's *Travels* were concerned, the Academy Commission decided in 1776 to reprint the title pages of these volumes and put them on sale in the Academy bookshop until the Society's printing bill had been paid off.[25]

The failure of Novikov's first attempt to found a company must be attributed in the first place to a lack of finance, and an optimist's misjudgement of the magnitude of the task he had set himself. Society as a whole proved to be too under-developed culturally and too unprepared for serious reading. But paradoxically it was the cultural over-development of a certain section of the embryonic Russian intelligentsia that stood in the way of success: those who gave their wholehearted support to the activities of both the Translating and the Printing Society, from the empress down, were well enough able to read European literature, and certainly French literature, in the original. As Pushkin was to complain many years later, their fine liberal education was accursed in that, while opening up Western literature to lively young Russian intelligences, it tore them away from their native language. In this particular instance it surely acted as a barrier to the success of Novikov's Society. There was a possible reading public in the provinces as Novikov had sensed – lively in intelligence but lacking the knowledge of languages which was the key to Europe's cosmopolitan culture. However, the means of book distribution were at this time rudimentary, and the Society lacked the human and financial resources to create a workable book-distribution system.

Against the heavy inertia of the existing situation, Novikov had undoubtedly been sustained in his optimism by the patronage of the empress and her court. The force of this patronage was nowhere made more apparent than in Novikov's despair and sense of loss when it was temporarily removed from him when the court moved to Moscow in January 1775 to celebrate the peace of Kuchuk Kainardzhi. In a letter to Kozitsky on 26 March 1775 Novikov requested him to pass on to Catherine the announcement of a new edition of his *Ancient Russian Library*. 'I cannot give you any news from here other than that the departure of the Court has created such turmoil in my business that I do not know how I shall be able to complete the *Library* this year, for not only are new subscribers not forthcoming but also other books are hardly being sold at all.' Novikov begged Kozitsky to petition the empress to support his new edition: 'Without this help I shall be under an extreme compulsion to abandon all my business uncompleted. What is to be done when my zeal in rendering service to my fatherland is so badly received by my compatriots?'[26]

Although disappointed by his first attempt to organise a publishing company, Novikov did not abandon his vision. Circumstances were to change radically in eleven short years and in 1784 he was to enjoy much greater success with his Typographical Company in Moscow. But the Society for the Printing of Books had undoubtedly been an instructive forerunner of this later enterprise.

The independent publisher

From his own observations Novikov should have had no reason to be sanguine about the success of his Society. Although the 'news from Millionnaya Street', quoted at the beginning of this chapter, had been good in respect of the availability of serious books, it had also been bad. These volumes remained unsold: and sales of *A Thousand and One Nights* continued to exceed those of Sumarokov's works.

This latter fact certainly did not escape Novikov, the private publisher. For at the same time as his involvement with his Society, he continued to publish independently in 1773 and 1774, and the following works appeared: *The Story of Monsieur de la Bédoyère and his wife written by his friend*, an anonymous translation of Baculard d'Arnaud in four volumes; *An Appreciation of the Sovereign Boris Fedorovich Godunov* composed by K. Fiedler (1603), translated from the Latin by Sergey Voronov (1773); a translation from the French of William Walsh's *Aesculapius or the*

Hospital of Fools, that is 'a presentation in conversations of human follies of various sorts', added the Russian title; *A Short Account of Past Pretenders in Russia* by Mikhail Shcherbatov; and the fourth part of Feofan Prokopovich's *Works of Divinity*, a continuation of three volumes which had appeared in 1760, 1761 and 1765 respectively in a large print of 5,000 copies. This work had a preface signed by the initials N. N. – presumably Novikov.

The nature of these publications was very different from those with the imprint of the Society. Introducing Russian readers to the generally accepted European classics such as *Gulliver's Travels* or Goldoni's comedies, and the solid works on classical history, such as Radishchev's translation of Mably's *Observations sur les Grecs*, was the Society's purpose.[27] Propped up by patronage, as it was in the activities of the Society, the enlightened spirit could prevail over mean commercialism. But in Novikov's private ventures the commercial instinct was predominant: in publishing Walsh's *Hospital of Fools* and Baculard d'Arnaud's *Tales*, Novikov was clearly more confident of his appeal to the main Russian reading audience of merchants with their taste for strongly spiced plots and the macabre and outlandish which both Walsh and Baculard d'Arnaud were able to supply. In presenting the latter in particular to Russian readers, Novikov proved that his instinct for what the readers demanded was sound, for before the close of the century thirty-one works by Baculard d'Arnaud had appeared.[28]

In both cases Novikov also appealed to that growing taste for things English which was supplanting French influence. Despite the fact that Baculard d'Arnaud was French, from the time when Denis Fonvizin entitled his translation from the Frenchman *Sidney and Silli, or Virtue and Gratitude, An English Tale* in 1769, he was considered as a purveyor of English tales (ten of the thirty-one works were sub-titled as 'English Tales') whose 'Englishness' consisted of a mingling of the macabre and the sentimental. Many of Baculard d'Arnaud's works were also sub-titled 'historical tales' and this, as well as placing them in line with the tradition of Russian folk 'historical tales', reflected the new European taste for old, unhappy, far-off things. The growing historical consciousness of the citizen in the eighteenth century was, in its vulgar aspect, reflected in the popularity of d'Arnaud's sentimental historicism.

If his choice of Walsh and Baculard d'Arnaud was guided by the predilections of readers obliged to read in Russian, then in selecting his historical titles he chose subjects on which one was obliged by the nature of the subjects to write in Russian. In the first case, the readers had to read Russian through their lack of French; in the second, one read in Russian because the stuff of the book was Russian. Many young educated Russian noblemen must have found it as unnatural to read Mably in Radishchev's Russian, as Tolstoy's Pierre in *War and Peace* was to find it unnatural to use Russian to treat abstractions during his induction into a masonic lodge. This sense of linguistic embarrassment would be removed when the subject was Boris Godunov or the past pretenders to the Russian throne.

It is not that Novikov's interest in the past of his country must be seen as merely stemming from his commercial instinct as a would-be bookseller. But neither must it be ignored. This was a vigorous strand which was interwoven with a genuine concern for one's own history, an apparent need to balance the dissemination of the new experience of the West with an awareness of one's own traditions. Novikov's commercialism was to bring these vague aspirations into the market-place where they could prosper in the rough-and-tumble as surely as the ideas of the Enlightenment prospered through being traded vigorously in the commercial enterprise of the *Encyclopédie*. In a curious way, in his publishing activities of 1773–4 Novikov, by dividing his energies between the Society for the Printing of Books and his own independent publishing, acted out the division of Russian thought into Westernising and Slavophile tendencies in the following century: in the Society, Novikov was a Westerniser, as a private publisher he was a Slavophile.

6

Disillusions and doubts (1774)

... the members of the English Club are besides that fact sons of the fatherland too ...

Tolstoy in *War and Peace*

The 'Bag' (1774)

From the disappointments and strivings of the official and independent publisher sprang his fourth satirical periodical, the *Bag*, announced in the *St Petersburg News* of 8 July 1774. Indeed, the magazine can only be fully understood in the context of Novikov's concurrent tribulations. Experience was forcing him to give deeper consideration to issues which had been to the fore in the preceding magazines, such as the elaboration of the social paragon, linguistic purity and the nature of the Russian national character. Had his present publishing, and his growing understanding of Russia's past, caused him to modify his previous views, or had they been confirmed and consolidated by his commercial activities and scholarship? In the *Bag* Novikov seemed to have taken the opportunity of clarifying his own thoughts on these matters. This he did, however, not by any close, logical analysis, but again by mock dialogues and dramatised debates reminiscent of his earlier writings. And having done so with much success and no little entertainment in nine monthly issues, he brought the *Bag* – its sole purpose seemingly having been served – to an abrupt end in September.

Novikov's doubts were reflected in the tantalising riddle carried by the title – 'the turning of a Russian bag into a French one'. What was this bag? 'It was understood ... that gentlemen should be dressed in bags', wrote Thomas Jefferson in 1793,[1] and Thomas Carlyle in his *Life of Frederick the Great* – aware of the symbolism of bags – described an embarrassing moment for his subject: 'But, alas, he cannot undo the French hairdressing; cannot change the graceful French bag into the strict Prussian queue in a moment.'[2] Even if the elegant gentleman editor of the *Spectator* type of journals had finally left the stage, his grace and gentility were still reflected in the title of the *Bag*, that essential part of a gentleman's attire – the little silken pouch which gathered the back hair of a wig. The metonymy, however, took a critical turn in Novikov's pun. Vain Russian noblemen were only too ready to exchange one bag for another: that is, their substantial money-bags for the fashionable article of clothing. Real Russian wealth, it was suggested, was being squandered on everything for which the bag stood. Did the setting of the riddle show that Novikov was beginning to revolt against the enlightened elegance of manners and thought emanating from the West? The aim of the new publication seemed to be to answer that question.

The son of the fatherland

The basic impulse to create the pattern of a social paragon remained: he was the patriot, 'the son of the fatherland'. The *Bag*, dedicated 'To My Fatherland', began with a discussion of him based on the *Encyclopédie*'s article 'Patriote' and echoing the latter's affirmation: 'Servir sa patrie n'est point un devoir chimérique, c'est une obligation réelle.'

With his relish for attack, Novikov then proceeded not by attempting to define his patriot further, but by scornfully demolishing the non-patriot in a long sustained period ending in a satirical shaft calculatedly thrust home before 'the whole of Europe', which clearly was to stand in judgement over the non-patriot.

> I have never followed the rules of those people who, without examination of inner gifts, but seduced by some externally glittering gifts from foreigners, not only prefer foreign lands to their fatherland, but yet, to the shame of all Russia, even shun their compatriots and believe that a Russian should procure everything from foreigners even unto their characters; as if nature, having arranged all things with such great wisdom and conferring on all regions gifts and customs suited to their climates, would be as unjust as to deny to Russia alone a particular character to her people and bid her roam over all regions and take up scraps of various customs of various peoples in order to compose from this mixture a new character not fitting to any people and least of all to the Russian, excepting those alone who voluntarily turn themselves from men of reason into senseless apes and make themselves the laughing-stock of the whole of Europe.[3]

It was not French or Western influence in itself that Novikov found repulsive, but the blind, uncritical acceptance of the superficial emanations of Western culture by his compatriots and their disdain for the real worth of their own culture. He was no more anti-French than Fonvizin was in his portrayal of the Gallomanic Ivanushka in his comedy *Brigadir*, where again the satire was directed against the Russian aping of foreign fashions rather than against foreign culture itself. He was certainly no more anti-French than Diderot himself who found himself full of Francophobia in St Petersburg. 'La plupart des français qui y sont', he wrote home, 'se déchirent et se haïssent, se font mépriser et rendent la nation méprisable; c'est la plus indigne racaille que vous puissiez imaginer.' And again, 'La canaille française languit dans l'indigence et le mépris, comme elle le mérite. Les gens honnêtes et instruits y sont bien placés.'[4]

The failure of Novikov's recent enterprises had evidently deepened his distaste for the anti-patriots: his Society's books had not been bought by those with a veneer of Western sophistication but no understanding of the real worth of the Enlightenment. And their eyes remained closed to the ancient Russian virtues, whereas Novikov's recent concern with history had opened his own. 'And this is not surprising', explained the *Bag*, 'for we have long abandoned the real precious gems favoured by our ancestors as worthless and not used in France, and avariciously taken to buying false ones; but I would boldly state: if France had had as many gems as Russia, then she would never have begun to design beads: necessity is the mother of invention.'

Novikov has been seen by many as caught in a paradox here, torn between his keen appreciation of the European Enlightenment on the one hand, and by his high regard for the ancient Russian virtues on the other. 'Novikov could not unite into a definite view', wrote Pypin, 'his ideas on the historical past [*starina*], on the Russian national character, on the Enlightenment, and on the modern collapse of morals'.[5] Novikov, for Pypin, was unsure of himself, vacillating between the new Enlightenment and the old morality: the attraction of Freemasonry for him at this time was in its offer of a way out of the paradox to a firm moral standpoint.

In my view, the cast of Novikov's mind has here been misunderstood and a paradox seen where none exists. Regard for the staunch moral virtues of the past, the *starina*, was part of the *philosophe* concept of the patriot, and in the *Encyclopédie* article Cato's regard for the virtues of Republican Rome illustrated this belief. Novikov, following this picture, was not so much concerned with the Russianness of the past – their being Russian did not prevent him flaying Ivanushka's uncle in the *Drone* and Falaley's father in the *Painter* for their old vices – as with a past which was a repository of virtues. The son of the fatherland might accept the inheritance of these virtues as a member of a human family; any differences in virtue from land to land were to be accounted for by Montesquieu's climatic relativity. The test of virtues was in their antiquity and consonance with the Enlightenment, and not in their national exclusivity. The image of the patriot that Novikov held, therefore, was not riven with ambiguities but was all of a piece; for the interest in the past virtues of the local society was as integral to the Enlightenment's concept of the patriot, 'Who makes the welfare of mankind his care', as was the stress on the use of the local vernacular to carry the message of the universal Enlightenment.

The mother tongue

Problems of the vernacular were addressed in the *Bag*'s first issue. In the earlier journals, a correct use of the language had been merely one important mark of the true noble man, but the language of Novikov's books – after his experience in publishing – was now held in focus for its own sake. Being the bearer of enlightenment to Russia, the vernacular had to be enriched; otherwise it would be the enlightenment itself that would suffer.

Russian, it was felt, would not develop its full expressiveness until the common habit of using foreign words was kept within bounds. However, Novikov was not a purist in his outlook, but had a sensible middle-of-the-road attitude to the vocabulary of literary Russian: as well as searching out real Russian words and coining new ones from Russian roots 'following the example of German', one could employ foreign words but 'only with extreme care'. The main trouble would be to persuade people to use such a refined Russian vocabulary in colloquial speech, and the *Bag* reported how one group of acquaintances had established a forfeit-box for fines on those who, 'without extreme need', slipped foreign words into their Russian speech. Monthly proceeds from the box were to go to a foundlings' home. This might well be the same forfeit-box which reappeared in Julie Drubetskoy's salon in Tolstoy's *War and Peace* where society people decided – Tolstoy was scathing about the self-consciousness of the decision – that French was out of fashion after Napoleon's invasion of their country.[6]

The editor's own attitude to the forfeit-box was one of wry amusement; even if the Russian language would not benefit much, he thought, at least the coffers of the foundlings' home would swell. Nevertheless, there was a new and acute self-consciousness about the Russian language.

Although the forfeit-box might be a ludicrous way of developing the use of Russian, as the *Bag* suggested, at least it was as likely to be as efficacious as any bureaucratic scheme designed for the same purpose. The animus against bureaucratic formalism was, from the beginning, a mark of Novikov's social paragon: we may recall the scornful and exasperated account of frustrating visits to a passport office by N.N. of the *Drone*, which has been seen as the forerunner of the satirical portrayals of offices and officialdom so common in Russian literature of the following century.[7] As well as smiling wryly at the forfeit-box, Novikov mocked – with perhaps the melancholy experience of the Society for the Translation of Foreign Books in mind – a committee project for increasing the use of Russian.

> Some will say that the fatherland's language should not be developed and enriched in this way [i.e. the forfeit-box]. They say that to this end there are specially established places which concern themselves day and night with the matter, or at least should concern themselves; that three, five or ten young men, and only amateurs at that, are no more to an assembly of scholars than one in a thousand; that this is how such important business should be approached: some years of thought, some years of discussion, some years of making a scheme, some years of looking at it; many years of preparing material, many years of gathering it, many years of putting it into order, many years of making a note of what has been brought into order, many years of writing from the notes, and then, above all, many years of reviewing the work and preparing it for the press; that the workers should be given large salaries, quiet chambers, good desks etc. in order that all that might sweeten their feelings and bring their patriotic spirits into action; finally, that the treasury should lose completely some tens of thousands of roubles before society sees some dozen lines of this important work sent to the press.[8]

Once more apparently Novikov failed to come to a decision: neither state nor private enterprise was especially favoured as a means of promoting the national language. His sense of toiling in a cultural wilderness came over strongly in his sardonic picture of contemporary concern at the state of Russian. But lack of theoretical decision did not lead to practical indecisiveness. While the *Bag* might speak of cynical indifference, Novikov's actions in his Russian-language publishing were much more telling.

Views of the national character

Although bereft of a directing editorial *persona* the *Bag* was still dominated by human characters rather than unfleshed ideas, and much of it consisted of dialogues between a Frenchman and a Russian, and the same Frenchman and a German.

At first the impression might have been created that the *Bag* was inveighing against French influence in the satirical portrait of the Frenchman, revealed in his conversations as an unprincipled, fawning gambler, a confidence trickster duping the gullible Russian. The use of the generalisations of Frenchman, Russian and German seemed to invite readers to imagine a representative national type. But the Frenchman – eventually particularised as the Chevalier de Mensonge – was definitely not such a type. He was only representative of the breed of French mountebanks which Diderot found so distasteful in St Petersburg. In a sort of denouement to the drama in the penultimate issue of the *Bag* which contained a father's letter from Marseilles, the Frenchman proved to be a humble tradesman's prodigal son who had left to seek his fortune in Russia, 'which is justly considered the India of France'.[9] A note spelt this out: our Chevalier de Mensonge had 'demeaned himself to become a tutor to a middling Russian nobleman at a mere 500 roubles per annum plus board, servant and carriage'.[10] But since his duties were light he sold off cheap tobacco as a superior grade at five or ten roubles a pound; this was far better than being the hairdresser he had been in Holland, and his humble beginnings as son of a cook. It was these details, taken from life, that chipped away at the generalised figure in Novikov's satires and made entertaining individual characters of them.

Less a Frenchman than the Frenchman-in-Russia, he was used, not principally to allow Novikov to attack French influence, but to satirise the gullibility and lax self-deception of the Russian who handed over money to a gambler while convincing himself that this was a virtuous act prompted by the expansive Russian soul. The latter left the stage free for a dialogue between the Frenchman and the German, who represented two different sorts of Western influence in Russia, or rather two different modes of acceptance of Western influence by Russians. Again, the German was made into an individualised *dramatis persona* with biographical details: born the son of a country priest, he had a university education and, aware of his solid worth, had no pretensions to give himself a noble title and had come to Russia 'firstly to see this Empire under the rule of the Most Wise Empress renowned throughout Europe and secondly to seek out a position in keeping with my station'.[11] Here, then, in contrast to the self-seeking Frenchman, was the true patriot who could remain a patriot in Russia by affirming, as he did, 'for the man of learning, as they say, the whole world is his fatherland'.

The moral of the satirical dialogue was that Russians were not able to discriminate between true and false models. That the Russian was indeed the aim of the satire was made plain towards the end of the dialogue when the Frenchman was asked his frank opinion of him.

> Frank? – gladly. Frankly speaking, I consider him a simple-hearted, gullible and stupid man . . . How could he put his trust in the approval of a young rascal, who had left his fatherland, only in order to roam the taverns and public haunts of another, and waste senselessly his earnings in his fatherland? How could he believe everything I said about my breeding; and finally how could it not enter his head that if I was indeed of that birth which I gave myself and had the smallest real income, then would I have left my fatherland, and have left the known to chase after the unknown? – From all that, I draw the following conclusion that my new friend is nothing more than a good machine to be used for good and ill. And I have noticed this vice in many of my friend's compatriots: they rely too much on honesty and cannot distinguish truth from cunning; but it is very worthy of note in this context that although the German and Englishman do not deceive them and behave truthfully and honourably with them, yet they are not liked, their customs are not taken over and if the former wished to deceive them, they would never be taken in; yet the innermost heart and soul of the Russian is open to the Frenchman.[12]

The German patriot reacted to this cynical view of the gullible Russian by presenting the view of the true son of the fatherland. He was not an exclusive nationalist but was careful to discriminate between the French fop and the universal culture borne by the French language, 'be sure that reasonable Russians, unlike the giddy heads, do not respect you, as a Frenchman, but the French language'. The German continued with an elegant defence of the reasonable Russians:

> Russians in their comprehension of the arts and sciences . . . have as much wit, reason and perspicacity as the French, but have much more steadfastness, patience and diligence; the whole difference between the Frenchman and the Russian in the comprehension of science is that the one has taken to science much later than the other. France is obliged to the age of Louis XIV for the spread of arts and sciences, while in Russia this honour has fallen on Catherine the Great who astonishes the whole world with her deeds.[13]

Russia was a late starter in the Enlightenment, but the German already saw her overtaking and racing ahead of the cultural leader, France.

Novikov could be taxed here again with an inability to find a 'definite viewpoint' on the national character. However, this criticism would be unfair, since he was not primarily interested in elaborating one. As in the preceding magazines, his main concern was to demonstrate the breadth and complexity of views in Russian society. What the reader had been presented with were two extreme views of the Russian's particular character. Of course, Novikov would have preferred to accept the German's indulgent appreciation; he would indeed hope that his views might in time prove to be correct. Of course the Frenchman's cynicism was abhorrent; but unfortunately it was a cynicism based on the Russian reality so well portrayed in all Novikov's journals and confirmed by the failure of the Society for the Printing of Books. Of the two witnesses, it was the German with his wishful thinking who was the less reliable.

The shadow of Rousseau

It is hardly surprising that the arguments of both the German and his opponent had revolved around the question of national mores. In one of the most influential historical works of the century, the *Essai sur l'histoire générale et sur les mœurs et l'esprit des nations*, Voltaire had made *mœurs* (as the usual abbreviated title, *Essai sur les mœurs*, makes plain) one of the central interests of the historian. His concern was with a 'social pattern', which could be one translation of *mœurs*; and, despite the anachronism, the modern sociological jargon word 'mores' might well catch Voltaire's understanding of the word.

In following the *Bag*'s historical discussions 'mores' will be used deliberately as an equivalent for Novikov's *nravy*. Whereas English lacked a single word to encapsulate the full range of meaning of the French *mœurs*, Russian at the time had the equivalent in *nravy*. When the *Bag* taunted its Gallomanic readers with only being able to understand Russian by translating it mentally into French as they read, Novikov was not being over-fanciful: when many Russians read *nravy*, they understood the word as the French *mœurs*. Translation from the French at that time rarely sprang from a genuine need; rather it was a demonstrative mark of approbation for a French work.[14] Thus, when confronted with the title of Pavel Potemkin's translation of Rousseau's first discourse, *Vosstanovleniye nauk i khudozhestv sposobstvovalo li ko ispravleniyu nravov*, most of its Russian readers must have recognised the full French title, *Si le rétablissement des sciences et des arts a contribué à épurer les mœurs*, and would have read *nravy* as *mœurs*.

Rousseau, as the translations from him indicated, was already influential and in the discourses of the *Bag* one is very conscious of his thinking, already chafing away at previous ideas of the perfectibility of social mores. The earlier journals, the *Drone*, the *Tattler*, the *Painter*, had an assurance about the ideal social pattern for which they were meant to be a level, undistorting mirror. That self-confidence had broken down in the *Bag*. Perhaps it is significant that this was the first journal without a confident editorial *persona* enshrined in its title. And the title itself, with its pun on the meaning of 'bag', was a cracked looking-glass. Previously, one feels that there would have been no question of mocking the graceful wig bag which would have been a prescribed part of the 'clean costume' of the *Drone*'s socially immaculate merchant and, as the German's opponent argued, part of the outward display of support for Peter the Great's reforms. It was Rousseau and his interpreters who helped to shake Novikov's faith – which was also the common faith of his age – in the external symbols of mores. 'How pleasant it would be to live among us if the external countenance were always the image of the heart's feelings; if decency were virtue; if our maxims were our rules; if real philosophy was inseparable from the title of *philosophe*! but so many qualities rarely go together, and virtue hardly ever proceeds with such great pomp.'[15]

Rousseau's thesis had appeared in the essay which won the prize at the Dijon Academy in 1750 and made his reputation. It had been a common topic set by a number of French learned societies during the previous decade and there was nothing radically new in the thesis that virtues had declined with the growth of luxury; this had been a commonplace from the ancients onwards, the theme being part of the myth of the Golden Age.[16] The Dijon topic turned on two words, *rétablissement* and *mœurs*, and Rousseau immediately addressed them. The former, the re-establishing of the arts and sciences, was clear in its meaning; it meant the Renaissance, and in two sentences the accepted historical view was summarised: 'The fall of Constantine's throne carried the remnants of ancient Greece into Italy. France in turn was enriched by these fine remains.'[17]

Mœurs were less clearly defined. After dealing with the 're-establishment', Rousseau went on to describe his view of the mores, the distinctive social pattern which had developed from the Renaissance: '. . . and the main advantage of the trafficking of the muses began to be felt, that of making men more sociable by making them wish to please each other with works worthy of their mutual appreciation'.[18] He was prepared to admit that the surface manners of his bewigged and powdered society were exemplary. But Rousseau's insight was to recognise the falsity of this outward show.

What the *Bag* seemed to echo was the growing unease at the worth of mores, the feeling that they were a mirage and, at worst, a deceitful mask which, as Rousseau argued, would delude the citizens of distant countries. He caused the idea of mores to crumble by dividing mores into external manifestations and true inner qualities: *mœurs* are split – as the English language prefers them to be – into manners and morals. These two were not interdependent, but manners were used to mask man's morals, which led, maintained Rousseau, to confusion. 'What train of vices will not accompany this confusion! No more sincere friendships; no more true esteem; no more firm confidence. Suspicion, umbrage, fear, cold, reserve, hate, treachery, will constantly be hidden under the uniform perfidious veil of civility, under that urbanity, so highly thought of, that we owe to the lights of our age.'[19]

Novikov reacted to the new insight, as the title of the *Bag* proclaimed: the graceful French bag did not necessarily contain graceful morals. It was another image for Rousseau's 'perfidious veil'.

It has been argued that the fount of his first discourse was

Rousseau's spleen against the *beau monde* of Paris which had not recognised his learning and literary art. Yet that cultivated society was too well established, too sure of itself to react with more than amusement to a paradoxical attempt to prove by wit the folly of learning.[20] This amusement at Rousseau's impudence had been reflected in the *Painter*'s third paper when, addressing the philistine obscurantists of Russia, the editor expressed surprise at the identity of their views with 'Jean-Jacques Rousseau of most illustrious human wisdom in our age: he by reason, and you by ignorance, prove that sciences are useless'.[21] But in Russia the amusement could not have been so gay. Whereas Rousseau could argue perversely from a city possessing those comfortable, civilised mores which he belittled, the situation in Russia was very different. When Bolotov came to the city, he had to learn painstakingly how to behave in society, for the simple courtesies of life were not firmly rooted: in that situation where the little common decencies could form a much needed social cement, it was perplexing to read of Rousseau's apparent attack on mores. There was no firmly established *beau monde* to laugh aside his paradoxes: the brittleness of the fabric of high society, the chasm between town and country, demonstrated by the recent brutality of the Pugachev rebellion, was the Russian reality.[22] There was a hint of foreboding in the *Painter*'s smile, and in the identity of Rousseau's thesis with the stubborn conservative belief that Russian mores had been better before Peter's reforms. The thesis, seen in a benign light in Paris, was viewed in a much harsher glare in St Petersburg and Moscow.

The historical significance of the first discourse was also understood in a different way in Russia. The Academy of Dijon, it is true, had set its topic with a historical limitation; but, although Rousseau began by observing this, and addressed himself to learning re-established by the Renaissance, he soon ignored the limitation and drew widely and haphazardly on history to prove his thesis. For him, therefore, arts and sciences had not come from any particular direction; he was concerned with a general case. Virtue would recede with the certainty of a tide as the moon of enlightenment rose – 'and the same phenomenon is observed at all times and in all places'.[23] That the Renaissance came from the East was of little import.

Direction, however, was extremely important for Russians. For them, arts and sciences came from the West. Were a Frenchman to accept that his learning was injurious to his mores, he could not indicate any point of the compass which was to blame. Russians had a direction; they could indicate that the wind that blasted their mores gusted through Peter's window into Europe or Catherine's wide-open door. The distrust of the West, deeply embedded in the Russian consciousness, had been without a theoretical basis since the elaboration of the concept of 'Moscow the Third Rome' in the sixteenth century. Suddenly that distrust had such a theoretical foundation. 'Beautiful morality, unanswerable proofs, a new truth is revealed to the world!' – the *Painter* mocked the sense of joyful revelation felt by the conservative bigots on reading Rousseau.[24]

They would be further heartened by Rousseau's criticism of Peter the Great's reforms in his *Social Contract* where, in comparing the maturing of a nation to that of a person, he argued that Russia had been spoiled by being forced into a civilised state too soon, as a child is spoilt by being made to shine momentarily by his tutor:

> The Russians will never be really civilised, because they were civilised too soon. Peter was an imitative genius; he was not a real genius, one who can create and make something out of nothing. Some of the things he did were for the good, most were out of place. He saw that his people were barbarous, he did not see that they were not ripe for a civilising force [*la Police*]; he had wanted to civilise them when they should only have been disciplined. He wanted first to make Germans and English when he should have begun with Russians: he prevented his subjects from ever becoming what they could be, by persuading them that they were what they were not.[25]

In a way, Rousseau would cleave Russians into Slavophiles and Westernisers. By giving Rousseau's 'arts and sciences' a direction (significantly Novikov's German had by his very name stressed their Western origin) subsequent Russian social thought would make something new of the concept of the corruption of mores. Slavophiles would follow Rousseau in dividing mores into manners and morals which were inimical; they would argue that Western attitudes had brought with them corrupt manners which masked the true morals, the virtues of Russia. Tear away the corruption of manners and the underlying virtues would be revealed in their pristine beauty. The Westernisers would remain convinced that mores were indivisible: after all, there was the indivisible word *nravy* which had been used constantly as a standard of social behaviour. For them, in this word, manners and morals were woven into one: tear away Western manners and the virtue of the Enlightenment would be rent; restore the woof of Muscovite manners and the warp of their barbarous morals would be restored too.

Novikov, aware of Rousseau's new revelation and its significance, was a perturbed man, and this attitude pervaded the *Bag*. For years he had used mores as an indivisible standard in his attempt to create a valid self-image for Russian citizens. Now, without abandoning his view, he was in doubt. For the moment he would persist in demonstrating and extolling the manners of his forefathers through his historical researches and publications. But one action revealed his preparedness to turn aside from the manners of the external world and search for moral virtues within the inner man: in 1775 Novikov entered his first masonic lodge. History and freemasonry, however contradictory the impulses behind Novikov's enthusiasm for them, were both to engross him in the years ahead; he would soon prove to be an eminent historian and fervent freemason.

7
The historian
(1773–91)

History is the account of facts taken to be true ...

Voltaire

... history is philosophy teaching by examples how to conduct ourselves in all the situations of private and public life ...

Bolingbroke

A sense of history

The first edition of the *Ancient Russian Library* was published from 1773 to 1775; the *Bag* appeared alongside it. Not only was the latter a reaction to the failure of the Society for the Printing of Books. For a full understanding of the weekly, it is also necessary to read it in the context of Novikov's historical researches. While the *Ancient Russian Library* published essential archival material, it did not attempt to find solutions for, or even formulate, historiographical problems. However, the *Bag* provides a valuable glimpse of the prevailing attitudes to Russian history which should be considered before examining the *Ancient Russian Library* itself. Again no definite viewpoint can be said to have emerged from the *Bag*. Once more two extremist positions were given: one by the German, the graduate of a German university, and the other, not by the Chevalier de Mensonge (whose background would not have allowed him to deal seriously with history: again Novikov's scrupulous care with the validity of his 'characters' is apparent), but by a 'correspondent' outraged by the German's arguments.

Consciously idealising the past, the German considered it wise of the Muscovite rulers to have resisted the influx of arts and sciences from the West, since they held that the mores of Russia – which might suffer from such importations – were of greater value. 'It seems to me that the wise old Russian sovereigns seemed to foresee that through the introduction into Russia of sciences and arts, the most precious treasure of Russia, her mores, would perish irretrievably; and so they preferred to see their subjects in some respects ignorant of sciences, but with good mores, virtuous men, faithful to God, sovereign and fatherland.'[1] And it is interesting to see the German concluding his argument by anticipating Russia's official nineteenth-century nationalism, formulated as 'Orthodoxy, Autocracy, Patriotism'.

Novikov, fresh from his acquaintanceship with old Russian documents, might be expected to share these conservative views. But the German, as we have seen, had been portrayed as a somewhat naive and consequently unreliable witness. Not only had Novikov prefaced the dramatic dialogue with an editorial disclaimer, but he immediately supplied a corrective to the German's views in the form of an angry response from a correspondent. Although his letter was allegedly written in a mixture of French and Russian, the editor explained that he had translated the French; significantly, not out of any puristic principle which would have guided his friends with their linguistic forfeit-boxes, but on practical grounds, 'for I am under an obligation to do this for those of my readers who do not understand French.[2] If one had to define Novikov's own position, it would probably be one illustrated in the treatment of this correspondent's French: while leaning in sympathy towards the nationalists – after all he does expunge the French – his stance was one of pragmatic neutrality. The same uncommitted position was assumed in the conclusion to the editorial disclaimer: while not stating his own attitudes clearly, he asked the reader to suspend his judgement until an editorial reply was made. As previously with Falaley in the *Painter*, no reply was forthcoming. Again Novikov might have felt that silence was the most eloquent rejoinder to extremist positions.[3]

At first the 'correspondent' seemed to be in agreement with Novikov's own previous views. In the portraits of the older generation in the *Drone* and the *Painter*, a regard for tradition and the ancient mores often amounted to an apologia for vice; this was little different from the line now taken by the German's opponent who mocked the obscurantism of pre-Petrine times 'when all virtues depended on the thickness of the beard'.[4] Aware of the significance of Peter the Great's reforms of Russian dress, the correspondent was upset by the joke in the title of the *Bag*. Shaving off the beard and adopting Western dress were still felt as a sign of the Russians' change 'from barbarians to Europeans'. Would the editor of the *Bag* really prefer to see the comfortable old Muscovite dress readopted so that men 'could visit ladies in their night attire' and, presumably, revert to barbarism?

However, although the 'correspondent' was allowed to advance a reasonable and strongly argued case against the German's position – a case with which the Novikov of the earlier journals might have been expected to concur – he soon revealed himself as too extremist in his pro-Western attitudes for 1774. First, he proved to be an admirer of the Abbé Chappe d'Auteroche and accepted uncritically the distorted view of Russian history prevalent in the West.[5] Secondly, he was unmasked as one of those educated Russians who never read their own language. Attitudes like his explained the failure of the Society for the Translation of Foreign Books and the Society for the Printing of Books. For he only possessed a single volume in Russia, *Les Œuvres de Mr. Lomonosoff*: 'This book is known under the title of the Works of Lomonosov but in order to avoid the shame of having a Russian book seen in my library, I ordered the bookbinder to put its title in French.'[6] This stage property of a book on the stage set of an educated Russian's library is another excellent illustration of Novikov's ability to mount little dramas of social and literary controversies in his journals: it was by this means, rather than by abstract reasoning, that he encouraged men to recognise and examine their roles in society.

What gave support to the correspondent's rejection of any respect for the Russian past was a potted history, through French eyes, centred on social behaviour: it began with the *philosophe*'s view of the introduction of Christianity as being positive in its softening of wild barbarity, but regrettable in its encouragement of superstition. Ivan IV, whose title of 'le Tyran' or 'le Terrible' in French histories was replaced by ellipses, might have thrown off the Tartar yoke, 'but Russian mores remained the same and ignorance was as strong as before. For mores can never be reformed by flogging, the yoke or the sword.'[7] If under later tsars there had been some civilising process, then it amounted to nothing more than recognising foreigners as human beings. At this point, Novikov used his often-exploited device of breaking off his correspondent's letter and explaining in a footnote that decorum had forced him to suppress parts: 'Here I was obliged against my will to exclude much from this letter. However I can assure my reader that there were here the most ridiculous slanders which Russia's enemies could have invented.'[8] As for the tentative beginnings of Russian literature, the correspondent's view was one that still tends to be generally held: 'one is amazed as by a child who, taking pen in hand, begins however clumsily to trace on paper'.

Even Peter's reforms were not recognised as true enlightenment, since, for the correspondent, enlightenment was measured not in technological progress, but by the refinement of mores. For him it was 'the bag' as a graceful fashionable article of dress that was important, and not 'the bag' that represented material wealth. Peter's approach to enlightenment was therefore incorrect: 'he took on the enlightenment of mores from the wrong direction: for the Germans, Dutch and English would never have enlightened our mores. To the French alone was this honour reserved.'

At this point, the correspondent, who until now had been allowed to argue his case cogently and reasonably according to his lights, suddenly degenerated into one of the absurd Frenchified fops who had populated the pages of the earlier magazines. The enlightened ways of which he had spoken turned out to be no more illuminating than the fashionable bag; they consisted of knowing the tricks of salon behaviour, of knowing 'how to make an entrance, to bow, to perfume oneself, to take one's hat and with it alone express various passions and show the condition of our hearts and souls'. Soon he was condemning himself with a recital of those mildly corrupt mores which were fair game for all the satirical journals – the imperative of marrying, not by arrangement, but 'for love, or affection for money'; the need to praise Parisian fashions and mock old Russian customs; the ability to have 'apart from a wife, ten mistresses and deceive them all'; and the putting on of a show of learning: 'by means of my intercourse with Frenchmen, without studying anything I have become a scholar and can discuss and criticise military, civil and political affairs, ridicule state institutions and, pretending to know all, be surprised at nothing'.[9]

The concept of mores had been brought down to a meaningless bundle of social conceits. After showing himself to be a cogent advocate of Westernisation, the 'correspondent' himself had degenerated into an absurd fop. Finally the devaluation of mores, and the degeneration of an educated Russian, were capped by Novikov's favourite device of 'translation' when the editor, deliberately avoiding the term 'son of the fatherland', referred to him ironically with the French borrowing, *patriot*.

In many ways the *Ancient Russian Library* was to be a scholar's reply to both the German and his 'correspondent'.

The 'Ancient Russian Library'

'The favourable reception by society of some of my insignificant works has heartened me and been an encouragement to more important labours.' In the first sentence of his preface to his scholarly historical series *Ancient Russian Library*, Novikov acknowledged the debt he owed to his satirical journals which had established him as a publisher by providing him with the necessary finance and patronage. He was now ready to capitalise on this by publishing scholarly works to which he was prepared to give his name, and so to emerge from the guarded anonymity of his earlier ventures. After the disappointments of his first well-organised attempts to found a state-sponsored society for publishing in Russian Novikov, we have noted, guided by a mixture of social need and self-interest, moved towards history. And this movement was given added momentum by a push from the West, which seemed to be more intrigued by Russian history than the Russians themselves. Novikov's incursions into history were, in no small part, defensive in nature – the understandable urge by a Russian patriot to defend his homeland against unconscious misrepresentation and deliberate libel from abroad. There was a sense of strain in his protestations of Russia's present greatness for, on the whole, the history he wrote was not a self-confident chronicling: it came close to being apologetic. Yet, given the circumstances, it was not surprising that Russian historiography should at this early stage be shot through with a sense of defensiveness.

A protective concern for Russian literature had inspired Novikov's *Essay at an Historical Dictionary of Russian Writers*. A similar defensive posture was also proclaimed in the preface to the work which now capped his endeavours of the previous two years, his *Ancient Russian Library* which appeared as a periodical publication from January 1773 to 1775.[10] The work which followed, he suggested with some passion, would be a defence against those Gallomanic Russians whose shame it was to disdain their own country and fall in with the libel of the Abbé Chappe d'Auteroche.

In examining, collating and selecting from the riches of archive material made available to him through Catherine's pleasure, what did Novikov look for? What did he consider suitable for his *Ancient Russian Library*? What did he seek to counter above all in Abbé Chappe d'Auteroche's libel? There is no need to look further than the first few lines of Novikov's preface:

> Not all of us yet, thank God!, are contaminated by France; on the contrary there are many who with great curiosity would read descriptions of ceremonials used in the society of our forefathers, and with no less interest would like to see an outline of their mores and customs, and with enthusiasm would learn of their greatness of spirit enhanced by simplicity. It is useful to know the mores, customs and ceremonials of ancient foreign peoples; but it is much more useful to have knowledge of one's forefathers...[11]

To see customs and ceremonials in this way as the main stuff of history may seem naive to the twentieth century, but for Novikov's time it might well be the prevailing view in accord with Lord Chesterfield's opinion on Voltaire's *Le Siècle de Louis XIV* that it 'showed how history should be written. It is the history of the human understanding, written by a man of parts for the use of men of parts.'[12]

The concern for the outward decorum of social behaviour which was central to the impulse behind the *Ancient Russian Library* meant that the venture was not a new departure in Novikov's creative life, but a continuation of the aim of his satirical journals to promote the decorous image of the civilised man in Russia. It was in the *Bag* that Novikov could be seen most clearly to be stepping over from the field of the *Spectator* type of magazines to that of history; but in all his satirical magazines from 1769 to 1774 there were numerous excursions into history, the abiding interest in history being signalled at the close of the *Drone* in his epitaph to Fedor Emin.[13] The Abbé Chappe d'Auteroche's strictures on the barbarity of the old Russia, which had been caricatured in the *Bag* as descriptions of how the Russian tsars were married in sauna baths and smeared their hair with honey, were now countered by many examples of ancient Russian mores, customs and ceremonials designed to show their venerated seemliness. Much space was given to church literature describing religious ceremonials and Orthodox symbolism, and the sacrosanct nature of these was probably intended to spill over into the numerous descriptions of secular prescribed behaviour and ceremonial mostly appertaining to the court. They contained detailed accounts of rituals such as the coronations of the Grand Dukes and Tsars of Muscovy, the marriages of tsars such as Ivan the Terrible, Mikhail and Aleksey Romanov, the birth, christening and burials of members of the royal family and a description of the noble ceremonials of falconry at the tsar's court. Alongside this display of old customs went a keen interest in genealogy. This affirmation of the importance of the old-fashioned princely and noble families might seem to go against Novikov's constant stress in his journals that true nobility did not spring merely from accident of birth. Indeed he seemed uncertain in his request to Catherine for permission to publish genealogical material whether his aim would also be acceptable to her. Novikov clearly did not wish to flatter individual noblemen, but he realised that a demonstration of the traditional worth of Russia's principal families could be another refutation of Chappe d'Auteroche's libel. Noble birth in itself was never a negative quality for Novikov: his only quarrel was with those degenerated noblemen who had lost their sense of obligation and *ipso facto* lost their claim to true noble rank in the eyes of other enlightened gentlemen. Furthermore, the historian's antiquarian instinct had been well roused in Novikov as his gathering of material for the *Ancient Russian Library* progressed. 'This seems to me to be a very important and useful subject', wrote Novikov to Catherine's secretary, Kozitsky, towards the end of October 1773, 'especially since no better means can be found of managing to collect a full genealogical book than by this publication. Many noblemen from Moscow have asked me to do this and have promised to send genealogical records which at any other time would be impossible to obtain.'[14] As a result, the *Ancient Russian Library* published the family trees of the Golitsyns, Kurakins, Shcherbatovs, Repnins, Sontsovs and the Odoyevskys amongst others; in particular many documents and material supplied to Novikov by G. F. Müller dealt with the life and work of V. V. Golitsyn (1643–1714), one of the most impressive, educated, 'Westernising' noblemen of the seventeenth century.[15]

So often in his journals Novikov had managed to bring abstract considerations firmly into contemporary society. In a charming way he managed to do this in the course of the publication of the *Ancient Russian Library* as well, and affirm the point that his recollection of ancient Russian decorum was not an empty exercise, but a spur to contemporary civilised seemliness capable of binding society with bonds of gentility. On his nameday, 9 May 1773,

Novikov, in a letter to Kozitsky, recalled that it was an ancient Russian custom for noblemen to present the sovereign with a suitable gift on their nameday, and so he wrote:

> as a publisher of rare manuscripts, I venture on the day of my Angel, through you to present to Her Imperial Majesty as a gift a printed book remarkable for its rarity. Through you I have been provided by Her Imperial Majesty with rare manuscripts for the continuation of my journal and so been sustained in my labours; through you I wish to express to Her Majesty my most humble gratitude. I will be completely overjoyed on this day, if you will take upon yourself this trouble and if it be pleasing to Her Majesty.[16]

This awareness by Novikov that a study of ancient mores could provide a pedigree for the seemly social behaviour of contemporary Russians appears to have given him a necessary sense of balance when faced with the bewildering quantity of material in the archives. For, at first, there seemed to be no definite system for arranging the material either on a chronological or thematic basis. Only in the second edition of the *Ancient Russian Library* of 1788–91 was Novikov able to collate the material more rationally, 'bringing them into a possible chronological order in each volume', as he explained in his preface, 'at least grouping pieces by subject'.[17] Documents were, in the earlier edition, printed as they were discovered and the contents of the journal were, therefore, extremely rich and varied. The journal covered Russian history from Kievan times to the contemporary close of the eighteenth century. The earliest document was a tenth-century *ustav* of Prince Vladimir Svyatoslavich on church affairs and there were three thirteenth-century Novgorod documents, but most of the material came from the sixteenth and seventeenth centuries, with eighteenth-century documents taking up very little space. The variety of the material acceptable to the publication was reflected in its first full title *Ancient Russian Library, or a collection of various ancient compositions such as Russian embassies into foreign states, rare documents, descriptions of marriage ceremonies and other historical and geographical curiosities and many compositions of the ancient Russian versifiers, published monthly by Nikolay Novikov.*

Pride of place in the journal naturally went to documents and material on internal Russian history, but great attention was also paid to documents on external affairs and memoirs of Russian diplomatic dealings with foreign states, as promised in the journal's full title. Much attention was paid to lists and descriptions of embassies, the most interesting among them being those of V. S. Plemyannikov and the interpreter Istoma Maly to the Emperor Maximilian in 1518, Trifon Korobeynikov to Constantinople, Alexandria, Antioch and Jerusalem in 1593; A. Vlas'yev to the Emperor Rudolph II in 1599; M. G. Saltykov-Morozov, V. T. Pleshcheyev and A. Vlas'yev to Poland in 1601; F. I. Baykov to China in 1654; I. I. Chemodanov to Venice in 1656; V. Likhachev to Florence in 1659; P. I. Potemkin to France and Spain in 1667–8; Izbrant Ides to China in 1692; B. P. Sheremetev to Cracow, Venice, Rome and Malta in 1697. Descriptions were also included of the receptions given to embassies from abroad, including those of the Papal Nuncio A. Possevino in 1580, the ambassadors of the Holy Roman Empire in 1661 and a Swedish embassy of 1683. These descriptions of embassies were accompanied by a large quantity of diplomatic material. All this spoke of the wide-ranging diplomatic links which Russia had with the outside world, with the Holy Roman Empire, France, England, the Papal *Curia*, Sweden, Spain, Venice and the Turkish Sultanate. Sufficient material was printed to enable readers to form a clear impression of the organisation of the diplomatic service and of diplomatic ceremonial in Muscovy. As well as stressing the ancient civilities of Russian life Novikov, through the bulk of this diplomatic material, sought to imply the long experience of Russia in the comity of nations. Manners between the Russian nation and others were as important as manners between men within the nation.

Principles of editing historical material

One had to wait until 1788 and the second edition of the *Ancient Russian Library* for a more scholarly marshalling of the material and the first critical historical articles, such as the two on 'Ancient Muscovite Departments (Prikazy)' and 'An Historical Report on the Mentioned Ancient Ranks in Russia', which appeared in the twentieth part of the journal. But, as his work on history progressed, Novikov did not limit himself to the mere publishing of antiquarian material. He also worked out the methods necessary for their publication; and this at a time when the historian lacked the auxiliary support of archivists and paleographers, when he considered that it was justifiable for a source to be 'corrected', often with the aim of supporting the views of the publisher. Given the undeveloped condition of historical science and that Novikov had no special training, he was obliged to work out his own procedures. However, in the same year as the launching of the *Ancient Russian Library*, Novikov showed in his preface to an edition of the *Ancient Russian Hydrography*, a work composed in the previous century, his scrupulous care as an editor. He wished to publish the work, he declared, for the two reasons that as well as being a useful historical document, it would dispel the widespread opinion that no secular works had been written in pre-Petrine Russia. It would, therefore, be another argument for the defence against the supporters of Chappe d'Auteroche's view of Russian history. He received a copy of the work from P. K. Khlebnikov but did not set about publishing it until he had compared it with other manuscript copies. His thoroughness led him to locate and consult five further copies: two in the Academy of Sciences Library, one in the old and one in the new orthography; a further three were found through 'the endeavours of my friend' in Moscow, two from the library of the late A. G. Sabakin and one marked 'a copy from a copy in the Patriarchate Sacristy'. After evaluating the six copies, Novikov came to the conclusion that Khlebnikov's copy was the oldest and so used this as his basic text, consulting the other copies only to correct obvious copyist errors and mistakes. At a time when historians still tended to deal with texts in cavalier fashion, it is interesting to see Novikov from the beginning refuse to meddle with his sources even when that source was clearly corrupt; 'In some places', he explained, 'the names of streams are not given, while in others the same river is indicated by two names; but I have left these mistakes just as they appear in the copies for fear of transgressing more than the copyist himself by corrections.'[18]

These procedures seem to have been refined as the work on the *Library* progressed. In the first issues he was content to list documents or give short resumés of their content, but later he was to print the text in full and as the original, except for the correction of obvious scribal errors and the restoration of lost passages from other material. Only in time did Novikov attach essential notes to the documents published, together with a paleographical description. But noting this growing professionalism of Novikov as a publisher of historical documents makes one aware of the speed with which he assimilated the craft in a field in which he had very few predecessors in Russian. By 1777 his scholarly, bibliographical journal *St Petersburg Academic News* demonstrated his ability to approach texts critically, fix their chronology, refine the transcription of proper names and explain the linguistic and paleographical characteristics of his sources. In that journal there is an article on the art of publishing documents which shows how much Novikov had learnt during his work on the *Ancient Russian Library*. The publisher of documents had to ensure

> that there should be attached to each section an alphabetical list of material included in that section which is very necessary for books of that sort for searching out desired things; that as far as possible notes should be made on obscure and unintelligible passages and words; that in dating, the Year of Our Lord should always be added; that ancient orthography should not be changed to the new and above all that nothing be added, subtracted or corrected, but that it should be printed exactly as it was found in the original; and finally that it should be precisely indicated from where the copy was received, where the original is to be found and in what hand it is written, old or new.[19]

The contribution to Russian historiography

Novikov's contribution to the development of history in Russia was extremely significant on two counts. For the first time would-be Russian historians had at their disposal a monumental collection of ancient Russian documents among which were historical sources of prime importance. In the works of such foremost eighteenth-century historians as G. F. Müller, Shcherbatov and Boltin there are frequent references to Novikov's historical publications and in particular to his *Ancient Russian Library*. For many generations of Russian historians, the latter work was to remain a prime source. Not only did Novikov make this valuable material available to them, but, equally significantly, at a time when Russian antiquarian interest was merely burgeoning, Novikov laid a firm basis for a scholarly approach to archive material and established, as we have seen, both in practice and in theory the procedures necessary for publishing sources which anticipated by half a century the efforts of later historians.

With his historical editions Novikov not only began to nurture an interest in reading history in Russian among the enlightened Russian public, but his example served as an encouragement to other Russian antiquarians, such as V. G. Ruban, F. O. Tumansky and I. I. Golikov. Even before the second edition of the *Ancient Russian Library* appeared in 1788, S. Ya. Rumovsky, a pupil of Lomonosov's, had begun to publish at the St Petersburg Academy of Sciences the multi-volume *Continuation of the Ancient Russian Library*, of which eleven parts were published from 1786 to 1801. Not surprisingly Novikov was to be singled out as one of the main practitioners by William Coxe in his short review of Russian historiography.[20]

The response of the reading public

The growing availability of material for the *Ancient Russian Library* was shown by the organisation of the publication. Initially in 1773 it was published monthly in comparatively small volumes (five printed sheets) and six of these made up one part. The following year the monthly issues were doubled in size and so each part comprised three issues; therefore parts III–VI appeared in that year. In 1775 the parts were published separately at two-monthly intervals, but Novikov only managed to produce four of the intended six parts, and without warning the journal ceased to appear after the tenth part in the second half of 1775.

Unfortunately, as the material increased, so the number of subscribers fell. At first the *Ancient Russian Library*, considering its scholarly nature, was suprisingly popular. It circulated not only in the capitals but in the provinces and among various sections of the population. Initially there were 198 subscribers to 246 copies.[21] The list published by the editor showed that they covered the whole of Russian society, from Catherine who received ten copies down to one peasant subscriber, a certain Aleksey Banev from the Kholmogory district. The principal noblemen followed their sovereign's lead and among them were K. G. Razumovsky, A. M. Golitsyn, G. A. Potemkin, G. G. Orlov, P. B. Sheremetev, P. I. Repnin, R. L. Vorontsov, Z. G. Chernyshev, F. A. Apraksin and A. V. Kurakin. The church hierarchy was well represented by Archbishop Plato of Moscow and Tver′, Archbishop Innocent of Pskov and Theophylact, Rector of the Moscow Academy. The spread of the work through the provinces was due mainly to its subscribers from the merchant class and ennobled entrepreneurs, which included Anan′yev from Rostov, Gebgard from Revel and the Demidovs from the Urals. Naturally the work found favour among literary men such as Radishchev, Dmitrevsky, Kheraskov, Maykov, Shcherbatov and Ruban. However, after an encouraging start, interest in the publication abated and in 1774 the number of subscribers had fallen to 133 for 167 copies, and finally in 1775 it sank disastrously to a hard core of 57 subscribers for 77 copies. Possibly the inflation that followed the Turkish war and Pugachev rebellion had had a particularly adverse effect on book buying.[22]

The enterprise certainly could not have prospered without the active support of Catherine who, in response to Novikov's request,[23] issued personal directives for archive material to be released to Novikov, as her letter of 26 October 1773 to G. F. Müller shows,[24] and also gave Novikov a handsome financial subsidy. A receipt signed by him on 3 November 1773 attested to 1,000 roubles received from Kozitsky and another receipt of 1 January 1774 acknowledged a further gift of 200 Dutch *chervontsy*.[25] Nevertheless Novikov, who during 1774 not only pressed on with the publication of the *Ancient Russian Library*, but was also deeply involved in the Society for the Printing of Books and even launched the *Bag*, was also harassed by the undeveloped state of the Russian printing industry and its lack of discipline which had already been reflected in the lags in his previous periodical publications. On 17 November 1773 he apologised to Catherine through Kozitsky for not being able to supply that month's issue of the *Library* bound in satin: 'I was in great haste with the publication this month', he excused himself, 'but the Academy Press was too much for my endeavours.'[26] The following year in a letter of 6 July, his impatience showed itself in his unceremonious bluntness: 'My dear Grigoriy Vasil'yevich', he wrote to Kozitsky, 'I enclose two copies for July which were only printed yesterday, and the reason for that is the drunkenness of the compositors.'[27]

The final catastrophic slump in the number of subscribers for 1775 was due to the departure of the court from St Petersburg; in March Novikov had to warn Kozitsky that he saw little hope of being able to complete the projected issues of the *Library* for that year. Despite the appeal made by the publication initially to various classes of the population and Novikov's continued hopes for support from the provinces, it is clear that in St Petersburg the reading public for Russian history books was identified with the society around the court which followed the clear lead given by Catherine. Not only had the temporary migration of the court deprived the *Ancient Russian Library* of its subscribers, complained Novikov in his letter to Kozitsky, but it had become apparent in St Petersburg that book-buyers generally had been absent as a result.[28]

The 'Library''s successors: attempts at popular history

In the same letter Novikov explained that he had spent a hard winter, having suffered with eye and chest complaints for over two months. Yet, despite his ailments, the confusion of his affairs and the cruel lack of real interest shown in his patriotic publishing ventures by Russian society in general, Novikov demonstrated his resilience and refusal to bow down to misfortune. In the same breath as he announced his inability to continue with the publication of his *Library* – and the work of compiling material did not cease, as the second edition showed – he proposed a new historical publication which he wished to be drawn to the empress' attention in the hope of gaining further patronage. This new successor journal was to be called the *Treasurehouse of Russian Antiquities* and Novikov indicated that plans for publication were well advanced by including in his letter to Kozitsky an engraving which was intended for it.[29] It aimed to be more popular in its appeal than the more scholarly *Library*. As well as including a medallion engraving of one of the Russian sovereigns with a short biographical note in each of its issues, the *Treasurehouse* was to have architectural notes on Russian cathedrals, monasteries and churches accompanied by choice grave inscriptions. There would also be a section on heraldry describing the devices of Russian principalities and towns, and a section on ancient Russian coins. Although it was promised that each section would be accompanied by historical and geographical notes, clearly the new journal was intended to appeal by being an antiquarian pot-pourri, and only the fifth section had other aims. This was to be 'notices of books published in Russian on the History and Geography of Russia'. Although Catherine gave her lead by subscribing for six copies of the new venture, other subscribers could not have been forthcoming in sufficient numbers, for the *Treasurehouse* only appeared once.[30] Even then, Novikov did not cast his ideas aside. The sketch of a bibliographical section reappeared as a specialist bibliographical journal – the first in Russia – in the *St Petersburg Academic News* of 1777, and a historical journal designed to capture the popular taste was published in 1776, the *Narrator of Russian Antiquities, or a collection of various curious notes for the benefit of Russian History and Geography*. The overriding aim of the publication was much the same as the *Library*'s in making Russians aware of the 'mores, customs and rituals of our famous forefathers', but Novikov mocked the seriousness of his *Library* in much the same way as he had been ironic at the expense of his own choice of the archaic word *Vivliofika* for the journal in the *Bag*. The self-mocking was an attempt to reassure readers, who must have been more than a little confounded by the documentary diet provided in the *Ancient Russian Library*. 'You will not be repulsed', Novikov told his readers, 'by an ancient style, dry, coarse and strange for us; you will not be tortured so much by the frequent repetition of words found in almost all old compositions; your ear will not be rent by the articulation of the wise, strange and absurd word, *Vivliofika*; and you will not suffer, from our reasoning, either apoplexy or frequent and severe fainting fits.' Furthermore, readers are ironically assured that the dust and decay of ancient documents will not harm the sweet perfume of their powder and pomade.[31]

Two further historical works were published by Novikov in the same year of 1776. One was the popular history, A. Lyzlov's *Scythian History* of 1692, which Novikov claimed was taken from the best extant copy in the Moscow Library of the Patriarchate. The other, *The History of the Innocent Incarceration of the Blizhny Boyar Artemon Sergeyevich Matveyev*, was clearly intended as an exemplary work depicting a true son of the fatherland of the previous century. Novikov had four copies of the work at his disposal: one from the Academy of Sciences Library, one received from P. K. Khlebnikov, and one collected by Novikov himself; but it was with pride that he stated in his preface that the manuscript was brought to his attention by Catherine, and that the copy used in the edition was the one received from Her Imperial Majesty's personal library. In retrospect there is a cruel irony in Novikov's enthusiasm for Matveyev's biography, and for a man on whom he must have wished to model himself. Matveyev seemed to be a perfect historical reflection of that self-image of the social paragon that Novikov had been promoting for the previous seven years in his satirical journals and historical works; a man of humble pretensions with his 'small and cramped little house', but loyal to the person of his sovereign Aleksey Mikhaylovich Romanov, replete with a sense of service to his fatherland and obligation to the common people, educated and enlightened. While fiercely patriotic, Matveyev was not afraid to welcome Western culture, demonstrating his taste and knowledge of the liberal arts by having the iconostasis of his domestic church decorated by the best available Italian artists and enjoying the company of foreign men of learning in order to further his own love of learning. Novikov was to follow Matveyev in obeisance to the fine arts by decorating his own domestic church at Avdot'ino, and in a just and generous appreciation of Western culture. But in 1776, he could not have dreamt that in fifteen short years – with Catherine, who had passed the exemplary biography of Matveyev to his attention, still on the throne – he, like Matveyev, 'in the face of Christian and civil laws' and partly because of 'social intercourse with foreign men of learning' would be dispatched into 'innocent incarceration'. The historical image, it seemed, would return to devour the image-maker.

8
The freemason
(1775–80)

And Pierre began to expound Freemasonry to Prince Andrey as he understood it. He declared that Freemasonry was the doctrine of Christianity freed from political and religious dogmatic bonds: the doctrine of equality, fraternity and charity.

War and Peace

Russian freemasonry

In all his activities, as journalist, publisher and historian, Novikov's desire had been not to act in isolation. Preface after preface had called on Russian writers and patriots to help him in his ventures, and that help had been forthcoming. The journals had drawn the young literary men, many of them graduates of Moscow University, into an embryonic literary society, and the *Ancient Russian Library* had obliged Novikov to form strong bonds of interest with men like Gerhard Müller and P. K. Khlebnikov. This urge for collectivism had been fostered by Catherine, as was evident in the organisation of the combined literary endeavours of the minute-writers of the Legislative Commission, and of her 'family' of satirical periodicals. By acknowledging at every turn the lead given to him by his sovereign, Novikov was showing how abiding an influence were the ancient presumptions of Muscovite centralisation. In Catherine's age the old system of tutelage (*opeka*) was still alive: indeed it had not really passed from the Russian scene for, as Pypin argued, even the enforced character of the Petrine reforms, although condemned by the Slavophiles for being enforced, was itself the heritage of ancient state practice. Under the influence of the ideas of the Enlightenment, the traditional tutelage was now directed with enthusiasm on the part of Catherine to the moral improvement of society, but again only to the prescriptions of the autocratic authority. Tutelage was now inevitably exerted on the inner life of subjects as well as its outer modes of behaviour, and Pypin recognised the contradiction which was not apparent to Catherine's contemporaries: the moral improvement of society implied a freedom of individual initiative which could quickly lead to a clash with the entrenched moral authority of the state.[1]

Novikov moved outside the tutelage of the autocrat with his entry into a freemasonic lodge in 1775. Yet he could not have seen the act in those terms at the time. In the 1770s the outlook of the Russian freemasons was broadly that of the approved *philosophes*, and indeed the masons' contemporaries of the eighteenth and early nineteenth centuries did not differentiate between the two terms. For them 'Voltairean' and 'freemason' were synonyms, very often used as a mild reproach of eccentricity, or as abuse. Catherine's Society for the Translation of Foreign Books, which was seconded by Novikov's Society for the Printing of Books, gathered together many prominent masons of the present and future: I. A. Alekseyev, S. I. Gamaleya, I. A. Dmitrevsky, A. M. Kutuzov, V. A. Levshin, M. I. Popov, A. N. Radishchev and others. It was these literary groupings and influential circles at court, all enjoying the favour of Catherine, which formed the first gatherings of widespread masonry in Russia: Novikov, when forced to review his masonic activities at his interrogation after his arrest on suspicion of subversion in 1792, stressed in justification of his entry into masonry that at that time, 1775, the gatherings of the brotherhood were to all intents and purposes public, and that it was the influential principal noblemen who were the most prominent masons.[2]

In eighteenth-century Europe masonic lodges had spread along the main trade routes, for one of the functions soon discovered for masonry was to provide a social outlet for expatriate businessmen, and presumably to offer them a forum for making business contacts.[3] It was among expatriates that masonry spread initially in Catherine's Russia, and the lodges were a meeting-place for a society of exiles. Many of Russia's masons were probably Germans, and one of the St Petersburg lodges, Perfect Union, was exclusively English.[4] German and English influence was revealed in the languages used in the lodges: the Urania lodge, which initially conducted its business in Russian only, began to employ German as well from 1775 and in the eighties and nineties German and English were its official languages. The lodge of Archangel also used German and English in its business.[5]

The first widespread national Russian manifestation of masonry uniting a number of lodges was at the beginning of the seventies under Ivan Perfil'yevich Yelagin, whose authorisation as provincial grand master was signed in London on 28 February 1772 by the Duke of Beaufort.[6] It was a lodge of this 'English' system that Novikov was invited to join in 1775 and, like Voltaire who became a member of the Nine Sisters lodge in Paris three years later, he did not submit to any oaths or rites of initiation.[7] The first three degrees were revealed to him beforehand, lest the cautious Novikov should find something in them 'against his conscience'.[8] The fourteen lodges in Yelagin's English system – in St Petersburg, Moscow, Archangel, Vladimir as well as the military ones in Jassy and Sadogury in Moldavia – carried on the tradition of acting as suitable resting-places for itinerant men on business, and recommending their members to a new lodge when they transferred to another post in another region. Links were also maintained with foreign lodges and the Urania lodge frequently entertained visitors with letters of introduction from English, Dutch and German lodges. Apart from the ceremonial initiation – which was fairly accurately described by Tolstoy in the case of Pierre in *War and Peace* – Yelagin's lodges were little more than agreeable social clubs (one of the constant members of Urania was F. Gardner, the founder of the famous English Club, in St Petersburg in 1770).[9] The lodges flourished as excellent places to dine and enjoy good company; the club-like *bonhomie* was fostered with the playing of cards and in September 1774 the Urania lodge even decided to install a billiards table for members' use.[10] Even in the more bacchanalian lodges, it is true that despite the mocking of the masonic mumbo-jumbo, lip-service was still paid to the moral side of masonry and its philanthropic interests, although the extent of the charity may be gauged by the accounts of one Il'in, who recorded a rouble entrance fee, five kopecks for the poor-box and ten for a glass of punch.[11] In 1769 Novikov, while patterning his Drone on the clubbable Mr Spectator, did not have a suitable home for his Russian idler: a few years later that idler would have had plenty of Russian clubs in which to pen his social portraits.

The mood of Novikov, now older and a scholarly man of letters, had changed, however, and he recalled his dissatisfaction with the superficial high life of the 'English' masonry.[12] Mere shallow *bonhomie* was rejected as it would be even in its country of origin, the further one went in time from the taverns of The Goose and Gridiron, The Crown, The Appletree, The Roman and Grapes, whose lodges united in the Grand Lodge of London on 24 June 1717. In the general unease about the authenticity of the masonry practised, there emerged new varieties to meet the demands for a revelation of the true and original craft of free masonry which might provide a panacea for the world's ills. Yelagin himself was one of the first to have doubts about the system of masonry over which he presided in Russia, and he turned his attention to a parallel system of masonry established by Baron Reichel, an expatriate German who was an adherent of the Swedish–Prussian system of Dr Zinnendorf, also known as Lax Observance. The title was paradoxical. This brand of masonry deliberately underplayed the strict observances of the hierarchic masonic ritual – hence the title – but it was certainly not lax in its moral commitment, demanding strict moral discipline from its practitioners. On 12 March 1771 Reichel opened the Apollo lodge in Petersburg and in a letter to Zinnendorf acknowledged his dependence on the latter's Berlin lodge. Reichel was the master of this lodge which had only one Russian, General S. K. Naryshkin, among its founders. Seven other lodges followed Apollo's system; two were opened in Riga and Revel, while the others were established in St Petersburg. Of these, three are of particular interest, since they proved to be training-grounds for the future masonic groupings in Moscow in the 1780s which were to be so influential in Novikov's life. On 15 May 1773, the Garpokrat lodge was established with Prince N. N. Trubetskoy as its first master, directly appointed by Reichel; on 2 December 1775 the Laton lodge was established with I. P. Chaadayev as its first master (later its master would be Novikov); the following year the Osiris lodge was established in St Petersburg, but then moved to Moscow. Osiris was commonly known as the lodge of princes, since its master N. N. Trubetskoy and a number of its members were princes.[13]

From their beginning Reichel's lodges sought a merger with Yelagin's, and many members of the latter's lodges went over to Reichel's side. When Yelagin himself finally agreed to accept Reichel's system in September 1776, he became state grand master of eighteen united lodges, with only Apollo and Osiris of the old Reichel lodges remaining outside the agreement. However, Novikov had already anticipated Yelagin's move. After helping to create a new lodge headed by Yakov Fedorovich Dubyansky in 1775, Novikov seems to have become almost immediately dissatisfied with the masonry practised in the 'English' system. The decisiveness and energy of the man which had obviously been essential for his publishing now made themselves apparent in the new venture; the man who had entered masonry cautiously, by invitation, and only when reassured of its social and political respectability, now embraced the new craft with enthusiasm. 'Usage led to habit, habit to an attachment for and interest in masonic teaching and the explanation of hieroglyphics and allegories',[14] recalled Novikov at his interrogation, and one sees perhaps the newly fledged historian fascinated by the ancient mysteries as many were, before the discovery of the Rosetta stone finally broke the code of the Egyptian hieroglyphics. Novikov seems to have taken an active part in the search for the true masonic alternative to the convivial 'English' lodges; during the absence of Reichel in Moscow, contact was made with his deputy Rosenberg who arranged for the Novikov group to form a new lodge headed by Ivan Petrovich Chaadayev. There was a clear distinction between the two systems; 'between these acts and the previous English ones', noted Novikov, 'we noticed a great difference, for in them everything was based on morality and self-knowledge, the speeches and addresses produced great respect and sympathy'.[15] Meanwhile in Moscow, Yelagin had agreed with Reichel to unite their lodges, but not all masons approved the agreement and among them was Chaadayev, who withdrew to ally himself with Rosenberg. His replacement as master of the lodge was Novikov who was elected by the other members. Therefore, in a short while from his timorous joining, Novikov found himself moving into the hierarchy of Russian freemasonry, meanwhile making the masonic acquaintances which were to determine his future career: with Prince Nikolay Trubetskoy, one of the oldest Reichelian masons, Mikhail Kheraskov, Prince Gagarin, Prince Kurakin.

Now that they had begun the search for the Holy Grail of true freemasonry, the Russian masons could not rest content with the four or five degrees which Reichel could offer them, a mere degree or two above the three basic degrees of apprentice, fellow craftsman and master. Less than a month after the union of Yelagin's and Reichel's lodges, Prince Alexander Kurakin was sent to Stockholm to inform the Swedish king of the tsarevich's marriage. The Provincial lodge – which had as Yelagin's deputy Count N. I. Panin, a relative of Kurakin and to all intents and purposes Minister of Foreign Affairs – entrusted Kurakin with the task of receiving 'true masonry' from the Stockholm grand lodge. Kurakin and his colleague Gagarin were inducted into the higher degrees of Swedish masonry and returned with their secrets to St Petersburg in the spring of 1777, but without the essential documents necessary to establish the orders in Russia. These were to be brought to St Petersburg in the summer by none other than the King of Sweden himself, Gustav III, who duly arrived at the end of July.[16] However, in the Swedish system the need for the lower ranks to submit unconditionally to those above them (which in practice would mean the unconditional submission of Russian masons to Swedish masters), the personal interest of the Swedish king, the fact that the negotiations had been carried out by Alexander Kurakin, a close personal friend of the tsarevich, and Grand Duke Paul's own interest in masonry, all ensured that Catherine would look askance at this new enthusiasm. For Catherine, the innocuous conviviality of the earlier lodges was supportable although, as a woman, she could not enthuse over the delights of men's clubs: now, however, the masonic brotherhood seemed to be taking on a distinctly political colouring. The coolness of court circles was reflected in Yelagin's prevarications and eventual rejection of the offer to become a grand master in the Swedish system.[17] Novikov, too, was shrewd enough at the time not to follow the majority who rallied to Gagarin as the head of the new 'higher order' masonry. His own lodge, as well as that of Trubetskoy in Moscow, remained in alliance with Yelagin. However, there was no clear demarcation between the lodges in practice, since blood ties and personal friendships meant that men would visit lodges as guests where they were not necessarily members, and the cautious minority under Yelagin were irresistibly drawn to Gagarin's higher order masonry which united the glamour and good living of Yelagin's masonry with a decidedly more intense intellectual and philanthropic activity. In 1778 Trubetskoy and his lodge united with the Gagarin lodges 'on certain conditions', and, since Novikov was at that time in Moscow, he was pressed to accept the high seventh Swedish degree. Once again, however, Novikov had qualms about the wisdom of this action and, on reflection, remained aloof from the Swedish system.[18] For the present he could avoid choosing sides for his St Petersburg lodge: since he had decided to move to Moscow his lodge in the capital was consequently disbanded.

This ended, on his own admission, Novikov's first period as a mason. On his entry to the brotherhood in 1775, it must have seemed to him that he was entering a society with broad aims similar to those of his own literary activities.[19] Masonry was concerned with the moral training of the citizen, and the initiate to Yelagin's lodge took an oath which bound him to the image of the good citizen which had been promoted in Novikov's journals:

> I swear on my honour before the Most High Creator of the world, that on entering through my sincere desire the virtuous society of masons, I shall always remain an honest and humble man, a good, obedient and peaceful member of it, an unshakeable witness to the majesty and great wisdom of my Maker Most High, a loyal subject of my gracious Sovereign, a straightforward and worthy son of my dear fatherland, a peaceful and good citizen. That I at this moment will extirpate from my heart not only vengeance but also my indignation against those who despise and insult me in my life, that through my authority and my own property I shall always endeavour to help the poor, comfort the unhappy, defend the oppressed, not only among the masonic brotherhood but all worthy men.[20]

Novikov further refined his ideas on the nature of masonry in conversation with Reichel whose advice, accepted gratefully, he used in justification of his attitudes at his interrogation. Novikov saw masonry as seeking moral perfection by means of self-knowledge and enlightenment in the light of Christian doctrine; Reichel agreed, adding only that false masonry could be recognised by carousing and meddling in politics: 'every masonry having political aspects is false; and if you note even the shadow of political aspects, links and the affirmation of the words equality and liberty, then you can consider it false'.[21] The warning against politics was meant for the ears of his interrogators, but also Novikov's actions at the time would seem to prove that he heeded his superior's advice on that score. More decisive for the development of Novikov's and Russia's social thought was the stress placed on personal moral regeneration by means of self-knowledge.

In the moral weeklies, it could be argued that two protagonists had emerged: on one hand there was the 'club', the model of the desirable social organism which had to fit into the existing framework of official attitudes, and on the other, there emerged the social outsider – his position on the sidelines indicated by his name of Spectator, Idler, Drone or Painter – who, by the demands of the genre, was self-conscious and aware of the moral freedom of his personality. In Yelagin's initiation oath, the demands of the 'club', 'the virtuous society of masons', are still paramount. After becoming acquainted with Reichel's masonry, Novikov's emphasis is on the individual personality and the mason's own personal regeneration. For Reichel, masonry was an elite movement, withdrawn from the pomp of the world, non-proselytising, reserved and reticent.

This did not mean that the mason abandoned the world. One of the main and most easily documented results of the attempt at moral self-discipline was the charitable efforts of the Russian freemasons, rich and powerful as many of them were, to aid the weak of the world. Philanthropy came to dominate the social activity of the masons who developed a restless social conscience based on Christian charity. Charity was written into the masonic handbooks and was a favourite subject for speeches and addresses in the lodges.

When Reichel warned Novikov against political involvement, he had in mind the political implications of forging links with foreign powers and the possibility that masonic lodges might become clubs which would attempt to change the political framework of society by their 'affirmation of the words equality and liberty'. Novikov no doubt thought that he could avoid this involvement by limiting masonry to personal regeneration. Yet, on this point Catherine's political acumen was probably more acute. She looked askance at the foreign links of her principal noblemen through masonry, but she also disdained the idea of masonry. With her strongly developed political intuition, she probably sensed what the more naive could not comprehend: that the man who searched for his own fulfilment and moral perfection, as soon as he turned, animated by these desires, towards the outside world, became inevitably involved in political life. Political initiative was encouraged as long as it took place within the bounds of that traditional *opeka*, the state tutelage which was deeply engrained in the body of the Russian state; so Novikov had been encouraged and supported as a satirist and historian, working for the same general ends as his sovereign. Now, for the first time, and unconsciously, he had found another channel to mediate his energies and impulses, a channel outside the traditional ones of the autocracy. George Vernadsky doubtless overstated his case when he said that in implying that the whole state should be concerned with morality and the welfare of the people, 'philanthropy was being transformed into socialism' by the masons.[22] But there is a glimmer of truth in the suggestion. If one accepts that British socialism owes as much to Methodism as to Marx, then Russian socialism's similar debt to masonicism must not be ignored. There is little doubt that, from her point of view, Catherine's distrust of any form of freemasonry – even the least 'political' manifestation – was shrewd.

The St Petersburg Academic News

From 1777 onwards, Novikov was no longer to work alone – even with the patronage of Catherine – but with the support of a society of like-minded persons ready to support him materially and, more important, with a ready-made readership. Part of the plan for the *Treasurehouse of Russian Antiquities* which Catherine had approved two years previously, the projected critical and bibliographical section, was finally realised in a weekly publication, the *St Petersburg Academic News*. From Novikov's introduction to the new journal it is also clear that he wished to continue the work begun in his *Historical Dictionary of Russian Writers*: 'We intend also to include in our papers matter pertaining to the description of the lives of Russian Writers which could serve as an aid in bringing to full perfection The Essay at an Historical Dictionary of Russian Writers (composed by Mr Novikov) and printed in St Petersburg in 1772.'[23] It was to be published by K. V. Müller on Fridays, and an announcement by him explained the cavalier attitude to periodisation which was general among the editors of journals in Russian at this time. It was intended to publish fifty-two weekly numbers of the *Academic News* in 1777, but since two months of the year had elapsed before the appearance of the first issue, the first numbers would be backdated and, by publishing twice weekly through the months of March and April, it would be possible to bring the journal out on the correct date from May onwards to the close of the year. In the event, the journal for some reason did not survive its twenty-second issue, dated 2 June 1777. Most probably the journal did not win enough support, and did not have a sufficiently large output of scholarly works on which to feed.

If previously Novikov in his prefaces had made appeals for help from readers – appeals which met with little practical response – the *St Petersburg Academic News* seems from the beginning to have been a collective venture. The introduction to the journal, written by Novikov, began with a declaration: 'Our society, consisting of several persons, has undertaken the publication this year of periodical papers under the title *St Petersburg Academic News*.' His moral weeklies, as we have seen, attempted in part to create a readership, to arbitrate the bounds of that readership and delineate its self-image. In this new venture the target readership was more clearly defined: it was to be *Uchenyy Svet* – Learned Society. Here was the new source of patronage on which Novikov was to draw, a world to which the compiler of the *Essay at an Historical Dictionary* and the editor of the *Ancient Russian Library* had gained entry. An insight into that world is provided by the letters sent regularly by the 21-year-old Mikhaylo Murav'yev, newly arrived in the capital, to his father and sister in Tver'.[24] Immediately captivated by Novikov's personal charm and enthusiasm for literature,[25] Murav'yev was soon pressed into translating Boethius[26] and would solicit subscribers for Novikov's publications in his provincial home. Both had an entrée to Mikhail Kheraskov's salon and were among the twenty-five or so who celebrated Kheraskov's birthday on 25 October 1777.[27] The bonds fashioned there were made more secure by the ties of Masonic brotherhood and soon Novikov was able to demonstrate his reliance on this new world. After Kheraskov's move to Moscow as curator of its University early in 1778, Novikov too left the more open and frivolous society of St Petersburg to follow Kheraskov to the old capital of Moscow.

Novikov had a clear picture both of the Learned Society invited to contribute to the new journal and of the type of journal which would serve it. As with the earlier moral weeklies, Western Europe had many examples of such journals which Russia lacked and which Novikov now intended to provide. However, while admitting that his new venture would imitate these models, which concerned themselves with 'information on books printed throughout Europe together with a critical review of them; the inclusion of Maps and Charts, Prints etc.; news of the work of Scholars and their successes in the Sciences will also have their place: in short, whatever happens in *Learned Society* will find a place in these compositions'.[28] One proviso was made: initially the new journal would only concern itself with the Learned Society of Russia. In this, Novikov was following the principle which he had already learnt. He could in no way compete with the European scholarly journals with their charts and prints in gaining the attention of Russian scholars by content alone. But he could monopolise the small corner of the market where things Russian were perforce to be discussed in Russian; therefore aspiring correspondents were invited to compose inscriptions to thoroughly Russian subjects: Prokopovich, Antiokh Kantemir and Nikolay Popovsky, 'men renowned in the Sciences', and Anton Pavlovich Losenko and Yegraf Petrovich Chemezov, 'men excelling in the Arts'.

The new journal was to contain a critical section and Novikov, concerned, perhaps, that his previous satiric sprightliness in the *Drone* might be taken amiss by his new and more sober readership, hastened to stress the 'extreme moderation' of that criticism; 'it will with the utmost strictness be kept within the bounds of decency and decorum'. The doctrine of *ad hominem* satire which had been defended so vigorously in the *Drone* was now expressly excluded by a man who had meanwhile perfected his literary manners. 'Nothing satirical pertaining to a person will have a place in our *News*; but we shall speak exclusively of books without touching on their Writers.'[29]

Although Novikov indicated a special society of private citizens as the source of his patronage in this venture, yet he was still prepared to acknowledge Catherine as the real force of the Russian enlightenment. This he did in a fine, controlled piece of rhetoric in the second issue which demonstrated Novikov's mastery of Russian prose, despite his constant self-disparagement and references to his 'feeble pen':

> There ascended to the Russian throne wise CATHERINE, there ascended along with HER a sun on the horizon of Learned Society: warm, pleasant, fresh days arrived; the Arts and Sciences warmed by HER patronage flourish, ripen and bring forth rich fruits; their roots, watered by streams of Generosity and Mercy from the Throne of the REANIMATOR of the Russian Muses, have swollen, taken and put out many shoots. Skilled Gardeners take cuttings, which have grown in these happy days, and transplant them to other places: and this little garden soon grows into great and handsome parks. – Wise CATHERINE rules in Russia: the Arts and Sciences rule in our happy Fatherland. Learned Men from all lands flock to the centre of the World of Learning, and in Russia discover the Fatherland of Science. What the Augusti of Rome, and what the Louis of France took centuries to approach, Our Wise AUTOCRAT has achieved in a decade and a half . . .[30]

There was no hint here that the now confirmed mason wished to shake himself free from imperial patronage. Rather he seemed to be casting the mason in the part of the 'skilled gardener' who happily takes cuttings of approved enlightenment under the solicitous eyes of the autocrat. Catherine's pre-eminence was stressed by her *Nakaz* (Instruction) being the first scholarly work to be described in the *St Petersburg Academic News.* In promoting the *Nakaz*, Novikov was not reaching back for material to the time of the Legislative Commission in the previous decade, for in 1777 a work entitled *Russian Apophthegms* was issued which consisted largely of edifying selections from the *Nakaz.* Once more Novikov had put himself in a position where he seemed to be directly supporting a literary initiative of Catherine. This was underlined in introductory remarks to his own *Ancient Russian Library* stressing the close relationship between Catherine and Novikov in their concern for the historical publication. Readers were informed that it was the empress herself who, immediately on hearing of Novikov's intention, ordered manuscripts from her court library to be sent to him through Kozitsky, and commanded G. F. Müller to supply him with manuscripts from the archives of the Moscow College of Foreign Affairs. The handsome subsidy received from the empress was also made public knowledge.

Yet this demonstration of homage also suggested that despite its high-sounding expectations, the journal would not have much scholarly material in Russian on which to base itself. It was Novikov's own *Ancient Russian Library* which in fact managed to fill out the pages of the journal, no fewer than seven of the twenty-two numbers referring to it, and two of his other historical works provided the material for one more issue: No. 16 described his edition of Andrey Lyzlov's *Scythian History* and also the sequel to the *Library*, the *Narrator of Russian Antiquities*.

It is very possible that Novikov in this journal was obliged to write bibliographical notes on his own works in order to find material which was not forthcoming from any contributors. Again, Novikov may have underestimated the reluctance of Russia's world of learning to provide him with the wherewithal for a learned journal. It is striking that Novikov, who promised to sign the journal's articles with an initial letter to tease, as he playfully put it, inquisitive readers, and duly put his own N. after dedication and introduction, failed to carry out his promise in later numbers. The reason for this may well be that he was supplying most of the material himself. The journal did, it is true, cavil at Novikov's wrong dating in the *Ancient Library* and failure to supply an index to the first part of Lyzlov's *Scythian History*, but this mild reproach also gave the opportunity for the writer, whoever he might have been, to suggest that an index would appear in the latter parts of the *History*, and to recommend these works to amateurs of Russian history. Indexing, indeed, seems to be a preoccupation of the journal: the critic of the *Ancient Russian Library*, while regretting the passing of that journal, called for a successor who would follow certain essential procedures, the first being an index to each section, 'an alphabetical list of materials in each part which is very necessary in books of this sort to find desired things'. Again, an important review article on Stritter's *Russian History* of 1770 which gave the author – possibly Novikov – an opportunity to review Russian historiography, ended with a note of deep regret at the absence of an index to the work.

Few initials point to contributors other than Novikov. In the eighth and ninth issues L. reviews Mikhail Popov's *Leisures* and praises him as a model writer for the young. Showing a catholicity of taste, I. in the fifth issue reviews Ruban's translation of Virgil's *Georgics* and an Italian comic opera by Giovanni Paisiello, Catherine's *maestro di cappella.* In both cases he was fairly severe on the shaky spelling and insecure grammar of the translations, and was faintly ironical at Ruban's excuses in his preface that this was the fault of the compositors and 'their weak knowledge of Russian'. The social arbitrator of the moral weeklies who had used knowledge of good Russian as one of the touchstones of the good citizen had stepped over into the *St Petersburg Academic News.* A telling example was the harsh review of an anonymous translation of Marmontel's *Alceste* of 1777 whose translator had so disfigured the clear wit of Marmontel's characters that 'although they speak in Russian, yet in such a strange style and so obscurely and inarticulately that nobody can understand them'.[31] Tyro translators were advised to consult as models the translation of Marmontel's *Contes Moraux* by P. I. Fonvizin (1764) and – another obeisance to the throne – that of *Bélisaire*, translated by Catherine and her retinue on her regal progress down the Volga to Kazan in 1767.

In many ways the *St Petersburg Academic News* looked to the past. But there are indications in it of the turn that Novikov's publishing was to take in the near future to a committed masonic journal. In the twelfth issue, a short notice of a devotional work standing out strangely in the journal was an indication of Novikov's growing interest in the religious life. This was a translation from the Greek by Stepan Pisarev of *Lenten Confection* – a meditation on death – dedicated by the publisher Vasiliy Mitropol'sky to Irina Yakovlevna Khlebnikova, the wife of Novikov's collaborator, P. L. Khlebnikov.

In its last two numbers before its untimely disappearance, the *St Petersburg Academic News* dealt with a small book of maxims which appeared in London in November 1750 and proved to be one of the minor literary successes of the eighteenth century. This was a collection of moral aphorisms that could be easily understood and appreciated by even the less well-read, couched in a slightly archaic language with deliberate biblical cadences, and sufficiently diffuse in its precepts so that it would repel no sect. The anonymous *Oeconomy of Human Life; translated from an Indian manuscript, written by an ancient Bramin: to which is prefixed an account of the manner in which the said manuscript was discover'd. In a letter from an English gentleman now residing in China to the Earl of* **** which rapidly took its place amongst the most important productions of the time has been ascribed to Lord Chesterfield, but it was almost certainly the work of its publisher, a man who Novikov might have been had he been born an Englishman – Robert Dodsley. The work quickly spread across Europe in translation. Two French translations appeared in the following year: one was made by the Prince of Orange's chaplain for the use of his daughter Princess Caroline, but it was forestalled by some weeks by another translation issued by Paul Vaillant, a Strand bookseller specialising in French literature.[32] The *Oeconomy of Human Life* duly made its appearance in Russia, as the *Academic News* reminded its readers, with a translation from the French by Prince Yegor and Prince Paul Tsitsiyanov published at the Moscow University Press in 1765 and reissued in three further editions in Moscow in 1769, 1781 and 1791.[33] The *Academic News*, however, preferred Ruban's St Petersburg version which appeared under a title which stressed the mysterious Eastern provenance of the moral handbook: *The Chinese Sage, or the Science of living well in society, consisting of the most useful moral rules composed by an ancient Eastern Brahmin. Translated from Chinese into English, then French and then Russian with the addition of the history of the finding of this work in the East and with the supplement of a discourse on Christian Law by a*

European Sage. The 'European sage' was Jean-Jacques Rousseau, and the supplement was made up of three articles from the first chapter of his *Esprit, maximes et principes*: 'De Dieu', 'De la spiritualité de l'âme' and 'De l'Evangile'. Novikov in 1786 was to publish yet another version with the more sober title, stripped of the chinoiserie, *A book of wisdom and virtue, or the Condition of human life. An Indian moral work. Translated from English into German, and from German to Russian*. In all, the *Oeconomy of Human Life* was printed in nine editions in the thirty years from its first Russian appearance in 1765.[34]

Where lay, for the readers of Russian, the appeal of this work which the *St Petersburg Academic News* heartily recommended to men of all ages? It seemed to be in the corrective it made to the more extreme radical views of the contemporary *philosophes*, dealing as it did not with abstract social theory, but with the human personality and man's duty as a social being, with the sober virtues of diligence, steadfastness and tolerance, with society seen in terms of personal relationships within the family, between master and servant, sovereign and subject. Public morality was based on the personal virtues of justice, philanthropy, gratitude and sincerity. The reviewer supported the quietist, reflective posture of the Chinese sage – an attitude which was also that of his European counterpart – against the combative criticism and effect-seeking of the modern *philosophes*, and gave the former a respectable veneer of age, an attractive Eastern lacquer which it did not really possess. 'It must be admitted that the ancient Philosophers far surpass the modern ones in their writings; the former enhanced their works with the purest morality, true divine reverence, and that most difficult of all sciences, self-knowledge; most of the moderns are only concerned with the beauty and effect of their style, with their literary wit and with destruction.'[35]

'Morning Light'

All these positive virtues which the reviewer saw with innocent eyes in Dodsley's captivating but distorted moral mirror were to be displayed in Novikov's next venture, whose title *Morning Light* beckoned to the East. That journal, a committed masonic one, would suggest that there was a mysterious lode of knowledge that had been lost, that the ancient philosophers were superior to the smartly cynical *philosophes*, and above all it stressed self-knowledge; self-knowledge was not only the most difficult of sciences but also the most important and rewarding.

Morning Light, which found a spirited response from the Russian reading public, was a monthly which appeared regularly from September 1777 to August 1780, at first in St Petersburg and from May 1779 in Moscow. Being a journal which was guided by an informal, collective editorship of a group of literary friends of Novikov – Maykov, Aleksey Kutuzov, Ivan Turgenev, Mikhail Kheraskov and Mikhaylo Murav'yev, it cannot be said to be a publication which at all times reflected Novikov's views. But there is little doubt of his general sympathy with its moral aims: the propagation of a Christian humanism. In its refutation of the free-thinking of the *philosophes*, *Morning Light* made much use of the ancient philosphers Socrates, Plato, Epicurus, Zeno, and called also on those whom it considered to be their allies among the moderns, Bacon, Grotius, Christian Wolff and particularly Pascal. In this attack on free-thinkers through selections from older philosophers *Morning Light* saw itself in alliance with the church, and Novikov noted with pride in his conclusion to the journal in 1780 that clergymen, on being asked the source of their most appreciated sermons, would admit frankly the debt owed to *Morning Light*.[36] In general *Morning Light* was opposed to the prevailing *philosophe* ideas on natural law, but upheld the authority of religion and state which had checked the base instincts of the natural savage and made him into a gentleman of society. But it would be going too far to see Novikov and his group as being opposed to the totality of *philosophe* thought, and forming a clear-cut anti-enlightenment party.[37] They had assimilated many of the currents of new philosophic thought: the dependence of man and his culture on his physical environment, the great importance of climate, the feeling that there was a meaningful process at work in the unfolding of historical events, that history was not the recounting of the acts of individual personalities. In many ways, the stance of *Morning Light* was that of the moderate enlightenment which had refused to become anti-Christian and which towards the end of the 1770s was beating a cautious retreat from libertarian excesses in favour of order.

If one agrees that the Enlightenment may be described as 'the commitment on the part of a group of writers to a dual task – liberation and reconstruction',[38] then *Morning Light* supported, up to a point, the liberating aim of the Enlightenment. It did not waver from Novikov's previous conviction that the obscurantism of churchmen, identified as superstition, had prevented progress from spreading into Russia; 'This was hindered not by our capabilities but by a sort of prejudiced superstition as if secular knowledge was not kindred with Christian piety or could be a cause for the corruption of mores.'[39] By the application of extreme logic this awareness could develop, as the history of philosophic thought in France had shown, into convinced atheism. But a more moderate enlightenment could exist without necessarily being anti-Christian in its stance, as German and English writers had demonstrated, and it is this moderation that was adopted by *Morning Light*.

The essential humanism of the Enlightenment was retained. From the basis of Christian morality, the journal brought its readers to the same conclusions as those implied by the idea of natural law: the freedom of the human personality was acknowledged, the freedom of conscience, the moral equality of men, the awareness of the brotherhood of man. Moral sense could be conveyed not only by the sustained, eloquent arguments of the great names of the Enlightenment, but by such minor works as the *Oeconomy of Human Life* whose influence must be measured by the breadth of their appeal rather than by the depth of influence left on a small number of sophisticated minds. The call to 'know thyself', so characteristic an aim of Novikov's masonry, rang out loudly in the introduction to *Morning Light*: 'Nothing could be more beneficial, pleasant and more worthy of our labours than what is bound to man by the closest union, and to have his virtue, welfare and happiness as our subject.'[40]

The inscription on the temple at Delphi – 'Know Thyself' – was being understood in another sense at this time. The stress was no longer on the austere classical conception of the beauty of knowledge for its own sake. Rather, the purpose of self-knowledge was to know one's sins and failings through restless self-analysis, and by means of this knowledge to correct those failings. The call to 'know thyself' had above all a moral aim, and *Morning Light* was seen as an attempt to illumine and develop that moral sense which Novikov and his colleagues considered to be an essential part of the enlightenment. Mr Spectator and Mr Drone had, it seemed, by eyeing society from the sidelines, become aware of their own isolation and their own impotence in the attempt to cast the society they contemplated into a desirable moral mould. It now seemed that the Spectators had turned their gaze inwards into their own natures, and that the Idlers had become more acutely aware of their otiose lotus-eating. Russia, shaken by the excesses of the Pugachev rebellion, which had threatened the basic framework of society, was clearly not in a mood to be swayed by moral exhortation; the retreat to the self was perhaps the only way to turn. The appeal to a moral self-knowledge in *Morning Light* hastened the literary shift to sentimentalism in Russian literature which was to flower – particularly in the works of Karamzin – in the closing decade of the century.

Addison and Steele could not have foreseen that their clubbable inventions would lead by the close of their century to the strange sentimental egoist. Yet the metamorphosis can be witnessed at the beginning of *Morning Light* which, although a miscellany periodical with no need for a directing editorial *persona*, presented a token *persona* at the beginning as an acknowledgement of its descent from the old genre. Strikingly, this ghost from past literary practice was formally endowed with the main characterising trait of the original Mr Spectator – his massive taciturnity.[41] Equally strange was the metamorphosis of those visitors from the Orient who had arrived in Western literature to challenge with naive common sense the entrenched assumptions of Western society. They had been a literary device, figures to manipulate: the focus of attention was squarely on the European culture against which they were directed. Slowly, however, their authority had grown, and the Orient was seen, not as a source of debunkers, but as a repository of pristine wisdom. Robert Dodsley, who had invented the *Oeconomy of Human Life*, no doubt had his tongue in his cheek when he described his work as 'translated from an Indian manuscript, written by an ancient Bramin: to which is prefixed an account of the manner in which the said manuscript was discover'd. In a letter from an English gentleman now residing in China to the Earl of ****.' But that commercial title, as well as appealing to the snobbery of readers wishing to cast their eyes over a letter addressed to an earl, sought also to catch the faith they had in the philosophic authority of the ancients and, in particular, Oriental ancients typified by his 'ancient Bramin'. A translation of Francis Bacon's *De sapientia veterum*[42] enabled *Morning Light* to state that ancient wisdom was often cast in the form of symbols, fables and myths. It has been argued that by including this piece in the journal Novikov was criticising the masonic penchant for the symbolic and stressing the importance of a modern, scientific approach,[43] but Bacon's observations could also be read as reason for reinforcing the respect paid by masons to symbols, ritual and secret signs.[44] This tendency to admit the necessity of a mystical approach to ancient mysteries, including those of Holy Scripture, becomes more marked in the closing issues.

The 'Morning Light' charity schools

Morning Light, which has been called with some justification Russia's first masonic journal,[45] showed its adherence to freemasonry not only in its contents, for it was not intended to be merely a literary magazine. Its first issue declared its aim to be a charitable one, to use the proceeds from its sale to establish 'a well-run and permanent School in which children could study by the best and shortest means, be trained in piety and for further study for the sake of themselves and their Fatherland'. Although the subscription was 3 roubles 50 kopecks, in view of its charitable aim many subscribers paid 5 roubles and over, to as much as 100 roubles,[46] and P. K. Khlebnikov, Novikov's constant associate, paid for a year's supply of paper. The stress on moral self-knowledge, the turning in on one's own moral condition, had led oddly enough to the need to show concern for one's fellow man. The process was not new, for the *Painter*'s 'English Promenade' had pictured a traveller driven by his own moral sensitivity to an act of charity towards the oppressed peasants around him. But that had been an isolated act of social responsibility. What was strikingly new about the *Morning Light* initiative was its organised nature, its attempt to draw a whole society into social action. The initiative was novel, but was also the result of a long, if perhaps unplanned, preparation by Novikov. Much of the force of his early journals had come from an apparent urgent need to 'translate' abstractions and platitudes into real life. The establishment of the *Morning Light* schools continued this translation of literature into life. The two sides of the editorial *persona* of the moral journals were brought into action: the side which was self-regarding, and self-conscious of its moral condition, and the side which sought to mould society and suggest the image of the truly noble man. Literature was also translated into life in another sense: Novikov had, as a publisher, editor of journals, historian and antiquarian, been involved in literature of a collective kind and he had reaffirmed his faith in collective ventures in the various prefaces which had attempted to rally men of letters to his side. Literary collectivism was now deployed in a collective social endeavour.

An attempt to maintain schools at this juncture on the proceeds of publishing edifying material might have seemed foolhardy, as Novikov's recent experiences with the Society for the Printing of Books would have suggested. It is true that he would hope to be sustained by his newly acquired masonic brotherhood, but on the other hand such avowedly voluntary public enterprise might meet with the disapproval of the authorities. However Novikov, as in all his previous ventures, was probably assured that he was once more moving in tandem with Catherine's wishes. From January 1778 onwards the official *Sanktpeterburgskiye vedomosti* (St Petersburg News) published a monthly supplement for benefactors of the Imperial Foundlings Home and this *Izvestiya Imperatorskogo vospitatel'nogo doma* might well have acted as a guide, or a least a justification, for *Morning Light*'s communications with the patrons of its own schools.[47] The absence of Catherine's name from the latter's subscription lists has prompted the erroneous view that she looked askance at this private masonic enterprise,[48] but more eloquent is the handsome support for the schools forthcoming from prominent courtiers and the choice of the empress' nameday, 24 November 1777, for the formal incorporation of St Catherine's School at the Church of the Vladimir Mother of God. A significant part was played by the orthodox church in the charity from the beginning and, while freemasonry undoubtedly inspired the project, the promoters of the charity were careful to channel it into the orbit of the national church. The second school, St Alexander's, was also opened, at the Church of the Annunciation on Vasil'yevsky Ostrov, on the carefully selected date of 30 August 1778 which was the first nameday enjoyed by Grand Duke Alexander, Catherine's first grandson on whom she doted.[49] In 1780 the account books of the two schools would only be balanced by a substantial subscription of 200 roubles (a tenth of the total expenses) in the name of the infant Grand Duke Alexander, which must have been seen by readers as a form of governmental subvention for a laudable public initiative.[50]

The necessity for such a gift demonstrates that the schools could not have been sustained by the publishing profits of *Morning Light* alone.[51] In fact the accounts of the schools and magazine show that whereas *Morning Light* certainly set the schools on their feet, by 1780 the charitable benefactions flowing into the schools were subsidising the publication of the magazine. With *Morning Light* not making a material contribution to its schools any longer, it was politic for it to close. One reason for the closure may have been the one given by Novikov that he wished to begin a successor magazine, the *Moscow Monthly*, from January 1781. More pressing was his second reason that 'not having made contact with some of our benefactors, we did not dare continue this Publication in view of such a small sum of money remaining with us'.[52]

There is no doubt that the schools had helped to restore Novikov's fortunes as a publisher of periodicals at a critical moment in his career. By persuading acquaintances to act as charity agents in drumming up subscriptions, Novikov was able to seek out and organise a new Russian reading public beyond St Petersburg. At the end of its third part *Morning Light* was able to list as many as 789 subscribers and had found its way to distant towns such as Archangel, Poltava and Orenburg. Provincial administrators and clergymen in particular were attracted to *Morning Light*, and Novikov gained valuable experience in distributing literature through the Empire.[53] His actions as publisher and educator combined must have played their part in obtaining for him shortly the lucrative lease of Moscow University Press through his masonic connections.

What of the schools themselves? Can it be said that Novikov left his mark on the development of schooling in Russia? With no habit of school-going established and no immediate advantage apparent to school-leavers, it is not surprising that the initial charitable ideal of providing a day school was frustrated by the casual and disorderly attitude of pupils, parents and guardians. St Alexander's, where cohesion was maintained by having half the pupils as boarders, soon eclipsed the St Catherine's day school. Patrons, among whom was Nicholas Cavanagh, the English owner of a sugar factory, enabled the number of boarders to rise to 34 after two years, and when *Morning Light* closed, the two institutions had become capable of existing on their own. The *Morning Light* of November 1779 explained why this was so: it acknowledged the encouragement of many illustrious personages, the help given by compassionate, charitable souls and the philanthropic efforts of many people in gathering subscribers for the journal. This was a shrewd assessment of the elements needed to be brought together to create a successful public charity: a dynamic compound of sentiment, hard work and more than a dash of snobbery.

One important effect of Novikov's schools may have been negative, but salutary. It was possibly the sluggish public response to the example of *Morning Light*'s subscription schools that convinced Catherine that only a state-directed system of schooling was possible in Russian conditions. In 1782 her National Schools Commission was established and St Catherine's and St Alexander's were perforce absorbed, probably to the relief of their public-spirited benefactors, into the new, uniform imperial system and surrendered their independence. However, that surrender was the result of a new educational policy and not of Catherine's animosity to Novikov. The latter's schools, as well as others established before 1782, contributed to the modest programme of the National Schools Commission. Thanks to them, the public mind had been prepared for elementary, secular schooling. Furthermore they provided a basis on which the Commission, by adaptation, could construct its uniform model. It is significant that a contemporary witness, Ivan Dmitriyev, believed that the role of the *Morning Light* schools was more positive than that of forming an inert physical foundation. A brief reference to their fate in his memoirs suggests that it was from Novikov's schools that Catherine's system of national schools was developed in provincial Russia.[54]

9

A move to Moscow (1779–83)

... the court is usually in Petersburg and not Moscow, but Moscow is farther from Petersburg than Versailles from Paris.

Sumarokov.

Lessee of Moscow University Press

The need to secure the family estate took Novikov in the summer of 1778 to Moscow, where he took advantage of his visit to renew some of his St Petersburg masonic acquaintances who met at Prince Nikolay Trubetskoy's. It was during this visit that Novikov was persuaded against his better instinct to accept the seventh degree of the Swedish system of masonry, but the offer of a place in the masonic hierarchy to him suggests that he was regarded as an influential visitor, worthy of cultivation. Kheraskov, as curator of the University, must have hoped that Novikov, as a man knowledgeable about publishing, might help him to restore the fortunes of the ailing Moscow University Press, and the question was discussed at gatherings with Trubetskoy, his half-brother. Later, at Novikov's interrogation, Sheshkovsky attempted to force Novikov to admit that there had been underhand dealings at this point, an exploitation of personal masonic links to the disadvantage of the University and the public interest. There is little doubt that it was through his new masonic acquaintances that Novikov was presented with a possible business proposition in 1778. But at that time few, apart from Novikov, could have realised the great opportunity behind the proposition.

On inspecting the University Press, Novikov found a press which was extremely run-down and with a total circulation for its newspapers of some 500–600 copies. He proposed an annual rent of 4,500 roubles to the University, whose income from the Press at that time was little more than half that amount, so that Ivan Shuvalov, Director of the University, was happy to assign to

Novikov on his return to St Petersburg a ten-year lease of the Press from April 1779.[1]

Novikov for his part had seen a timely opportunity. The recent departure of the court from St Petersburg had reminded him forcibly of the shakiness of his base there, and had created havoc in his business.[2] The unsavoury suicide of Kozitsky had also deprived him of an influential friend at court.[3] He was now offered a secure base, when the success of *Morning Light* would have brought home to him that Russian masonry might replace the court as a source of literary patronage. The run-down state of the Press at Moscow enabled him to acquire cheaply as part of a fair bargain – for the officials of Moscow University considered the assignment of the lease in 1779 to be very advantageous to them – a situation which could make him a rich man. He would acquire not only the prestige of a University Press, but the only press in the whole of Moscow, the alternative and senior capital, with a population twice that of St Petersburg and with less French to frustrate the sale of books in Russian. Novikov hoped that at the expiry of the ten-year lease he would be able to retire gracefully to the life of a well-off gentleman. These business calculations which were the paramount ones for his move to Moscow were more than well-founded. Within four years he had made – on his own admission – a profit of 150,000 roubles.[4]

Not only a business opportunity drew him to Moscow. As a man of letters who was increasingly absorbed in scholarly affairs, Novikov would look upon his old University, from which many of his literary collaborators had graduated, as a centre of Russian intellectual life. From 1776, on the title pages of those historical works to which he gave his name, he had announced himself as 'Fellow of the Free Russian Society of the Imperial University of Moscow'. In making the move from St Petersburg to Moscow he would be following in the footsteps of not only Kheraskov, but also of his literary mentor and paragon, Sumarokov, who had bewailed in 1769 that a hundred Molières would be needed to flay the vices of the inhabitants of Moscow and that, alas, there was only one Molière there – himself.[5] That brimming self-confidence of Sumarokov now seemed to have passed to Novikov. As he returned to the Russian heartland, not as an amateur publisher but as the controller of a university press, Novikov must have been conscious that the move from the new to the old capital had been done before. Catherine herself, aware of the symbolism of the journey, had demonstratively returned to the old capital for her coronation and the first meetings of her Legislative Commission. Towards the end of her reign, the symbolic import of the journey in this direction was echoed when Alexander Radishchev, in a literary exercise which portrayed an innocent traveller coming to self-knowledge on the state of Russian society, had him travel not from Moscow to the political centre of Petersburg, but from Petersburg to Moscow: Radishchev's traveller left Petersburg in naivety – it was in Moscow that he arrived full of knowledge of Russia.

The under-used Press at Moscow was immediately given more work by the transplanting of Novikov's Petersburg journals to Moscow. Responding as it did to the aspirations of the influential masonic societies of the old capital, *Morning Light* naturally served as a literary bridge for Novikov's move. From May Day 1779, the commencing date of Novikov's lease, it was published in Moscow and its closure in August 1780 to make way for a successor journal, *Moscow Monthly*, emphasised the Moscow connection.

There was another bridge as well of a more calculated commercial nature. As the *Drone* drew to its close in 1770 a 'correspondent' had written to the journal asking for his advice on the projected publication by him of a magazine entitled *Fashion Monthly*. The *Drone* – with a year's experience behind it – offered some paternal advice: there would be troubles, much time and money wasted but, it added ironically, the projected title would probably save the tyro publisher from money losses and might even make periodicals fashionable again.[6] On his return to St Petersburg after the first negotiations on the lease of the Moscow University Press, Novikov began to publish in January 1779 a journal which was very different from his moral one. Its title, as in 1770, was probably designed to avoid the slightest possibility of money losses – *Fashion Monthly, or a Library of Ladies' Toilet*. As well as containing entertaining stories, songs, epigrams and puzzles, the journal also aimed to give its readers the latest intelligence of Parisian fashion, and with each number came an engraving – 'The Flirt on her Walk', 'The Happy Dandy', 'Charms Revealed', 'Toilette à la Poule'. From January to April, the *Fashion Monthly* was published in St Petersburg, and from May to December in Moscow. The commercialism of the venture should remind us again that Novikov was not a disinterested moralist and scholar, but that the commercial instinct, which had already shown itself as being beneficial in stiffening his patriotic desires to publish in Russian, had not been stifled by his newly formed enthusiasm for freemasonry. What gave the European Enlightenment its particular character was that it did not remain closeted in scholars' chambers or the gatherings of esoteric societies, but elbowed its way into the market-place. Without the commercial flair, the desire to prove by an accumulation of wealth that he was as resourceful as the best of merchants, Novikov would not have been a real man of the Enlightenment.

'Moscow News' and its supplements

As well as bringing these two journals to Moscow Novikov, on taking up the lease, took control of *Moscow News* which had first appeared on 26 April 1756 as a University journal edited by its professors. It appeared twice weekly on the post days – just as the eighteenth-century London weeklies were scheduled to catch the post for the provinces – initially on Tuesdays and Fridays, and later on Wednesdays and Saturdays. In its initial prospectus, the type of newspaper it was meant to be was explained by Ivan Shuvalov:

> The Moscow papers should begin with a St Petersburg section if there be material, and end with a Moscow one, in which there should be described the principal public happenings in the city, the public university examinations of its students and the winners of honours among them (this, of course, pertaining to the university students and the upper form pupils, and not of the lower ones) the arrival of professors with their names, publications from various places necessary for information, and also particulars of the sale of private homes etc. . . .[7]

The publication was an amalgam of a state gazette, a university gazette and a newspaper. In the early years Shuvalov himself was responsible for the court news and the *Moscow News* announced governmental decrees, new appointments and promotions in government service. Announcements were made of business from the University, the Academy of Sciences, the Free Economic Society and other similar institutions. News was taken from foreign papers and material from the *St Petersburg News* was widely used. If the material of any number overflowed its eight pages, then an article would be published in a special supplement to the paper. In 1778, the year before Novikov began his lease, supplements contained news of a gift by P. G. Demidov, the Urals ironmaster, of a collection of models 'pertaining to the art of mining and smelting' to a newly established 'Chamber of Models' at Moscow University, a report of Lord North's plan for peace with the North American states, instructions on the medicinal use of Saratov mineral waters, an account of the opening of an old people's home and a national school in Yaroslavl, and an article on removing gallstones by surgery in which the writer, Dr Ivan Venediktov, proposed the free treatment of needy patients.

The supplements continued under Novikov's management and the one on gallstones had a sequel in 1782 when an announcement from the burghers of Tver' thanked Dr Venediktov for successfully operating on seven citizens of that town.[8] But the supplements began to reflect new interests with articles on literature and art, and under Novikov the shape of the paper changed considerably, with a more vigorous editorial policy. Some articles were specially commissioned for the paper, which was a new departure for the time, and instead of relying chiefly on the *St Petersburg News* foreign news was taken directly from Hamburg, Leipzig and Königsberg papers; in 1783 (No. 28) the editors even apologised for foreign news having to be taken from the *St Petersburg News*, since the foreign newspapers had not arrived in time for the edition.

Under Novikov the paper also increased its size, improved its appearance and expanded its readership considerably. Up to 1784, each issue was normally of eight pages, but this was then increased. The quality of the typeface and the paper was also continually improved. There is no evidence of the exact circulation, but, according to Karamzin, no more than six hundred copies were published before Novikov's period as manager, and then the number of subscribers climbed to four thousand.

To the development of magazines already established Novikov, in the intense activity of the early months of his lease, hastened to add new publications. For Andrey Bolotov – an enthusiastic amateur of country life who had contributed articles to the *Proceedings* of the Free Economic Society of St Petersburg and from 1778 had published, with Ridiger, the University bookseller, a compendium of advice on agriculture and gardening, entitled *Country Dweller* – one of the most memorable days of his life was 2 September 1779 when he left Novikov's presence, so overwhelmed by the energetic personality of the manager of the University Press that he felt that he had been directed to him by the workings of Divine Providence.[10] The sharp vignette of that encounter left by

Bolotov in his memoirs tells us much about the personal charm of Novikov which helped to rally men of letters around him and his Press on the eve of the ten years in Russian history which Klyuchevsky was to label 'Novikov's decade'. Bolotov had called at the Press in order to enquire about copies of his *Children's Philosophy*, a moral journal which had appeared from 1776 to 1779, and to meet the new leaseholder whose name meant nothing to him at that time. It is a striking fact that Novikov – who, although his moral weeklies had appeared anonymously, had given his name to his more substantial works – should be unknown to a man like Bolotov, a bookworm who might have been expected to be one of the more enthusiastic readers of books in Russian and followers of Russian-language publishing. Yet, despite Bolotov's writing of his *Children's Philosophy* and *Country Dweller* in Russian for Russian readers, the sources of those productions were the foreign works in German and French which were Bolotov's staple reading.[11] Bolotov's ignorance of Novikov was symptomatic of the disinclination of cultivated Russians who had the key to Western literature in their thorough knowledge of French and German (Bolotov had been a staff interpreter at Königsberg during the Seven Years' War) to turn to books in their mother tongue. The constituency of Novikov's readers should have embraced Bolotov, and his absence from it emphasises even more the importance for Novikov's early publishing of the clients at court directed to buy Russian books at the behest of the autocrat.

A glimpse of the businessman

More important for Novikov, however, at a time when he would need writers to supply him with sufficient material for a Press he hoped would be hungry for it, was to know where he could find his manuscripts. Bolotov, who arrived at the Press unheralded, found a new manager who not only had read and appreciated his technical and moral works but clearly had formed a shrewd assessment of the abilities of the hard-working Bolotov. The meeting was between a man of letters, patronised by Catherine and the court, who had moved easily among the higher ranks of Russian society in St Petersburg, and a somewhat rough-hewn, ex-army provincial squire, but the latter was utterly charmed by Novikov's gentlemanly reception, his genuine pleasure at having the opportunity of meeting a fellow writer. So easy was the conversation that they talked, noted Bolotov, 'about everything under the sun so that in a few minutes not only did we know him well enough to have lived a lifetime together, but a friendship was formed between us which has lasted to this day'.[12]

The business which followed was made easier – as it must have been so often – by the charm and simplicity of manner. But it was not only a matter of charm. The terms offered to Bolotov for supplying material of the *Country Dweller* type were substantially better than Ridiger's. The latter's payment for a year's run was 200 roubles, for which Bolotov wrote and edited the journal. Novikov offered to double the fee, to give the author fifteen free copies and declared – to Bolotov's great relief – that he himself would see to the editing of the proposed *Economic Magazine*, which appeared as a successful supplement to *Moscow News* from 1780 onwards, and made Bolotov's reputation among his contemporaries.

By controlling the editing himself, Novikov intended to improve the appearance of Bolotov's work, and his concern to improve the quality of printing was expressed in his apology for the poor appearance of the collected *Children's Philosophy* which was the result of the poor workmanship of the Press. With the gentlemanly charm went a firm, disciplinarian grip. In his appeal to Kozitsky for help before his departure from St Petersburg, Novikov had expressed his exasperation at the drunken idleness of the compositors which delayed the appearance of his work.[13] There, the presses were not his, but now that he had full control of the University Press he intended to exert strict discipline on his workers. In 1784, when Novikov had joined the Rosicrucian form of masonry which demanded the submission of its lower degrees to higher ones, he had been directed by his superior to hand over control of the Typographical Company to a certain Schwarz. Novikov, although prepared to relinquish personal control over the stores, office and shop and also the accounts of the business, demurred at one point. He refused to transfer responsibility for the Press itself. The main reason was that Schwarz, with 'the tranquillity of his temper and tender sensibility', was temperamentally unsuited for the industrial side of the printing business. Novikov had another mason in mind for the post, an Alekseyev who knew how to handle men. From the time of accepting the leasehold of the University Press to 1784, Novikov had struggled hard to establish industrial discipline at the Press and he was not prepared to risk squandering his achievement on that score. He explained patiently:

> In looking after printing business, the main and most trying thing is to have constant watch over the working men, to make sure they come to work, work properly, that there be no pilfering, pointless time-wasting or stoppages; also their quarrels etc. must be constantly sorted out, for you, most worthy Leader, to some extent know that most of the working men, because of the previous lack of supervision, are spoilt and drunkards, so that their supervision should be strict and this with humility I put forward for your consideration.[14]

Here is a hint of Novikov's own capabilities as a manager of men: the list of works published by the presses under his management is alone proof of how he had ensured that the lackadaisical workers should do a fair day's work. It also suggests the firmness of the nobleman who had often inveighed against the lack of nobility shown in the maltreatment of serfs; but fair treatment in Novikov's eyes was allied with firmness.[15] In the machine shop of his Press he was as much a patriarchal entrepreneur as he was a patriarchal serf-owner on his estate of Avdot′ino, making a point of striding through the village on Midsummer's Eve to ensure that the bucolic pleasures of his serfs should remain within the bounds of decency.[16]

J. G. Schwarz, and the search for true masonry

Novikov was no doubt telling the plain truth when he explained to Sheshkovsky at his interrogation that so bound up was he with the cares of his new business in 1779 that he had no time for any masonic activities.[17] Yet his social connections inevitably brought him from time to time into the lodges of Trubetskoy and Gagarin, and at the former's he continued his friendship with Ivan Turgenev, who had been a member of Novikov's lodge in St Petersburg. At Trubetskoy's Novikov made an acquaintanceship which was to reawaken his interest in masonry. This was with Johann Georg Schwarz, a young German from Transylvania who had come to Russia as tutor for the children of Alexander Rakhmanov. During a stay in Moscow he had met Vasiliy Maykov, who had been introduced by him to Trubetskoy and had been made a member of the latter's lodge. Schwarz then returned to the Rakhmanov home at Mogilev with a new interest in masonry which he pursued there, eventually being sent by his lodge to Courland in search for true masonry, and from where he returned with the fourth or fifth degree of strict observance masonry. On the death of Rakhmanov, Schwarz returned to Moscow in 1780 to a post as professor of philosophy and literature at the University, and soon became friendly with Novikov who, although studiously avoiding the discussion of masonry with a member of the strict observance form against which his mentor Reichel had warned him, was attracted by the exceptional intellectual qualities of Schwarz. Their friendship flourished on the basis of their common interest in literature and the Press.[18]

Soon, however, Novikov and Schwarz found themselves members of the same lodge, although the latter had to agree not to talk about the higher degrees of strict observance masonry as a condition of his entering a new lodge formed under Trubetskoy. The new lodge was small in number and secret, following, as Novikov noted, the elitist principle of Reichel. The six other members, apart from Novikov and Schwarz, consisted of constant callers at the Trubetskoy house and collaborators on *Morning Light*: Prince Trubetskoy, Mikhail Kheraskov, Prince Alexander Cherkassky, Ivan Turgenev, Prince Yengalychev and Aleksey Kutuzov.[19] Although this lodge met informally for discussions, it seems that Schwarz's personality had a decisive influence in their deliberations and, despite Novikov's protestations that he remained loyal to Reichel's prescriptions, the new Trubetskoy grouping began to be seduced by the chimera of the higher degrees of 'true' masonry. Schwarz's appeal to the habitués of the Trubetskoy house was mainly intellectual: they were attracted by the classes which he gave at Moscow University and he agreed to lecture to the new masonic grouping in Russian on *belles-lettres* and antiquities. Friends who were interested in the matters under discussion were invited to join, and – out of politeness to their much-respected lecturer, Schwarz – Trubetskoy's lodge felt obliged to accede to a request of Schwarz's which, otherwise, they might not have contemplated; they made an overture to Tatishchev who controlled the Moscow lodges which owed allegiance to the Swedish system. As a result of Schwarz's energetic activities as a go-between, the two most significant branches of masonry in Moscow began to draw together. Tatishchev, while remaining in control of his previous 'Swedish' lodges, joined Trubetskoy's lodge which also accepted Prince Yuriy Trubetskoy, as an old mason, and two other men who were to be significant allies of Novikov in the years ahead – Ivan Lopukhin and the saintly Semen Gamaleya.[20]

Masonry, as much in its Russian manifestations as in other European countries, was often a family affair: Tatishchev's son was master of one of his father's lodges, and the two Trubetskoy brothers with their half-brother Kheraskov made their own lodge an extension of their home. Novikov's friendship for the brothers, his delight in the literary atmosphere of their house, made his involvement with their masonic activities as inevitable, perhaps, as any real enthusiasm he had for the mystique of the craft, genuine though that interest undoubtedly was. The bonds were strengthened in 1781 when Novikov himself made a blood alliance with the Trubetskoy family by marrying Nikolay Trubetskoy's niece and ward, Alexandra Yegorovna Rimskaya-Korsakova, who had been educated at the Smol′nyy Convent's Institution for Noble Girls in St Petersburg.[21]

The interest of the circle quickened at the thought that it was possible that at last the secret of true masonry was within their grasp. In 1781 it was agreed that Schwarz should go to the West, accompanied by Tatishchev's son, in search of the tablets of true masonry. The Trubetskoy circle gave the two of them 500 roubles for their expenses and 500 roubles for the purchase of books, while the elder Tatishchev contributed a similar sum.[22]

On their return, the Trubetskoy circle were extremely put out to find that the two envoys had apparently betrayed their interests. Schwarz and the younger Tatishchev had been instructed to discover a true masonry which was kindred to Reichel's system, and to avoid any entanglement with Swedish strict observance masonry, French masonry or any other which had the political colouring against which they had been expressly warned by Reichel. On reaching Courland, Schwarz was informed that the Duke of Brunswick had been recognised as the head of European masons, and that a congress was imminent, summoned by the duke to decide the basic question posed in a preliminary circular sent to his masonic lodges in 1780: 'Should the order be accepted as a mere convention, or can it be traced from an ancient society or order; what is that order?' The congress eventually held at Wilhelmsbad between 16 and 23 August 1782 decided that no, the masonic order was not a continuation of a medieval order. It had a mere 'historical' significance; 'historical' in this case having the significance that it had in the eighteenth century as being akin to 'allegorical'. Modern masonry, decided the congress, should retain the old forms and invest them with a new significance, which was chiefly the conception brought to the convention by French masons of a charitable order of chivalry expressed in the sentimental pathos of the *Règle des Francs Maçons* of the Lyons conference of French masons in 1778.[23]

There was also a reorganisation of the order: seven degrees of rank were established, and the provinces of masonry were redefined. Russia was to form a new and separate eighth province, and thus was enabled to break the impolitic link with Swedish masonry. Sweden, in fact, refused to renounce the old idea of the order as a direct continuation of the medieval Templars and left the Duke of Brunswick's jurisdiction.

Both in its commonsense view of masonry and in the reorganisation of the international order which was advantageous to Russian masonry, the Brunswick system of masonry might seem to have been suitable for Novikov's cast of mind. Why then were his friends so troubled by the news brought back from Germany by Schwarz? The reactions could possibly have had political causes, for at the beginning of the 1780s there was a shift in Russian foreign policy with the breaking of Panin's Prussian alliance by Catherine, who now attempted to reach an *entente* with Austria. In view of this, connections in Germany as well as in Sweden could have been considered inopportune. Novikov, however, indicated two sufficient reasons for their disappointment. One was a matter of personal pique. By allying the Moscow masons with the Duke of Brunswick, Schwarz had made it appear that it was Tatishchev, after all, who had been correct in his opting for strict obervance as the true masonry. Although the new lodge, formed by the alliance of Trubetskoy and Tatishchev, which had sent Schwarz as its emissary, was called Harmony, the appeasing title clearly masked a great deal of continuing factiousness. The other reason was that they baulked at the very conception of an order of chivalry. The idea of 'chivalry', of 'knights of chivalry' promoted by the Duke of Brunswick, seems to have been identified with the aristocracy of birth which had been so resolutely attacked by Novikov in his journals and which was so distrusted by the general drift of the century's enlightenment.[24]

Schwarz, however, was diplomatic enough to return to Moscow

with something which would please both the factions which had dispatched him Westwards in search of the true masonry. With Tatishchev happy to be linked to the chivalry of the Duke of Brunswick, Schwarz then told Trubetskoy and Novikov that, since he had surmised that they would not be pleased with the first outcome of his journey, he had also brought with him another system of masonry. The explanation that Schwarz gave for his returning with two versions of the one, true system was that his informant in Courland had declared that he would only supply the information of its source on condition that the Russians first accept the masonry of chivalry and that the Swedish connection be broken at the coming convention. Yet it transpired that the true masons in Berlin who accepted the same fashion of degrees as Reichel and worked 'in complete humility and tranquillity' had not sent delegates to the Wilhelmsbad convention; indeed they suggested to Schwarz that not only were there no true masons at the Duke of Brunswick's convention, but that it might have been infiltrated by the *illuminati*, the most redoubtable foes of valid masonry who had their stronghold in Bavaria. The holders to the key to true masonry in Berlin whom Schwarz had visited were Johann Christian Anton Theden, staff general surgeon at the Prussian court, and Johann Christoph von Wöllner[25] who was to be Minister of State in charge of spiritual affairs in the reign of Frederick William II, an obscurantist who is remembered as establishing the rigorous censorship which put an end to the tolerant enlightenment of Frederick the Great.

The sending of Schwarz abroad had done nothing to clear the miasma surrounding true masonry, and his return with the two versions had compounded the confusion. In some ways he seems to have deliberately misled the Moscow masons by withholding information about Wöllner, for it is reasonable to suppose that he knew from his observations in Berlin that Wöllner had long been an adherent of strict observance masonry.[26] The rank system which Novikov distrusted was, in fact, exploited to extreme lengths by Wöllner, who placed all subordinates under the control of unknown superiors to whom they had to owe unquestioning allegiance, whose orders they had to carry out unquestioningly and to whom they had to submit regular confessional reports on their own spiritual condition.

A hint of Wöllner's skilful organising power was immediately discernible. No attempt was made to win over the Moscow freemasons directly. Instead they were bidden to be patient and wait until they were mature enough to receive the new dispensation from Berlin.[27]

In the meantime the Duke of Brunswick's lodges were to be established. Two chapters were set up: one under Tatishchev and the other under Trubetskoy. Novikov at this time was also moving to the forefront of the masonic movement and, under his lodge, as many as four were established with Gamaleya, Kutuzov, Lopukhin and Klyucharev as their respective masters. Moscow masons formed a union, and both Trubetskoy and Novikov as their acknowledged leaders received complimentary letters from the duke himself. At about the same time Prince Gagarin, who had moved to Moscow from St Petersburg, broke the Swedish connection and allied his lodges with the others.

This arrangement, however, was only provisional, for the Trubetskoy grouping were clearly eager to hear that they were acceptable to Wöllner and to a system of masonry which, as they had been led to believe by Schwarz, was opposed to a regard for a strict hierarchy. As they waited for the hesitantly humble overture from Berlin to become a firm invitation – they were not to know that the apparent quiet hesitancy on the part of Berlin was probably a calculated piece of skilful angling on the part of Wöllner and his missionary Schwarz – the Moscow masons probably began to cast the arcane Berlin system in their own image. Behind the mysterious overtures, they probably wished to see a quietist, moral masonry opposed to pomp, political involvements and the things of this world. Schwarz, who seemed to be acting as a conscious evangelist of Wöllner's mysticism, worked hard to foster this image, and retired from his University post in the autumn of 1782 to devote himself wholly to the missionary cause.[28] Novikov at his interrogation recalled with naivety Schwarz's tactics. On his retirement, he lived at Novikov's house for six months and first announced that he had word on good authority from Berlin that it was most probable that the Moscow masons would be admitted to the true masonic order and that it had been decided to allow the leading Moscow masons to submit pleas of application! Applications were invited from Novikov, Turgenev, Kutuzov, Gamaleya, Vasiliy Chulkov (who had been a member of Novikov's lodge in St Petersburg), Novikov's brother Aleksey and Lopukhin.

Novikov gave a somewhat schematic account of an exchange

between him and Schwarz on the nature of the Berlin brand of masonry. Although this exchange must be read partly as an attempt by Novikov to justify his actions to his interrogator, yet one must see in it a probable reflection of continuing discussions between the two on the nature of masonry during Schwarz's stay at Novikov's. And Schwarz's explanations seemed designed to fit Novikov's predilections. Reported Novikov:

> I asked him to give a true idea of the order and the nature of its purpose, to which he replied: that its purpose is knowledge of God, nature and oneself by the shortest and surest way. I asked: Is there not something in the order contrary to Christian teaching? He replied: No! The order in its doctrine follows in the steps of Christian doctrine and demands from its members that they be better citizens, fathers etc. than they were before entering the order. I asked: Is there anything against sovereigns? He replied: No! and swore to that.[29]

It was inner piety that Novikov looked for in masonry, as did Ivan Turgenev, who indicated that it was the mysticism of Wöllner's system which appealed mainly to his friends. Likewise Trubetskoy who, in a series of letters in the summer of 1783 to Rzhevsky in St Petersburg, argued that the latter should join the Moscow masons in switching allegiance from Brunswick's 'chivalry' to the strict moral code flaunted by the 'theoretical degrees' of Wöllner.[30] The choice had already been faced by the masons in the 1770s: should they submit to a strict system of degrees of rank, or should they deliberately play down their importance (Lax Observance) and submit rather to the equally strict demands of inward piety? Differences of opinion on the observances of ranks of 'chivalry' also caused friction between Schwarz and Novikov, although the latter, as he was promoted in the masonic hierarchy, obviously did not find his high ranks of knighthood particularly uncongenial in practice.

In all this confusion of wishful thinking, what is certain is that the attitude to masonry of the Moscow fraternity chimed with the attitude to society at large fostered by Novikov in his moral weeklies. The social paragon inside and outside masonry was not the man who owed his position to rank or birth – Novikov's journals had stressed the positive value of a lax observance of the old Muscovite hierarchical, social structure. The patriot was a man disciplined by an inner code of morality, sustained by his sense of identification with a like-minded coherent group, guided by a sense of *noblesse oblige*, of deeply felt responsibility towards his society.

This image delineated in the pages of the journals could now act out its part in an apparently suitable masonic form. Trubetskoy, in one of his letters to Rzhevsky, stressed that the 'theoretical degree' of the new system was open, if not to all the talents, then certainly to all men of worth: 'And thereby you will have completely broken with chivalry, for, in order to enter the theoretical degree, it is not necessary to be a Knight, but worthy men enter directly from the Scottish Degree'[31] (i.e. the first rank above the original three masonic ranks).

Schwarz had not only asked Novikov and his closest intimates to send letters of application to Berlin, but had also approached the other leading masons, Tatishchev, Trubetskoy and Gagarin. However, it was only he, as the envoy of Wöllner in Moscow, who had full knowledge of the overtures being made. In six months' time news was received from Berlin that the letters of application had been approved. Provisionally the Moscow masons had already formed a union of four 'mother lodges' which had decided to break with 'chivalry': Three Banners under Tatishchev, Osiris under Trubetskoy, Laton under Novikov and Sphinx under Gagarin.

Meanwhile, the disaccord between Wöllner and the masonry which had issued from the Wilhelmsbad convention was formalised on 11 November 1783, when Wöllner's Three Globes lodge in Berlin declared its own independence and invited other lodges to acknowledge their own dependence on it. This letter was received in the Moscow lodge of Tatishchev's Three Banners at the beginning of 1784, and signalled the final turning-point in the Moscow mason's drift under Schwarz's encouragement away from the Knights of Chivalry to the later Rosicrucianism.[32]

As we have seen, Novikov's role in all this masonic manoeuvring for organisational pre-eminence was considerable. By virtue of his close friendship with Trubetskoy and Schwarz, he stood at the centre of the masonic hierarchy, and was himself prepared to step forward to assume a directing role in the movement. Yet it would be a mistake to see his outlook at this time being formed by the masonic movement. Not only was he impatient at the caste feeling to which 'chivalry' masonry pandered, but he was unable to throw himself wholeheartedly into masonic activities as the professionalised mason Schwarz was able to do. This was a point of friction between them. Novikov, a man of the world, immersed in business and the management of men, could look with some objectivity at

Schwarz's fervent proselytising and sought to restrain the latter's enthusiasm. Schwarz in turn chided Novikov for his coolness to the order and desultory practice, but for Novikov this was inevitable, since during these early years in Moscow he was fully occupied by his publishing and the task of setting the University Press on its feet.[33] Masonry for Novikov was not a force which would mould his outlook: rather Novikov found in the practice of masonry a convenient receptacle which suited the philosophy which he had already worked out for himself in a decade of energetic work and thought directed at the enlightenment of his country. That Novikov's outlook remained substantially unchanged is suggested by Schwarz's efforts to draw the energetic publisher – who would be so useful for proselytising masonry – into his organisation by presenting the masonry of Wöllner to Novikov in terms which he knew Novikov would approve.

To the end of 1783 Novikov's other activities were of far more importance than his masonry, although they were inevitably entwined with his connections in the lodges. Masonic connections had led to his marriage to Alexandra Rimskaya-Korsakova, but because of that it does not necessarily follow that his choice of wife was a masonic act. Similarly, his activities as a publisher and educator in Moscow need not necessarily have depended on masonry. No doubt if masonry had not existed, Novikov would still have been a publisher, an earnest social reformer and would have married Alexandra Rimskaya-Korsakova.

10
The Russian reader discovered (1779–82)

Novikov was not a bookseller: getting rich by selling books was never his aim.

Belinsky

He traded in books as a rich Dutch or English merchant trades in the produce of all lands . . .

Karamzin

As a publisher, bent on creating and serving an expanding market for books in Russian, Novikov's most immediate problem was to obtain sufficient copy to feed his presses. Until now he had always been able to produce his own material, but the scale of his new enterprise was too great for that. Translations – predictable in their appeal – formed the bulk of the output in his first few months to the end of 1779, and, although no definite plan of publishing was discernible by the year's end, the preponderance of translations was to persist until the end of the decade. The translators were found through the connections of his Moscow friends and soon among the students of the University. One early sign of the patronage that was later to flow to the students was the translation in 1779 of a German work, *Curiosities of Nature*, by Alexander Lyzhin, 'Student of the Moscow Imperial University'. Noteworthy among the translations the following year were the versions from the French by Ambrose, Prefect of the Moscow Academy, of Milton's *Paradise Lost* which was dedicated to Archbishop Plato, the translation of Blackstone on English law by S. Desnitsky who had graduated from Glasgow University, a work printed at the expense of Catherine's Cabinet, and also Desnitsky's translation of Thomas Bowden on agriculture. Ivan Lopukhin rendered Young's *Triumph of Faith over Love* into Russian. That septuagint of translators which Catherine had attempted to marshal to bring the gospel of the Enlightenment into Russia was set to work again, and Novikov was still able to utilise the early initiatives of the Society for the Translation of Foreign Books and his own Society for the Printing of Books to serve his press. Editions begun by the latter Society but not concluded were now taken up again: in 1780 *Gulliver's Travels* and the *Golden Hours* were at last completed.[1]

Set against the mass of translations, the number of original works of literature in Russian was insignificant. It is true that eleven out of forty-seven titles in 1779 were original, but eight of these were light comedies or comic operas, and this high ratio was not achieved again during the decade. In the following year there were only ten out of a hundred and seventy, only nine out of seventy-three in 1781. In 1782, if one leaves out *poèmes de circonstance*, such as Bogdanov's *Ode to Count Chernyshev*, the original literary works amounted to two plays by Kheraskov: *Idolators*, a tragedy, and a comic opera, *Good Soldiers*, which had already been published in 1779 – and one anonymous piece, *A Miser Cured by Love*. In 1783 there were only five original literary works.

The poor showing of *belles-lettres* was probably due more to the absence of creative writers than to any antipathy on Novikov's part. He was quite prepared to publish translated *belles-lettres* in quantity, and as soon as he had established control over the University Press he set to work to edit the complete works of his literary hero, and constant touchstone of literary taste, Sumarokov. To this edition he was prepared to attach his name and credentials, 'Nikolay Novikov, Fellow of the Free Russian Society at the Moscow Imperial University.'

The church hierarchy played a prominent part in supplying the reformed Press with material. Work after work was dedicated to them, and by the close of 1783 no fewer than five works had been dedicated to Archbishop Plato himself. The clergy, who had found meat for their sermons in the pages of *Morning Light*, responded by writing an increasing number of devotional works, and 1782 saw a significant increase in the number of religious works by churchmen coming out of the Press. The following year – which was one when Novikov obviously gave much thought to finding a Christian path in the labyrinthine passages of freemasonry – saw another increase in the percentage of religious and devotional works. In his publishing there seemed to be a shift to the inner life of man, a moving away from the social glitter of the light comedies and comic operas. Works which were associated with masonry, such as Charles Johnston's *Pilgrim* and John Mason's *Self-Knowledge*, made their appearance in this year. The latter work, in particular, became notorious in Russia as the epitome of dangerous and seditious masonic literature. Translated by Ivan Turgenev, it was the work of an English Congregational minister, whose conservative views contrasted sharply with the apocalyptic vision of his grandfather, the John Mason of Holy Ground fame. Why a moderate devotional book by an eighteenth-century English divine should have earned such a reputation as a seditious work in official circles in Russia is one of the curiosities of literary history. The main reason may have been a genuine and general confusion about the author's name: the inoffensive John Mason being understood in Russia as an authoritative and somewhat mysterious John *the* Mason. Whatever the real reason, the notorious legend persisted into the following century when a work by 'John the Mason' was one of the doubtful books harboured in the small provincial town depicted in Gogol's *Inspector General*[2].

Education: textbooks and institutions

The flood of devotional literature, of course, reflected the interests of the age, as did the number of textbooks retailing factual knowledge for which the readership was certain. The University Press functioned, to Novikov's great profit, as an educational publishing house. Language primers were particularly numerous: a German reader, a French grammer, a Russian version of Gesner's *Latin Lexicon*, a Latin syntax, a multilingual lexicon. Technical textbooks were published: an economic calendar, a geometry and trigonometry textbook. Knowledge and language-learning could be combined as in the trilingual geography textbook in Russian, French and German published in 1781. Novikov published a poetry primer for the seminarists at the Trinity Seminary, Barsov's *Russian Grammar* for use in the gymnasium. One of the first works published was Johann Schwarz's German rhetoric in 1780, and this signalled the close links between Novikov's publication of textbooks and his continuing interest in education.

It was their collaboration in setting up charitable educational groups alongside the University Press that brought Novikov and Schwarz together initially: education would, of course, increase the demand for printed works, but it would also nurture the knowledge of European languages among penurious young men who would be the hard-working hacks of the future needed by Novikov for his translations. Through *Morning Light* Novikov's friends continued their support for the schools in St Petersburg, but their main concern now switched to Moscow where their burgeoning zeal for education was encouraged by Schwarz, who happened to arrive in Moscow at the right time. It has been noticed that Eastern Europeans helped to foster public education in both capitals, for, while Novikov enjoyed the support of Schwarz, a Transylvanian German, in Moscow, Catherine in St Petersburg had called on the aid of Jankovic de Mirievo, an Austrian Serb, for her Commission for National Schools.[3] If in 1783 the Commission had absorbed *Morning Light*'s establishments and founded an institution for training teachers, the need for teacher-training had been anticipated in Moscow for, as early as 13 November 1779, Schwarz found himself the 'Inspector' of a Pedagogical Seminar in Moscow for the training of teachers. It was the first attempt to realise Schwarz's programme, which would 'spread among the public the rules of education, support Novikov's press enterprise by translating and publishing useful books; endeavour to attract to Russia foreigners who would be capable of giving education – or better still – educating on their own account teachers from among the Russians'.[4] The Pedagogical Seminar was founded by a donation of 20,000 roubles from P. A. Demidov, the interest on which was to support six students. By 1782 the number of students had risen to thirty, each one being supported by a sum of 100 roubles.

On 13 March 1781, again at Schwarz's instigation, the Society of University Alumni, which has been claimed as the first student society in Russia, was formed.[5] At his funeral – Schwarz was to die as a young man just turned thirty within two years – a member of the Society recalled the two kinds of salvation which it might achieve:

> ... first, concerning the enlightenment of reason, to practise in compositions of various sorts and translations of the best passages from ancient and modern writers and to publish annually a journal in aid of the poor, and secondly, in order to reform directly our perverted inclinations, to make a speech on morality to the other members at the beginning of each meeting in turn; and in this way, uniting together in the most tight knot of love and desire to achieve an aim so magnificent for young men, they could make themselves useful in time both for themselves and for their whole beloved fatherland.[6]

The practice of literary composition and translation which helped to supply Novikov's press with material was further encouraged by a special Translation Seminar, established at the University in the summer of 1782 with the aim of translating moral works into Russian.[7] Tatishchev agreed to support six students in this new seminar, and prevailed on his friends to support a further ten. Six students were then transferred from diocesan seminaries to the new Translation Seminar, among them one M. I. Nevzorov for whom, as we shall see, it was a fateful and, in due course, a most unfortunate turn. A house was bought near Menshikov Tower as a residence for the students in the Pedagogical and Translation Seminars, and Schwarz moved from Novikov's apartment to live with them.

It was time for the quickening philanthropic activity in Moscow to be trumpeted to the world at large. On 6 November 1782, Tatishchev at his house at Krasnyye Vorota played host to the principal nobles and scholars of Moscow who had been invited in Russian and Latin to attend the formal opening of the Friendly Learned Society which had been officially approved by the governor-general of Moscow, Count Z. G. Chernyshev, in October and been given the blessing of Archbishop Plato of Moscow.[8] Novikov could not have been without interest in the aims of the Society which reaffirmed with pomp and ceremony the initiatives of the Seminars: the Friendly Learned Society, it was explained, had already had printed and distributed *gratis* to seminaries and other educational establishments textbooks to the value of 3,000 roubles, and also it supported a Philological Seminar of thirty-five students – which presumably referred to the gathering of the previous Pedagogical and Translation Seminars under one roof.[9] It is hardly likely that Count Chernyshev and Archbishop Plato would have given their wholehearted support to this venture if they had had any inkling of the disapproval from St Petersburg for the individual initiative taken within the framework of Moscow University. The twin capitals for the meanwhile seemed to be acting in concord, for the official opening of the Friendly Learned Society almost coincided with the setting up of the Imperial Commission on National Schools.[10]

The 'Moscow Monthly Publication'

The practice of translating moral works for charitable ends was given an outlet in Novikov's *Moscow Monthly Publication* of 1781 which was advertised as a continuation of *Morning Light* and was still intended to support the St Petersburg charity schools. Gifts to the schools were acknowledged in the first number, and an 'inhabitant of Moscow', it was reported, would pay the fees of three graduates of the charity schools – Vasiliy Il'insky, Vasiliy Titov and Stepan D'yachkov – at Moscow University. The table of contents of the first number gave readers a fair idea of the moral earnestness of the journal: 'Mr Bickerstaff's Conversation with his Guardian Spirit' (due obeisance was made to the by now somewhat wan *persona* of the *Tatler* and *Spectator* type of journals), 'On Mankind's Secret Wishes,' 'The Melancholy Consequences of Fickleness', 'From the Moral Compositions of English and German Moralists'. But it would be wrong to assume from this that one had bid farewell to Novikov as a sprightly journalist, that the move to Moscow had in fact signalled a shift to sombre preaching. Novikov's own foreword announced that although the *Moscow Monthly* was to be a continuation of *Morning Light*, the new name would signify a new direction in editorial policy. Significantly, it was a change of direction away from the over-earnest moral tone of the previous journal – which gives the lie to the view of Novikov becoming more and more obsessed with moral teaching as he became embroiled with freemasonry. The commercial considerations of the publisher in full control of his own press seemed to have dictated a lighter tone, and Novikov admitted this; the change in direction was planned 'in order thereby to please both those who would be bored by material which was lofty and consequently not amusing or diverting for them, and those who feel the sweetness and wholesome benefit in moral teaching and lofty thought'.[11] Divertingly spiced material appeared in the journal with its second number, which contained pieces culled from German publications with a moral, it is true, but designed to capture the attention of the more prurient reader: the cautionary tales of Henry VIII and Anne Boleyn, and the story – under the heading 'Justice and Paternal Love' – of James Lynch Fitzstephen, Mayor of Galway, who in 1526 condemned his own son to death by hanging for murder.

A clear picture of Novikov's views, now trenchant and uncompromising, emerges from the foreword. A moderate enlightenment seems to match the middle way along which he directs his editorial pen. His aim is to guard the middle ground of the enlightenment against the obscurantists on one side and the extreme free-thinkers on the other. Along with the men of the enlightenment, he is happy to proclaim that 'the cause of all human error is ignorance, and of human perfection is knowledge'. This middling commonplace had to be defended against the obscurantists who argued that learning often led to atheism. Novikov does so: 'Quite so, but this is not the result of the sciences, but of ignorance in the sciences.' Mechanical learning, voided of any moral guideline, is abhorrent to his moderation, and Russian sophisticates are denounced for using their knowledge and education to mock Christianity, which is presumably what Novikov means by 'the law received from on high by the first people for the salvation of human kind and rendered unto us by tradition'. But he may also mean – for as a man of his age he seems more given to devotion than theology – a Christian masonry, since he also declares that there does exist an ancient mystery which has become obscured by the patina of man's 7,000 years of age. There is a sense of loss in the foreword, the loss of a firm synthetic philosophy. It leads him to a discussion of the hieroglyphic language whose importance was that it was the means of expression of the first man who, with his 'pure reason and excellent feelings', was able to penetrate to the nature of things and understand their relationship – the *analogia rerum* – 'in a word, he could read the whole of nature and wonder at the wisdom of the Creator'. Before the discovery of the Rosetta stone, hieroglyphics had fascinated better-trained intellects than Novikov's among contemporaries, and as a printer with a craftsman's high regard perhaps for the craft secrets on which freemasonry was supposedly based, he had reason to be more fascinated than most by the sacerdotal implications of the Egyptian hieroglyphics.

In this one respect, there is a difference here from the *Encyclopédie* with its sceptical article on 'Hieroglyphics', but in general it is worth noting how closely Novikov stood to the position of the *Encyclopédie* in its approach to philosophy and knowledge.[12] Novikov had a weighty precedent for his moderate Christian stance. If a man did not put his heart into learning, if he did not unite a moral view with his knowledge, then 'he is worthy of pity, and for all his knowledge is a complete ignoramus, harmful to himself, his neighbour and his society', argued Novikov, from the premise that 'the object of all branches of science is threefold: we ourselves, nature and the Creator of all things'. That premise echoed the *Encyclopédie*'s declaration in its article on 'Philosophie'

– 'Les objets de la philosophie sont les mêmes que ceux de nos connaissances en général, et forment la division naturelle de cette science. Ils se réduisent à trois principaux, Dieu, l'âme, et la matière.'

The message of the preface was supported in the March issue – significantly dedicated to Archbishop Samuel of Rostov and Yaroslavl as a 'lover and patron of the sciences' – by an article entitled 'Philosopher' which made plainer the identification of Novikov's general outlook with that promulgated in the *Encyclopédie*. The first part of the *Moscow Monthly* article was culled from the *Encyclopédie* article 'Philosophie', which had explained that the gulf between theology and philosophy had been bridged as theologians came to realise that reason – man's true guide – was a divine gift. English divines were mainly responsible for allowing in this way the name of the *philosophe* to be equated with the true Christian.[13] Again the free-thinkers – a sect which had the impudence to call themselves *philosophes* – were put firmly outside the philosophical pale.

To the parts gathered from the article on 'Philosophie' was added a translation by the student Nikolay Lava of the article 'Philosophe'. This article, long regarded as one of Diderot's best, was, in fact, a shortened version of one written by some unknown person and first printed in 1743, and possibly circulated in manuscript before that.[14] No one's property, it seems to have been a distillation of the general view of the *philosophe* which made it acceptable to a general audience, for the repeated printing of the article in the eighteenth century bore witness to its widespread popularity. Voltaire, who not only reworked the text twice, but published it repeatedly, claimed that it was 'dans le portefeuille de tous les curieux'. In choosing a general definition for the creature called *philosophe*, who was its own creator, the *Encyclopédie* would naturally choose such a text, but what is significant is that Diderot had made the *philosophe* in his *Encyclopédie* more aware of the value of faith than the one in *Les Nouvelles Libertés de penser* on which it was based. One reads Diderot as arguing that one must have a better idea of the *philosophe* than as a man who scorns religious faith. There is, indeed, criticism of such a man – roundly seconded by Novikov – 'en qui la liberté de penser tient lieu de raisonnement'.

But the *philosophe* whose definition so appealed to Novikov differed from older ideas of the philosopher in one crucial way. If older philosophers had sought for an ultimate truth to which society was bound to conform, and furthermore had sought that truth in withdrawal from the world, the new *philosophe* accepted society itself as his standard.[15] He had to accept society's mores as criteria for moral conduct and, far from withdrawing from society in search of truth, had rather to engage himself, mind and heart, in the workings of society. Society was no longer conceived, as with Hobbes or Bacon, in a general and abstract way, but as a concourse of patriots whose image could be reflected in moral journals. For this reason, despite the stress on philanthropic charity, the pleasures of society and wealth were not denied in Novikov's foreword to the *Moscow Monthly*.[16] But with his traditional habits of thought uprooted by the modern *philosophes*, the son of the fatherland, the thinking Russian, was left with no firm cornerstone: and so Novikov hankered after the absolute truth behind hieroglyphics and the foundation stone of masonry.

On the whole, the contents of the *Moscow Monthly Publication* responded to the lead given in the foreword and the *Encyclopédie*'s view of the *philosophe*. The moderate enlightenment which was not anti-Christian, and which seemed to the Russians to be disseminated in England and Germany, was stressed by the distinctive English and German presence in the magazine. This did not mean that French influence was excluded: the prescriptions of the *Encyclopédie* were followed by selections from even such disguised libertines as La Rochefoucauld and Madame de Lambert. But the seeking of the credentials of enlightened authority in England and Germany was for the first time clearly evident in the *Moscow Monthly*. An anonymous article 'On the Main Reasons for the Growth of the Arts and Sciences' seconded the due given by the *Encyclopédie* to English philosophers for managing to unite faith with philosophy: 'The English have had great successes in Philosophy; the reason for that I maintain to be the proud liberty of their thoughts and compositions which can be an example to the whole world.'[17] Climatic causes were also adduced for the present pre-eminence of English culture: '. . . the sciences first grew on the fertile banks of the Nile, whence they were received by the Athenians who enriched them, the Romans brought them to perfection, and Paris embellishes them; London, wishing to multiply them, gave them a serious and melancholy aspect, matching the air around them'.[18] Mr Spectator was referred to as a 'moral teacher' at the beginning of an article entitled 'A Christian at the Graveside', which also included a reference to the touching thoughts of Hervey and his edifying musing on the majesty of creation in gardens and fields. One of the students, Andrey Bryantsev, busily translated directly from the English short moral tracts on the need for temperance and industry, and – a constant concern of the *Spectator* – the folly of duelling.[19] If England and Germany provided an example of healthy moderation, Spain was used by the *Moscow Monthly* as a sorry example of a world where obscurantism was compounded of laziness, pride and superstition: characteristically, the source of the two pieces 'On the Mores of Spaniards' and 'On the Government and Monks in Spain' was German.

In August and September, the initials A. K. and I. T. appeared in the journal, and it seems as if at this time Novikov might have handed over the editorial control to Aleksey Kutuzov and Ivan Turgenev, for there was a distinct change in the complexion of the *Moscow Monthly* in the last third of the year. Kutuzov and Turgenev, not being disciplined by the hurly-burly of commerce as Novikov was, were more deeply pious, more committed to masonic mysticism than their friend, but it is striking that in their contributions they followed the main lines of Novikov's introduction. Kutuzov's first piece was a priggish, Polonius-like 'Father's Advice to His Son on Sending Him to the Academy' but it reaffirmed the need for a morally committed and socially relevant education; the father stressed that if his son returned 'with more learning but less goodness of heart, I will receive you very coldly, but if you have gathered useful mores, I will receive you full of delight. If you have the greatest intelligence but are not an honourable man, I will weep for having given you life.'[20] Authority was given to the piece with quotations from German poetry, and Turgenev too looked to Germany by choosing to translate the inaugural lecture of a Leipzig professor, 'On the Influence of the Sciences on Man's Heart and Character', which again illustrated Novikov's outlook, since it was a fervent address on the significance of the liberal arts in forming a social being; in modern terms, he stressed their relevance to society.

With the advent of Kutuzov and Turgenev, there were more items, shorter and more digestible, there was more sentimentalism, more poetry and more devotional, avowedly Christian literature. English influence was still marked, but in the latter months of the year the emphasis was subtly different. When Josiah Wedgwood supplied Catherine the Great with the Frog service which depicted scenes from Great Britain and Ireland, most of the plates and tureens carried the images of stately homes and parks into Russia. But a few pieces bore the exotica of the crude crofts of the Western Isles of Scotland. These images reflected the Russian curiosity in two sides of English literature: if the stately homes suggested in their handsome proportions the self-confident moderation of the English Enlightenment, the yeoman croft was no less appealing – as Wedgwood had rightly sensed. A tale in the last issue of December entitled 'The Hermit, or Amintor and Theodora' was set in the Hebrides where 'Quiet tranquillity, an ancient loyalty, the union of hearts, and innocence are the household gods.' Sentimentalism had established itself with its union of religion and love, and also an English pedigree, which was reinforced by a prose translation – from the French – of Pope's 'Messiah: a Sacred Eclogue' (which had first appeared in the *Spectator* on 14 May 1712), papers given in 'a Christian Society in England' on brotherly love, and a fulsome reference to Richardson's *Pamela* in a letter written by a father to his 17-year-old daughter from his death bed. 'Pamela', he wrote, 'is the most exalted name of woman, much more illustrious than the name of a Tsaritsa.'[21]

This kind of letter, written by one person to his beloved – father to daughter, husband to wife – was common in the later numbers and is an indication of a withdrawal into the self. Writing was no longer a social activity as it was in Novikov's early journals, when letters were written to a social arbitrator and addressed, through him, to society at large. The crowd has been whittled down to one, the tone of voice was quietly intimate and writing was seen as an emotional rather than a social activity. 'Here I sit', writes a husband to his wife, 'muse, feel, sigh, weep and write: for sighing, weeping and writing – alas! melancholy exercise! – are now the most pleasant which I have.'[22] This literary movement was imitated in the intimate gatherings and quiet discussions of the masonic lodges; the faith in England and Germany as the homelands of a moderate, wise and Christian enlightenment gave the links with the masonry of those countries a spurious – and in the case of the links with Wöllner – a completely unjustified authority. Earlier, Novikov had castigated his fellow countrymen for not being able to distinguish between true French culture and the trinkets and baubles of Paris; now his circle of friends were to show a similar lack of discrimination in their new enthusiasm for the Northern lands.

'*Evening Twilight*'

The *Moscow Monthly* was followed in 1782 by another monthly, *Evening Twilight*, whose editors were Schwarz's students in the Pedagogical Seminar. The formal division of each number reflected the inflexible, academic character of the undertaking which was to be the field for the literary exercises of Schwarz's students. *Evening Twilight* began with a philosophical article – 'Discourse on the Immortality of the Soul', 'On the Existence of God', 'On Conscience' etc. – and continued with a verse translation of a Psalm, translation of moralistic tales, a medley section of verses, madrigals, epigrams, riddles and finally a masonic article 'On Egyptian Teaching'. Although the journal was dated from January 1782, so that it apparently followed *Moscow Monthly* without a break, the first issue did not in fact appear until March,[23] after the return in February of Schwarz from his quest for true masonry. The latter's influence on the journal through his students must have been particularly strong. This did not mean that *Evening Twilight* would have appeared to its readers to break radically with its predecessors. The title *Evening Twilight* was not a riposte to *Morning Light*, but was, as the foreword explained, a statement of the condition of man's awareness; 'Comparing our present condition with that in which our forefathers shone with the midday light of wisdom, we find that the light of our reason is hardly comparable even with the light of evening.'[24] That was a restatement of Novikov's longing for the lost secret held by the hieroglyphics when man could read the world directly. And the means that the young editors of *Evening Twilight* proposed to lighten their darkness were still those of Wolff, as approved by the *Encyclopédie* – a study of oneself, nature and Holy Writ as God's Word. The moderate views of Germans like Wolff and the English moral thinkers were not rejected, but more stress was laid on devotions and mysticism, as the lay-out of the journal alone suggested. As a result *Evening Twilight* was a journal very different, in its ethos, from the journals it claimed as its forbears.

11
The Typographical Company (1784–91)

Masonic intervention in Novikov's publishing

After the efforts expended on setting the press of Moscow University on a firm footing, engineering a source of material to feed his presses, seeking out a securely based readership, and emerging by means of his masonic connections as an influential social figure in Moscow, the autumn and winter of 1783 dealt a cruel stroke to Novikov whose constitution was probably weakened by the labours of the preceding years. For four months he was seriously ill, but recovered in the following year. His colleague Schwarz, however, who also fell ill in the autumn of 1783, did not live to see the following spring and died in February 1784. His widow and two sons were given a home at Avdot'ino by Novikov. During his illness Novikov underwent a religious experience which he detailed fully in a confessional quarterly report submitted to his masonic superior:

Sincerely and frankly I confess before you, most worthy Leader, that the precious columns on which the holy order is based i.e. love of God and neighbour, were not understood by me, or rather, were badly and incorrectly understood, for I thought that man by himself could love God and neighbour; I was even mistaken in believing that I had executed them; then with tears thanks be to my Saviour that He allowed me to experience and recognise my blindness; that He allowed me to understand and experience that love is a Divine gift which He gives to His saints to experience and enjoy, this sweetest enjoyment of the lowliest sinners; there are minutes when they experience love for their neighbours and have the sweetest delight of loving God. But these minutes are fleeting. Daily, on rising and retiring, I offer to the Father of the world, in the name of His Son our Saviour, my unworthy prayer for a gift of this sweetest experience of love and I thank my merciful Saviour that He often bestows upon me in His mercy a strong desire to love my neighbour and God. Our Saviour in His holy writ explains to us that there is no greater love than laying down one's life for one's fellow men, and that He put the seal on his holy and divine truth by laying down His life for His fellow men, for all sinners – but how far am I still from this divine love! Often yet, very often I have no wish to rise early and retire late and go into the mire for my fellow man. With tears I write these lines; I thank my Saviour and will ever be grateful for and sing the praises of His mercy, that during my illness which is known to you, most worthy Leader, and afterwards, He bestowed upon me experiences and feelings to which I was alien. How sweet, joyful and exultant is the momentary feeling of peace followed by love.[1]

The confessor to whom Novikov submitted this report of his spiritual state was a certain Baron Schroeder who had been sent to Moscow the previous year by the Rosicrucian hierarchy in Berlin to act as an assistant for Schwarz. On Schwarz's death, Schroeder assumed the leadership of the Moscow Rosicrucians and Novikov, true to the demands of the order, obediently submitted himself to the authority of his new leader, as is clear from the length and frank confessional tone of his first quarterly report. The authority of his masonic superior was not limited to Novikov's spiritual condition, however, but extended to a direct intervention in his publishing; it is evident from the quarterly report that Schroeder in his solicitude for the affairs of the Press was continuing Schwarz's close involvement. Schroeder had asked for an inventory and full report on the state of the Press; an added burden with which Novikov was unable to cope. In the circumstances Novikov was prepared to hand over the business of the bookshop and the keeping of the accounts to a nominee of Schroeder's, a certain Schwarz (not the late collaborator who was referred to by his masonic name of Garganus), but he baulked at allowing him to manage the Press as well, explaining to Schroeder that Schwarz, whom he considered to be temperamentally unsuited to man-management, would be overwhelmed by work. For the Press itself, Novikov suggested that a certain Alekseyev would be a better appointment: but it is significant that Alekseyev is presented to Schroeder as first and foremost an adherent of the Rosicrucian order.[2] This masonic control was intended to be exercised on Novikov's general publishing, for the plan of establishing a special press to print mystical works exclusively for the masonic brotherhood was dealt with separately. Schroeder had intended to keep a close surveillance over its activities by requesting written reports of every decision taken, but again in a matter pertaining to the publishing business Novikov was emboldened by experience to query the request of his superior: he felt it his duty to point out that owing to the constant need to come to quick decisions, oral reports – with the permission of his superior – would have to suffice. Novikov was not naive enough, nor sufficiently broken by his illness, to yield his directorate; his powerful personality and entrepreneurial sense stood in the way of any possible attempt by the Berlin Rosicrucians through their agents to gain full control of Moscow's main publishing centre.[3] Outside the world of printing, however, Novikov was amenable to the Order's promptings. Schroeder, on taking control of the Moscow masons, was also concerned to maintain the discipline which was still threatened by the old rivalries between the followers of Trubetskoy and Tatishchev: Novikov was enjoined to warn his fellow masons against their 'jibes' at Tatishchev, and he duly reported that he had received apologies from the chief offenders, brothers Filus and Vivax, the masonic names for I. V. Lopukhin and his brother A. I. Novikov.[4] At the same time Novikov gave assurances that the identities of the hierarchy would be kept in complete secrecy.

The identification of Novikov's publishing with masonry was eventually formalised on 1 September 1784 by the establishing of the Typographical Company, a project initially inspired by Schwarz's prompting. The shareholders in this joint-stock company were the members of the Friendly Learned Society wearing different hats; as in England in the eighteenth century, a joint charitable enterprise seems to have trained men to work together for a common end and prepare them for a joint commercial enterprise.[5] The capital raised to launch the Typographical Company was exceptionally large: Novikov and his brother Aleksey put books to the value of 80,000 roubles at the disposal of the company, the Trubetskoy brothers invested 10,000 roubles, the Lopukhin brothers 20,000, Turgenev, Chulkov and Aleksey Ladyzhensky 5,000 each, Kutuzov 3,000 and Schroeder himself 3,500.

Possibly the formation of the Typographical Company was an attempt to resolve business difficulties which had pressed on Novikov during his headlong expansion of publishing after gaining control of the University Press. In his first report to Schroeder, Novikov listed reasons for not keeping promises, and infringing the Rosicrucian rule that an adherent had to be 'a slave to his word': the reply is presumably to a charge that the publisher had broken faith in matters dealing with the publication of masonic books. Novikov's response only gives us a glimpse of the difficulties: first, he claimed that there was continual interference in the press from the University authorities and Novikov's attempts to right matters, on his own admission, often augmented the resulting chaos. Furthermore, he found it hard to refuse 'unjust demands' which led to a failure to keep up with other, more justifiable orders. What is more, he was unable to 'make free manoeuvres in financial affairs'.[6] Novikov possibly welcomed the Typographical Company's foundation as a means of freeing him from these constraints, and as a source of moral support in the aftermath of his illness and the turmoil resulting from the death of Schwarz.[7]

The spiritual crisis and strains of the masonic society were reflected in the nature of Novikov's publishing.[8] A surge of religious and devotional books was evident in 1784 – no less than seven titles were dedicated to Archbishop Plato – and, together with language textbooks, they left room for only one original work *Leynard and Termiliya or the Unhappy Fate of Two Lovers* by N. A. Neyelova. The following year was a trough in Novikov's publishing, the number of titles dropping to thirty-eight, amongst which devotional and masonic works predominated. The single original literary work, Kheraskov's epic poem *Vladimir Reborn*, was itself an expression of Kheraskov's Christian faith.[9]

The demands made by Schroeder and Rosicrucianism on Novikov's energy and prestige seem to have distorted the progress of his publishing at a critical juncture in his career, and in retrospect at his interrogation Novikov recalled that personal relations between him and the baron were always strained, since he could not have confidence in Schroeder because of the latter's youth, and obvious lack of sympathy. Any understanding between them was impossible, since they had no common language in which they could converse freely and were forced to carry on conversations through an interpreter.[10]

The coolness which Novikov described to his interrogator in 1792 was not a fiction fabricated to defend himself against the charge of masonic zeal if one is to judge from the three confessional quarterly reports submitted to Schroeder by Novikov. In the first, he did confess with an open heart and demonstratively displayed his readiness to submit to the demands of the Order. But in the interval between the first and second reports, Novikov had come to realise that Schroeder was not a second Schwarz. The second report was much shorter, more circumspectly guarded and more pointedly businesslike than the first. Schroeder was politely informed that the inventory of Novikov's Press had been completed and was attached to the report in Russian and German. The new Press manager – presumably Alekseyev – had been appointed at a salary of 250 roubles per annum plus board and lodging. Finally, Novikov declared that the independent press for printing mystical books was now in being and that two books were at the press, *A Simplehearted Prayer Primer* and a translation of William Hutchinson's *Spirit of Masonry*.[11]

The brevity of these reports reflected not so much Novikov's disappointment with the idea of masonry as his lack of sympathy for Schroeder as a person and his lack of leisure to devote himself to masonic gatherings. Throughout 1785 he seems to have been unable to give any time to masonic affairs 'on account of my almost continuous bouts of illness and the business and cares of the Press',[12] and the result was that Schroeder showed his displeasure in Novikov's apparent lukewarmness by removing Turgenev, Kutuzov and Gamaleya from Novikov's control. Consequently, the only members of the Order who remained under Novikov's jurisdiction were Chulkov, who was absent from Moscow, Bagryansky who was in Leipzig and Novikov's brother. Rosicrucian activity as such, however, was not to continue much longer, for at the end of 1786 Schroeder was instructed from Berlin to proclaim a *silanum*, a temporary suspension of masonic activities. With the accession in Prussia of Frederick William II, himself a member of the Order, the Rosicrucian hierarchy found themselves in political power and Wöllner became a minister in the Prussian government. In those circumstances, further activity by the Order was doubtless considered a needless embarrassment. Wöllner's solution to the problem was to proclaim a *silanum* which also extended to his Russian subordinates.[13]

The cares of the Press which had prevented Novikov from devoting any time to masonic affairs had to a great extent been created by the rashness of Schroeder, who in 1785 on his own initiative bought for the Order a house belonging to Count Gendrikov in Sadovo-Spasskaya Street, the present-day Spasskiye Kazarmy. This proved to be a white elephant which eventually led to the financial ruin of the Typographical Company. Schroeder had grandiose ideas for making the Gendrikovskiy Dom, as it was called, a charitable institution by first establishing an apothecary's there and later a hospital and *pension* for the nobility. The capital for this venture was to be an inheritance of 50,000 roubles or more which Schroeder expected to receive from an uncle in Mecklenburg; meanwhile a mortgage was obtained guaranteed by Prince Cherkassky, and the work of restoring and converting the Gendrikovskiy Dom was entrusted to Prince Yengalychev.

All this was the work of naive amateurs, and when eventually Trubetskoy turned to Novikov as a professional businessman to survey the new building, the true position became clear. Novikov recalled how his heart sank on hearing the news of the mortgage, and his recognition, on surveying the property, that a great mistake had been made.[14] His fellow masons now asked Novikov if he could shoulder the responsibility of converting the property. Novikov was in the invidious position of either agreeing to take on a proposition which he knew would probably fail, or else by his refusal appearing to shun the responsibility of aiding business collaborators, and brothers in the same Order, to whom he owed so much. With his usual energy Novikov set to work and had rebuilt all the wooden outbuildings, built a small block for the apothecary's and reroofed the main house under Trubetskoy's supervision, when news was received from Schroeder in Germany that he had been cut out of his uncle's will and that he could only be saved financially by selling the Gendrikovskiy Dom. Since the mortgaged house could not be sold, the outcome was that the property was taken over as a rescue operation by the Typographical Company. As a consequence of this decision Novikov's presses and bookshop were moved to the Gendrikovskiy Dom which also served as living quarters for himself and his workers.[15]

It has been argued that Novikov, despite his adherence to masonic organisations, was not a supporter of the ideology of masonry: in fact he is claimed to be a 'bad mason' whose outlook was fundamentally opposed to masonic mysticism. As evidence, the strictures of Schwarz and Schroeder on Novikov's apparent lack of zeal are quoted.[16] Yet, in reality, Novikov maintained his faith in masonry despite pressures which would have made a less robust character recoil; he retained his faith in a Christianised masonry despite the lack of sympathy between him and Schroeder, despite the personal animosities which persisted within the unified Order, despite the commercial blunders of his brothers in the Order. When faced with the prospect of attempting to make something of the fiasco of the Gendrikovskiy Dom, he confessed that he vacillated:

but in the event he was prepared to court financial disaster and the ruin of all that he had achieved in the Moscow University Press for the sake of his friends and relatives, and the honour of the Rosicrucian Order.

Official disfavour

The troubles for Novikov by his collaborators within the Rosicrucian Order after the death of Schwarz were accompanied by growing external interference with his publishing. The first intimations of official disfavour with Novikov followed his reprinting in 1784, at the request of Count Chernyshev, the governor-general of Moscow, of two works issued by the Imperial National Schools' Commission, *A Short Catechism* (Sokrashchennyy Katekhiz) and *An Orthographical Primer* (Rukovodstvo k chistopisaniyu). Count Chernyshev's alleged aim was to produce these basic textbooks more cheaply for pupils in Moscow schools, but Novikov was accused by the National Schools' Commission of breaking its copyright, which had been granted for a term of six years to Breytkopf's press.[17] Although Novikov pleaded that he had merely carried out the command of the governor-general, the Commission's rights were upheld: all unsold copies of the books were confiscated – 790 copies remained of the 1,200 copies of the *Orthographical Primer* printed – and Novikov was obliged to reimburse the Commission for the books already sold. The case was presented by the Commission as a fight on behalf of the common good against a thrusting, undercutting private entrepreneur, and the incident may well illustrate the forcefulness of the commercial drive necessary to ensure the success of the Moscow publishing ventures and particularly necessary for Novikov in 1784. In attempting to print the Commission's textbooks, Novikov's commercial instinct was undoubtedly well tuned: the profitability of the *Orthographical Primer* can be judged from its reprinting by Breytkopf in St Petersburg in 1785, 1787 and 1790, each time in editions of 10,000.[18]

Novikov's defence against the charges, namely that he had been obliged to print these books, has the ring of an excuse about it, for the suggestion may well have come originally from Novikov: certainly his friends were well placed to inspire Chernyshev with the idea, for Novikov was supported in his defence by his closest masonic brothers who also happened to be Chernyshev's personal assistants: Gamaleya was the governor-general's chancellory secretary, and his adjutants were Ivan Turgenev and Rtishchev.[19]

For the first time Novikov had not been permitted to participate in a movement which enjoyed imperial patronage. The move to Moscow had deprived him of the access to the empress' feelings and wishes which he had manifestly enjoyed during his years in the St Petersburg metropolis: profitable though the twin capital of Moscow was on many accounts for Novikov's publishing, it had proved to be too far removed for imperial auspices.

In September 1784 Novikov received another rebuff when an imperial decree banned the publishing of a *History of the Jesuit Order* in the *Supplement* to the *Moscow News*.[20] This *History*, which mingled an objective account of the Jesuits' excellence in educational work with an objective appraisal of their faults – the fanaticism inculcated in their schools, the Order's shifting morality and pursuance of secret secular aims under a cloak of spirituality – might not seem sufficient to have brought censure in itself. But any account of the Jesuits had a concealed significance at the time. The Moscow masons could not have been unaware of the recent Jesuit campaigns against the *Illuminati* in Bavaria which had led to the banning by the Bavarian authorities of the orders of the *Illuminati* and all masonic lodges in 1784–5; Catherine must also have been aware of the way in which the Jesuits had acted in concert with the authorities against suspect independent groups. By publishing the *History of the Jesuit Order*, the Moscow masons might well have aimed to head off any trouble from that source. Their prudence is understandable, for the Jesuits – who had been given a refuge in Russia by Catherine – from their bases defending Catholicism against Orthodox ascendancy amongst the lower classes in Poland and Byelorussia, had spread their influence to the capitals where they found sympathy among the aristocracy; a relationship portrayed with some asperity by Tolstoy in *War and Peace*, where Hélène seeks Jesuit aid to help her procure a divorce from Pierre.[21] If the aim was to pre-empt Jesuit influence at court, then it failed. Indeed one may suspect that Jesuit influence had been exerted to prevent the publication of their *History*, for the decree's wording clearly shows that Catherine had come to her decision not on a study of the offending piece but on hearsay: 'It having come to our notice, that apparently a libellous history of the Jesuit Order is being printed in Moscow, we order this printing to be forbidden; and if it has been published, then to confiscate copies of it; for, having given our patronage to this Order, we cannot allow that anyone should show the slightest prejudice against it.'[22] If the ban was intended to be vindictive, then the decree would probably have lacked the almost apologetic reason given in explanation of the imperial degree. That reason, however, was probably sincere: Catherine had patronised the Jesuits whom she fondly called 'these rogues – the best people in the world'[23] and she would not tolerate criticism of them despite their roguery.

These two slips were not sufficient in themselves to sour Catherine's tolerance, but, as Bogolyubov pointed out, the Moscow masons had the misfortune to meddle in two fields which the authorities guarded jealously – education and spiritual affairs.[24] Official suspicion was intensified by the tales of masonic conspiracy from Europe, and the dangerous distance of Moscow from the supervision of the court at St Petersburg.

If the first steps taken against the Moscow masons were tentative and uncertain, then soon officialdom seemed to be on a resolute march. First, the distance between St Petersburg and Moscow was bridged by appointing a rigid careerist as governor-general, Count Ya. A. Bryus – a descendant of a Scottish mercenary, Bruce – in place of Count Chernyshev in 1784. The latter had been favourably disposed to masonry, and Novikov not only lost his influence but that of the other masons who had served under him and who now went into retirement: Gamaleya, Ivan Turgenev and Lopukhin, President of the Criminal Court.[25]

A decree of 7 October 1785 led to the setting up of a special Commission composed of two churchmen nominated by the Archbishop and two University professors to inspect the work of all the private schools in Moscow.[26] Particular attention was to be paid to the teaching of divinity and the textbooks employed, which were to be the same as those used in state schools – a directive which clearly would limit Novikov's book market. All schools henceforth had to be open to inspection from a government department and in a decree, issued at the same time to Archbishop Plato, it was explained that this decision was taken 'in order that all national schools should be founded on the rules of true piety, orderliness and fulfilment of civic duties, and that they should serve to extirpate superstition, depravity and temptations'.[27] This move need not necessarily be seen as directed against Moscow in particular, and certainly not against Novikov personally, for the decree to Bryus stressed that the review of the private schools in the second capital was to follow a similar review which had already taken place in St Petersburg. If it was hoped by officialdom that the masonic schools would need purging, then their hopes were in vain: on the whole, divinity did not figure prominently in the curriculum of the private schools.[28] Nevertheless, the private schools were warned of possible displeasure from the state by the setting up of the Commission, and the state's presence in education was underlined the following year with the establishment in Moscow of an official national school, to be followed by three more in 1787.

The move to establish a state monopoly of textbooks used in all Russian schools would injure one profitable side of Novikov's publishing. But a decision now to control his publishing became clearer when, on 23 December 1785, in decrees sent to Bryus and Archbishop Plato, Catherine ordered an inventory to be made of all the books published by Novikov on the grounds that his presses produced 'many strange books'. Archbishop Plato was enjoined to examine Novikov's faith and review his books to see 'whether there are concealed in them thoughts not in concord with the simple and pure rules of our Orthodox faith and civic obligations'.[29] Furthermore, all books which were concerned with spiritual matters should henceforward be submitted to an ecclesiastical as well as a secular censorship.

An inventory of 461 books on sale in Novikov's shop was accordingly drawn up by the Provincial Procurator which, apart from the publications of Novikov's University Press, included books published by Lopukhin's press, the Typographical Company and twelve books from St Petersburg presses. A copy of each of these books was sent to Archbishop Plato for review.

It was not a reactionary, obscurantist churchman, however, who received the suspected books for examination.[30] Plato – his family name was Levshin – was the son of a deacon from a village near Moscow who, after distinguishing himself at the old Moscow Academy from which he graduated in 1758, became teacher of rhetoric at the Trinity Seminary and shortly its Rector in 1761. His fame as a talented teacher reached Ivan Shuvalov, who wished to send him to the Sorbonne, but this decision was frustrated by Plato's superiors. On her visit to the Trinity Monastery shortly after her accession, Catherine was struck during his delivery of a loyal address by the eloquence and powerful figure of Plato and she decided to take the young priest back with her to St Petersburg as spiritual tutor to the heir, Paul, who subsequently retained a warm, filial affection for his instructor in the faith. Plato was not only employed as court tutor and preacher, but also as an ornament of the enlightened Russian Orthodox Church to dazzle important visitors to Russia. Fluent in Latin before coming to St Petersburg, he was soon also speaking competent French. When Joseph II of Austria visited Russia incognito as 'Count Falkenstein', Plato was the guide appointed to show him the antiquities of Moscow, and on being asked by Catherine what he had found most remarkable in Moscow, Joseph, without hesitation, replied 'Plato'. William Coxe, Fellow of King's College, Cambridge, and a future Archdeacon of the Church of England was also favourably impressed when entertained by his fellow clergyman who took him to an Orthodox service and then treated him to a banquet of a breakfast. Under the flowing beard and Eastern vestments, Coxe portrayed a man of the Western Enlightenment.[31] This is why Plato was introduced to Diderot during his visit to St Petersburg, and why Voltaire, knowing Catherine's pride in her impressive and enlightened churchman, responded so fulsomely to the translation of a speech made by Plato in the Peter and Paul Cathedral to celebrate the victory of the Russian fleet under Orlov against the Turks at Chesme Bay. 'I shall not fail to boast to her imperial majesty of a sermon worthy of Plato the Grecian himself', he wrote to Dashkova in English, and three days later Voltaire kept his promise. 'This speech', he informed Catherine, 'addressed to the founder of Petersburg and Your fleets is in my opinion the most famous monument in the world. I think that never did any orator have such a happy subject on which to base his words, including even the Greek Plato. As long as you have Your Plato in Petersburg, then I am certain that the Orlov Counts will replace the Miltiades and Themistocles of Greece.'[32]

His preferment was swift; as early as 1768 Plato had become a bishop and member of the Holy Synod, and in 1775 for his services was nominated Archbishop of Moscow. He was not content, however, to be a mere ornament of the church, and did much to improve the lot and image of the lower clergy, writing with pride later that 'I found the clergy in bast sandals but put them into boots, led them from the entrance lobbies into the halls of the gentry.' He took particular pains in improving the education provided by the church. Naturally he was an ally of Novikov in his publishing enterprises, and a number of the latter's publications bore dedications to Plato.

This then was the man who in January 1786 summoned Novikov to his examination in divine law and invited him to supply written answers to the following twelve questions: (1) did he acknowledge the existence of God, (2) the immortality of the soul, (3) the mystery of the Holy Trinity, (4) the divinity of Christ, (5) the mysteries of the church, (6) the symbol of faith (this was the term by which the creed was generally known in the Eastern church), (7) the validity of the Orthodox Church, (8) the divine inspiration of the Holy Scripture, (9) the decrees of the universal and local cathedrals, (10) the reverence of icons, relics, prayers and rites, (11) did he take communion and confess annually, (12) did he belong to the Society of Masons.

The last question, of course, was the crucial one, and it appears cut off from the others. There was no need to ask it in an examination of the orthodoxy of Novikov's Christian beliefs: an affirmative answer to the previous eleven should have satisfied the Metropolitan. Yet the twelfth question was the one which Plato knew that the authorities meant to ask. If he chose the questions himself, then it would seem that he had chosen the previous eleven to cushion the effect of the last. And it was only in the case of the last question that Novikov had to qualify his affirmative reply: he had entered freemasonry, he added, because there was nothing in it opposed to beliefs, laws and conscience, but he promised that if necessary he would stop frequenting masonic lodges.

These replies were sent by Plato to Catherine on 15 January and a little later he made his own conclusion on Novikov's religious views: 'Before the throne of God as well as before Thine, most merciful Sovereign and Empress, I am obliged to inform Thee by my conscience and position that I pray to the most munificent God that not only in the pasture of the Word entrusted to me by God and Thee, most merciful Sovereign, but in the whole world there should be such Christians as Novikov.'[33]

Novikov's books had not been reviewed in January, as the empress herself noted in a decree to P. V. Lopukhin, the governor of Moscow, on 11 February, and Plato did not complete his review until 26 February.

Meanwhile the campaign against the Moscow masons was maintained in St Petersburg, and again Novikov and his publishing activities were singled out for rebuke. Two new decrees were sent on 23 January to Bryus, the new governor-general of Moscow: (1) to inspect again the schools and hospitals, established by 'the mob of the new dissent' and (2) to explain to Novikov, the owner of the Press, 'that presses are established to produce books, useful and necessary to society, and not at all in order to facilitate the publication of works filled with the new dissent for the deception and seduction of ignoramuses'.[34] Masonry, of course, was now tarred with the brush of 'the new dissent'.

Moscow replied through its governor Lopukhin that there were no heretical schools or private hospitals in Moscow: the *politsmeyster* had discovered fifteen lodgers in the house of the Friendly Society but they were all students at the University and seminary, and rumours of unauthorised hospitals may have been due to Novikov's treatment of his own Press workers.[35] Novikov's reply to the second decree was that all his publications had been passed by the censor.[36]

When Plato eventually reported to the empress on his examination of Novikov's books, he divided them into three groups:

> In the first are books of literature and since our literature is hereunto extremely meagre in its productions then it is very desirable that books of this nature should be more and more widely disseminated to encourage education. In the second I place mystical books which I do not understand and therefore can pass no judgement on them. In the third group are most harmful books corrupting good mores and scheming to undermine the fortresses of our holy faith. These foul and pitiful growths of the so-called encyclopaedists should be torn out as pernicious weeds amongst good seeds.[37]

It was a strangely ambiguous verdict. Whether Plato passed up this preliminary judgement in all innocence or not, it is impossible to say. But as it stood, it was more an assault on Catherine's taste in books – after all she had demonstrated her patronage of the 'so-called' encyclopaedists – than a criticism of Novikov's mystical books.

Further examination by the Ecclesiastical Commission, however, managed to isolate 22 suspect works among the 461 reviewed. Six of these were overt masonic books: all were translations by Novikov's collaborators including Ivan Turgenev, Aleksey Kutuzov, A. A. Petrov and P. I. Strakhov. Three of them had been published by Lopukhin's private press specifically for the use of masons. Of the other sixteen works two could be considered as the 'pernicious weeds' of the 'so-called encyclopaedists': Voltaire's *L'Homme aux quarante écus* translated by P. I. Bogdanovich and published in St Petersburg by the Academy of Sciences, and Paul Jérémie Bitaubé's *Josèphe* translated by Denis Fonvizin in 1769 and reprinted by Novikov at the University Press in 1780. Of the remaining fourteen, eight were unexceptional moralising works, although they would have proved attractive to the Moscow masons, and six were merely works of entertainment and general interest. Curiously, one of these, a translation by M. I. Bagryansky of Millot's *Ancient and Modern History* published by the Typographical Company in 1785 was dedicated to no other than Bryus, the new governor-general. One more book was later added to the list of twenty-two by Plato in 1786, a translation by A. A. Petrov, on the grounds that it 'praises pagan mysteries which have been found by the church to be sinful and what is more affirms that Christianity derived not only its rites but also its mysteries from that source'.[38]

If, at the beginning of 1786, Catherine had wished to put an end to Novikov's activities, she could have done so simply by inaction. For while the investigations continued, Novikov's business was suspended and his bookshop closed. Meanwhile, deprived of income for three months, Novikov had to maintain the idle press and its workers, pay for stock and settle with his creditors. By March he was facing personal ruin and the Typographical Company was near bankruptcy. A month or two more of masterly inactivity by the empress, and Novikov would surely have had to abandon his publishing career. However, he still had influential friends at court: on 12 March he sent a letter to Count Alexander Bezborodko, explaining his circumstances and begging him to use his influence with Catherine to bring the matter to a speedy conclusion.[39] Within a fortnight the decision was made. On 27 March Bryus was sent instructions from the empress to release Novikov's stock of books from sequestration and permit him to resume his business. But the decree implied that Bryus should remain vigilant: the six masonic books were to be confiscated and Novikov and other private publishers were to be strictly warned 'to beware of publishing books executed with similar strange thoughts, or rather, real errors'.[40] Indeed, it has been suggested that Catherine, in asking her Moscow governor-generals to investigate Novikov's activities, was motivated not so much by a wish to eliminate the publisher, as by a desire to test the vigilance of her police authorities.[41] Investigating Novikov became a favoured tactical exercise for them.

There is little doubt, however, that Catherine was apprehensive of freemasonry. All masons – for she did not seem to differentiate between their varieties – were to her what they appeared to be in her anti-masonic plays: scoundrels and dupes. The lack of incriminating evidence from the investigations by the secular and ecclesiastical authorities might have only confirmed for her the wiles of the masons and their talent for secrecy. In 1786, although the decision was not publicised, the Moscow lodges were closed: four years later the then governor-general, Prince Prozorovsky, in correspondence with Catherine, indicated that this had taken place under his predecessor Count Bryus when the order had been given to 'disband the lodges'.[42]

The year 1786, with the closure of the lodges, the assuming by the state of a monopoly over profitable textbooks and the warning to the private presses, was a watershed in Novikov's publishing. Although there was now no hope of printing distinctly masonic books, nevertheless Novikov's circle continued to publish the devotional and moral works which it considered to be its *raison d'être*. In a way, there was now little danger of such books being attacked, since they had to pass through ecclesiastical as well as state censorship.

But Catherine did not let matters rest there. She decided to make religious and moral works a state monopoly as well as textbooks, and on 25 July 1787 she instructed her secretary Khrapovitsky 'to write to Moscow in order to ban the sale of all books related to religion which are not printed in the Synod Press'. This was drafted as a decree on 27 July:

According to the customs of our forefathers, the printing of church books and those relating generally to our Orthodox law is permitted exclusively to ecclesiastical presses. The freedom, granted by us to the printing of books in secular, public presses managed by private persons in no way contradicts this usage, for it extends to secular books serving the common good, and so we command you [the governor-general, Moscow] to ensure that no prayer-books printed by the Synod be on sale in any secular press or secular bookshop in Moscow; also church books or those relating to Holy Scripture, or to the exposition of law and religion, apart from those printed in the

Synod or other ecclesiastical presses under the control of our Synod, should henceforth be published from the National Schools' Commission with our permission. In consequence of this, in all bookshops where such books are found which are not published in the above mentioned ecclesiastical presses or by the National Schools' Commission, they should be given into the keeping of the Synod Office to await our future decision.[43]

Despite being cast in general terms, this retrospective legislation hit hardest at Novikov personally, for of the 313 books confiscated 166 were published by Novikov's University Press or the Typographical Company. This was a loss from which he could not hope to recover, since these books were his most profitable lines. And any lingering hopes of continuing his publishing business were finally dispelled by the news received on 17 October 1788, from Catherine, that the lease of the University Press, due to expire on 1 May 1789, would not be renewed to Novikov.[44]

The 'Diligent at Repose' – apprentice editors

Despite the disappointments and trials which threatened to bring Novikov's publishing to ruin in these years, he could not have considered that all was lost. The eighteenth century was remarkable for the way that it had organised thought and culture and created the institutions which could sustain intellectual pursuits: England had recently seen the establishment of the Society of Antiquaries, the Linnean Society, the Royal Academy, the Royal Botanic Gardens. In Russia, masonry supplied this organising force.[45] In 1784 and 1785 Novikov established two journals which demonstrated the way in which the Moscow Rosicrucians had already managed to create a cohort of young successors who would carry their strivings towards enlightenment over into the coming century.[46] These were *The Diligent at Repose* (Pokoyashchiysya trudolyubets) and *Children's Reading for Heart and Mind* (Detskoye chteniye dlya serdtsa i razuma).

The *Diligent at Repose* announced that it would be a vehicle for students at Moscow University – 'eleven in number' according to the preface.[47] One has an impression of great serious-mindedness and the appeal was to the man ready to contribute to society: the journal was dedicated to him, the 'son of the fatherland', the 'worthy patriot'. 'If you, dear reader', explained the preface, 'are among the lovers of your fatherland, if you are not a fruitless member of it, if your zealous regard for the common weal makes you worthy of the dearest name of son of the fatherland: to you, worthy patriot, among others is this book dedicated. To such we bear this small offering, for such we publish our works and in such hands we desire to see them.'[48]

The material would be primarily serious, although, as always, the pill would be sugared: 'theological, philosophic, moral and all kinds of both important and amusing material'. Among the amusing material were the occasional satirical pieces reminiscent of Novikov's own youthful squibs against the sins of greed and cruelty. The favourite butt of the venial bureaucrat even made a nostalgic reappearance in a fable 'The Vixen and the Eagle' where the vixen which has just caught a plump duck is compared with a clerk in state service:

> Being a lover of profit,
> Of course she had a clerk's mind.[49]

However, the squibs did not puncture the general tone of serious philosophising maintained by the journal. What sort of philosophy did the eleven student collaborators seek to popularise? Viewed from Moscow, Western Europe seemed to offer two warring world-views: there was a sharp-edged rationalism which, spurning the supernatural, put all natural phenomena to the test of reason, and there was a deeply felt mysticism with an unshakeable faith in a benign supernatural power and which saw the rationalists as corrupting the manners and morals of vain mortals in the passing show. At this juncture in Novikov's publishing, it might have seemed predictable that the young enthusiasts for masonry would have pressed the claims of the mystics and excoriated the rationalists. This, however, did not prove to be the case. Novikov's previous journals had not exalted mysticism at the expense of rationalism, and the *Diligent at Repose* is clearly recognisable as a successor to the *Moscow Monthly* which was also, to some extent, a 'student' publication. Even Schwarz's *Evening Twilight*, by constantly citing Locke as an ally, tempered its attacks on rationalism.

In the *Diligent at Repose* a key article on 'Enthusiasm' revealed the extent of Locke's influence, arguing as it did that greater weight should be given to reason than revelation on the grounds that no man has the right to elect himself as a recipient of divine revelation, that man's natural reason is the conduit to revelation with the aid of observations and proof.[50] 'Whosoever tries', we read, noting the scientific metaphor, 'to reduce the power of reason with the aim of exalting revelation, extinguishes the light of both and seems to deprive man of his eyes in order to let him observe with a telescope the rays of an invisible planet in the distance.'[51] This question of human reason, illumined by Western philosophising, obsessed the student collaborators in the *Diligent at Repose* and, throughout the journal, essays treated the subject in detail. Even some of the clerical hierarchy shared the views of their lay masonic friends on the primacy of reason over revelation: thus the Ieromonakh Viktor in his 'Reflections on Virtue' insisted that 'healthy reason and experience' were the only guide to human knowledge.[52]

This sober attitude to revelation as a source of knowledge was insisted upon at a moment when Novikov and his masonic circle were under attack as being obscurantists, and were being indirectly pilloried by Catherine in her anti-masonic plays, like *Siberian Shaman* (Shaman Sibirskiy). Curiously the *Diligent at Repose*, doubtless in an attempt to parry the satirical thrusts from the empress, echoed her expressions of disgust at the evils of fanaticism and superstition. If Novikov's circle was committed to piety – which they would not deny – then this piety was given a cast of reasonableness and sober common sense. Thus a 'Letter to the editors' from a like-thinking correspondent gave harsh treatment to the subject of 'Fanaticisim or Pseudo-holiness'. He attacked the haughty exclusiveness of religious bigots who were disdainful of virtuous men, and countered their attack on reason:

> despising the natural gift by which the connexion of things, their influences and causes may be correctly understood, they fix their minds on empty designs; instead of the valid way of comprehending things by natural reason, they seize on certain grandiose concepts which vary according to the variety of fickle minds which rely on these empty dreams and have no desire to spend a single moment on reasoning about anything. What is more, many mortals, led astray by stubborn superstition in the darkness of their unenlightened state, often revere these bigots as great men of wisdom, considering it a mark of great intelligence if someone makes absurd suppositions, announces false revelations, divine phenomena or any other vain dreams of their own.[53]

Clearly seen here is the rationalism of Locke and Toland, the scepticism of Voltaire battling against superstition and ignorance. Despite masonry's penchant for the arcane sciences, the *Diligent at*

Repose did not shrink from castigating alchemy and astrology which had no place in a reasonable world. The idea of a panacea was also attacked. 'A universal panacea', wrote the editors, 'also belongs to the chimeras whose adherents are either charlatans or those who are not yet detained in a madhouse. How can a thousand ills be cured by one medicine?'[54]

Not only did the student journal reject the hermetic sciences which were so favoured by the mason, but also in one article, 'A Dream', it seemed to attack masonic ritual directly in the favoured eighteenth-century mode of the allegorical dream. Various superstitious sects with their trappings of ornate ceremonial garb, occult books and skeletons gather around their divinity and invite others to follow them, but the triumphant appearance of Faith attended by Reason and Truth disperses the gloom around the worshipped deity to reveal a black crow. 'God – a reasonable and truthful being – ', announces Faith, 'demands a reasonable and true service.'[55]

From these attacks the conclusion has been drawn that Novikov and his young collaborators were 'bad masons' in that they looked askance at the outlandish ceremonial and superstitions of the masonic brotherhood while at the same time supporting the positive side of masonry, a striving to improve the common weal.[56] These 'bad masons' could be seen in alliance with the *philosophes* both putting the human personality at the centre of their world and demanding the liberty necessary for its development. The 'bad masons' and 'good *philosophes*' had common enemies: ignorance, prejudice, superstition. They used the same weapons in their assault on these enemies: enlightenment, education, organised initiative. Here lies the germ of the modern Soviet view of Novikov as a mason despite himself, an undercover rationalist who merely exploited the organisation of the masonic brotherhood for the attainment of his own radical ends.

Yet these stray shafts struck at spurious observances in the *Diligent at Repose*, set against the solid evidence of Novikov's wholehearted involvement in masonry, can cast no doubt on the view of Novikov as a committed 'good mason', sustained by its ceremonial, fascinated by its mysteries and hermetic science. A reading of his introduction to the *Moscow Monthly* and his enthusiastic acceptance of the concept of hieroglyphics as signs of true knowledge is proof of this. He would not have seen 'The Dream' as being directed against his own variant of masonry, being convinced that his own brotherhood would have been approved of by Faith, attended by Reason and Truth. It had, after all, taken much tortuous self-searching before he had come to be convinced that he stood at the head of the Russian branch of the one true universal form of masonry.

Seen in the context of 1784, the strong criticism of superstition and bogus sects is understandable as an attempt by Novikov to come to terms with the new outlook at court. Partly this must have been the reaction of an experienced publisher, who had enjoyed Catherine's literary favours for many years, to align himself with the author of *Deceiver* and *Siberian Shaman* while proving the loyalty of his own masonic society. Later in her reign, other masons in Novikov's circle were to attempt to disassociate themselves from the disreputable 'martinists' and protest their loyalty and true faith.[57] And there would have been nothing hypocritical in this support for Catherine who unfortunately, however, did not take the trouble of attempting to unravel one strand of masonry from another. Novikov's main motive in being a mason might well have been masonry's social concern, but that concern was closely interlocked with the ceremonial and ritual of the Order which gave a necessary shape to a generalised social conscience.

That conscience showed little sign of becoming more radical. True, the *Diligent at Repose* touched on the question of serfdom, which had not been aired in Novikov's journals since the *Painter*'s days. Once again, though, it was not the question of serfdom itself that concerned the students, but the paramount question of nobility whose validity can be weighed and measured by a correct attitude to its serf charges. A sketch, ironically entitled 'Boyar Generosity', told of a squire who wished to give a reward of half a rouble to a servant for saving his life, a servant whom he had previously beaten continually: the moral was that when might alone rules then virtue can only be found among the poor and oppressed.[58] The rich man 'rewards the unworthy ones who share with him his luxury, all that he gathers from groaning peasants who work his fields. He does not know men's needs, not having ever experienced them; he gives without pleasure and destroys without a twinge of conscience.'[59] The focus is centred, as with Lukin's preface to his *Haberdasher* a generation previously, on the rich man in his carriage. It has not shifted a whit to the labourer in the field: the latter remains aside, a mere counter to weigh *noblesse oblige* in the balance. There is no real criticism of the social contract implied between serf-owner and serf: rather it is a somewhat supercilious and haughty reminder that a true gentleman should honour a gentleman's agreement. Not caring for one's charges cannot be the hallmark of the gentry of modern times; in the old days things may have been different, suggested the author, who no doubt refers to a *boyar* generosity with deliberation.

Of particular interest in the journal was an article on Western and Russian writers, 'A letter to the editors', which revealed the considered opinion of the young collaborators towards literature, and showed that they were not prepared to be bound by the literary prescriptions of their mentors and seniors. There had been a shift in taste from the previous generation: no French writer was acclaimed as a modern master, but the towering figure of Lomonosov was flanked by two English poets – Milton and Shakespeare; though the latter, it is true, has to be explained in a footnote: 'Shakespeare – an Englishman.' Noteworthy too was the eclipse of Sumarokov: the letter considered only Kheraskov and Maykov to be worthy of mention alongside Lomonosov.[60]

Novikov had long ago realised the worth of using his journals as a place to argue the merits of his social initiatives; the *Painter* had demonstrated his skill as a publicist in promoting his Society for the Printing of Books. Another example of the spirited promotion of a worthwhile objective in the *Diligent at Repose* was an article propounding the advantages of European travel, 'General Observations on Journeys', which argued that travel was better than books since it acted on the heart and fired the imagination rather than ordered thoughts as the latter did. The essay's original author was the Marquis de Pezay but the French aristocrat, reflecting the *Drone*'s animus against the rich young man on his gilded tour, explained that travel was of little use to the children of the principal nobles 'who from birth have the right to be principal men which they exploit, and also the right to know little which they make even better use of'. Travel with a purpose was of most use to young men 'born with intelligence, but poor and obliged therefore to know more and be humble'. The article ended with an appeal to rich men to subsidise the European travels of these worthy young meritocrats.[61] And this proved to be not an academic essay, for the ideas expressed in it were put into practice by the Friendly Learned Society which sent abroad at its own expense a number of young Moscow University graduates.

Two of them, Kolokol'nikov and Nevzorov, had cause to rue their sponsored journey, since they were ideologically stranded by the outbreak of the French Revolution which caused the suspicions of the Russian administration to be raised in regard to them. Their sponsors, aware of their danger, attempted through letters to maintain control over their charges and prevent them from incriminating themselves by a visit to Paris at that particular time. So the two young men wandered in mental confusion through Europe like Rozencrantz and Guildenstern – and like the fictional pair they are fated to be remembered in literary history as a pair of characters – to return eventually to St Petersburg and inevitable imprisonment and disgrace; one was placed in an asylum and the other arrested.[62]

Another young protégé of the Friendly Learned Society, however, who may possibly have been sponsored by the Society on a European tour, was later to give his name to a crucial period of Russian literature. This was Karamzin who, although Prince Nikolay Trubetskoy denied at his interrogation that he was an envoy of the masons, is recorded in a note by F. N. Glinka as saying that 'the Society which sent me abroad gave me travelling expenses calculated for breakfast, dinner and supper'.[63] Karamzin's journey turned out to be a remarkable demonstration of the argument that travel for an intelligent man could well be more formative than the study of books.

It was not only an opportunity to travel, however important that was to be, that the Friendly Learned Society gave to Karamzin: it also gave him the opportunity to practise his early writing in the pages of another journal that was to provide an even more influential literary schooling than the *Diligent at Repose*. This was *Children's Reading for Heart and Mind* (Detskoye chteniye dlya serdtsa i razuma) which was issued as a weekly supplement to the *Moscow News* from 1785 to 1789. For Novikov the new supplement would have fulfilled the twofold aim of furthering education by out-of-school reading material now that he had been forbidden to publish schoolbooks, and also fostering a future reading public. That the journal did appeal to young readers there is little doubt, for *Children's Reading* was republished for the third time as late as 1819. Novikov was aided in the editing of the supplement by A. A. Petrov and A. A. Prokopovich-Antonsky, and its initial form owed much to the journalistic tradition which had taken root: a diverse mixture of factual and moral instruction sweetened with amusement and served by the *persona* of Dobroserd (Goodheart), introduced to the child readers as the editors' close friend. This attempt at a formal appeal to child readers did not continue when Karamzin became sole editor of *Children's Reading* in 1786, and decided to fill its pages with translations of James Thomson's *The Seasons* – a partial prose version – and the tales of Madame de Genlis. It has been suggested that Karamzin was guided in his choice of Mme de Genlis' work not only by their educational and moral intent but also by a personal identification with their protagonists who undertook travels through Europe to complete the education of their minds and hearts.[64] That interest in educational travel, as we have seen, was probably intense among the young students, to judge from the *Diligent at Repose* article.

A prosperous publisher

The story of the Moscow freemasons and their publishing is not one of a steadily mounting suppression from the state, and a steady decline of publishing in the course of the 1780s. If 1785 was the trough, then a new wave of publishing began for Novikov in 1786 which was soon to launch another edition of his collected works of Sumarokov and his revised edition of the *Ancient Russian Library*'.[65] Strangely, despite the recent anti-masonic moves, John Mason's *Self-Knowledge* appeared in a second edition, and other notable translations from English were the works of John Bunyan and Oliver Goldsmith's *Vicar of Wakefield*. The year (1787) that followed proved to be one of the most productive in Novikov's publishing career with the issuing of 132 titles. It was really an act of rejuvenation, for Novikov returned to the previous decade for his material, and a stream of second editions came from the presses, forty-seven titles being reprinted: the works of the Society for the Printing of Books and the Society for the Translation of Foreign Books were reissued together with the second edition of the complete Sumarokov. Although it has been suggested that in order to retrieve his business Novikov moved into the safe field of history, it would be truer to say that in the second half of the decade he moved to reprints. And these were accompanied by translations of the accepted European classics, such as Beaumarchais' *Marriage of Figaro*, Marmontel's *Tales*, Pope's *Essay on Man*, Fielding's *Tom Jones* and Karamzin's significant translation of *Julius Caesar*, a landmark in the Russian appreciation of Shakespeare.[66] With the increasing vigour of Novikov's publishing, the number of original literary works began slowly to multiply. The 1787 pattern was repeated in 1788, which saw the last flowering of Novikov's presses with 154 titles, of which 67 were reprints or the first printing of plays translated and performed many years previously, and many European classics: La Rochefoucauld, Beaumarchais, Lessing, Locke, Fénelon, Smollet's *Roderick Random* (wrongly attributed to Fielding), Swift's *Journey of Captain Samuel Brunt*, Diderot's *Le Bâtard* and Pope's *Rape of the Lock*. The issuing of the complete series of Sumarokov's plays in 1786 was imitated in 1788 by a series of translations from Molière. Since the lease of the University Press terminated in May 1789 only forty-five titles were published by Novikov in that year, of which ten were historical works, continuing a trend towards history which was apparent in the previous year when seventeen historical works were published. As throughout the decade, original works in Russian were not conspicuous: only one appeared, Kheraskov's *Kadm i Garmoniya*.

The continuing success of the publishing not only in maintaining a loyal readership, particularly for the journals, but in training young men of a similar cast of mind to continue with the work of enlightenment must have heartened Novikov and his friends. Certainly a rare glimpse of country life on Novikov's estate provided by an album of some twenty pages entitled 'Festive Days at Tikhvinskoye 1788' allows us to see a picture of contentment and prosperity during the 'festive days' enjoyed by a gathering of Novikov's Moscow intimates at his estate to celebrate midsummer as well as Ivan Turgenev's birthday on 21 June and his nameday on 28 June.[67]

The party, as they self-consciously and in the manner of sentimental nature lovers admired the sunset on 25 June, were attracted by a heavy, dark cloud shaped like a tall column which appeared ominously in the clear sky accompanied by flashes of summer lightning. One of the guests even sketched the sunset scene and presented it to his host.[68] But there was no hint in the serenity of that evening that this cloud presaged the storms that lay ahead.

Novikov had set off for his estate seven hours ahead of the main party so that he could meet his friends, who included A. A. Petrov,

G. M. Pokhodyashin, Vasiliy Chulkov and possibly F. P. Klyucharev as well as Ivan Turgenev, with due ceremony for a holiday similar to one which they had already enjoyed two years previously. Good use had been made by Novikov of his seven hour start: the guests were welcomed to his house with greeting verses written for the occasion, and during the next few days the energetic host treated the party to firework displays, built a flower-festooned bower on his terrace for after-dinner conversation, enhanced the pleasing view across the river with young orange and cherry trees in tubs and shaded the terrace with parasols which could be taken for palm trees from afar. For the church festival, Novikov busied himself all day with decorating his church with sweet-scented roses, stocks and lavender; garlands of cornflowers covered the iconostasis; a carpet of wild flowers and new-mown hay was put down on the floor and the belltower, porch and north and south entrances were illuminated. Particularly impressive were the arrangements made for the celebration of Ivan Turgenev's nameday party. After dinner, and a recital of congratulatory verses, Novikov's children, his 5-year-old daughter Varvara and the 6-year-old Ivan came into the dining-room hand-in-hand bearing garlands of roses, wearing flower chains as necklaces and bracelets, and cornflower crowns, to recite a short verse each to Ivan Turgenev:

Varvara: Live and enjoy yourself,
Enter the holy temple,
Ivan: And find in it love,
Be crowned with a garland of roses!

Host and guests then walked along a flower-strewn path to a bower specially constructed of woven birch boughs lined with flowers, and a magnificent firework display now began on the far bank of the Severka, which included a pyrotechnic poem in praise of Turgenev:

Love today through these fires depicts
The tender flame which our heart conceals for you.
It burns brightly within us
Akin to these flames . . .

Poetry had to appear among the fireworks even, for the guests at Avdot'ino accepted versifying as a natural part of the enjoyment of life. Turgenev was regaled with verses at his nameday party; verses also greeted the guests on their arrival at Novikov's, sent them to bed, and a series of expromptu verses – which identify some of the guests – bade them farewell.

The album allows us to see that the self-conscious rustic Arcadian simplicity of the retreat to the country was of a highly refined kind. Despite the formal closure of masonic lodges at this time, and the official *silanum* proclaimed from Berlin, the week at Avdot'ino-Tikhvinskoye reveals a group of men for whom masonry had set a certain social tone, a certain way of life, which could be pursued without the formal rites of the Order. The unknown compiler of the album in his foreword explained that the readers would 'see pleasant pictures of love, hear the sweet language of sincerity and feel the pure pleasures and innocent diversion of comradeship. You, united by the bond of love, friendship and brotherhood, sincere friends! You especially can partake in these pleasures of our friends, and so their description is dedicated to you.'[69] The sentimental piety shunned asceticism – clearly Novikov intended to follow his own precepts of moderation from the *Moscow Monthly* preface – yet among the delights of the high living of their summer vacation, the freemasons did not cease from high thinking, and hymns as well as elevated verses punctuated their pleasures. During the dinner on St John's day – one of the only three festivals of the Theoretical Gradus, celebrated with suitable humility 'so that our dining meetings should not resemble bacchanalian feasts as has happened in many masonic lodges through misuse'[70] – the first toast was drunk to the accompaniment of 'As the Lyres of the Heavenly Hosts' (Kak liry zhiteley nebesnykh), the second toast to the health of all Russian students and craftsmen was accompanied by 'Come has the Desired Day' (Nastal zhelannyy den'), while the third, to the masters of Russian craftsmen, was drunk to the shout of 'brotherhood united by friendship'. Then there followed 'other songs elevating the spirits and gladdening the hearts of friends united by a bond of love and brotherhood'.[71] During their admiration of sunsets which was a habit with them – A. A. Petrov had written with enthusiasm about the custom two years previously to Karamzin[72] – they would break into hymns, and the album records the inspiring singing of the anthem 'How Wondrous is the Lord in Zion' (Kol' slaven Gospod' v Sione) and the reciting by one of the party of the 148th Psalm 'Praise the Lord from the heavens'.

During these high-minded celebrations the serfs on the estate remained in the background but were not forgotten. *Noblesse oblige* compelled Novikov and his companions to take a stroll to the midsummer fair set up in the village to ensure that peasant jollity be kept within the bounds of decency, and the following day the opportunity was taken of exercising masonic philanthropy. As well as entertaining 38 guests at the church festival dinner, Novikov fed 'all the poor to the number of 904' and presented each one with a gift of ten kopecks.[73] The figure of 904 is surprising, since fewer than 300 of them could have been the Novikov brothers' own serfs;[74] however, the unexpectedly large number of serfs mentioned in the album was a fleeting hint of radical changes taking place on the estate at Avdot'ino.

Famine relief: a masonic charity

The 904 poor who had gathered around the philanthropic table were witnesses to the large-scale relief work which Novikov had energetically set in train in response to the famine that followed the drought of 1787. They were the neighbouring peasants of his acquaintances who shared his own supplies of corn handed out to his destitute peasants and 'other poor applicants' who came in search of sustenance on hearing news of Novikov's largesse. The famine gave the masonic brotherhood an opportunity of demonstrating their pietistic philanthropy: G. M. Pokhodyashin donated 50,000 roubles for the purchase of corn and Novikov – the manager as ever – spent the whole winter and spring on his estate, organising the purchase and distribution of food supplies to some hundred settlements in his district.[75] Under serfdom, which determined wealth by the number of 'souls' serving their master, famine relief on one's own estate would have been powerfully motivated by self-interest, but Novikov's relief work went far beyond the bounds of Avdot'ino. A comprehensive inventory of the estate following his arrest in 1792 – listing everything from land area and number of peasants to the kettles in his house – reveals the energetic reaction of the landowner to the crisis of the years following the 1787 drought.[76] The striking items in the inventory are that a large number – 127 of Novikov's 285 serfs – were classed as 'household serfs', that is, were not directly engaged on the land, that the seventeen peasant families numbering 158 people had seventy-eight horses at their disposal with no family having fewer than three horses and that the estate was intensively farmed with, on average, 15 desyatins (approximately 40 acres) per peasant household under crops. The peasant families, clearly, had the horsepower needed to work their fields and so it is surprising to find that the largest single building on the estate was for livestock, where Novikov had 67 horses of which 49 were work horses – with a correspondingly large number of harnesses and farm implements.[77] Nearby stood a large, well-stocked granary and threshing barn, which Novikov explained at his interrogation had always contained a reserve of from 5,000 to 10,000 roubles-worth of flour and grain since the first relief work of 1787.[78]

The agricultural improver

It is easy to explain the purpose of the granary, but why the vast building for livestock built from white stone which remained standing until 1968, and the great reserve of horsepower? The answer to this is again to be found in Novikov's interrogation where he explained that the settlements which had received relief from Avdot'ino and were unable to repay in money were expected to make restitution in terms of labour. This supply of debt labour – many of the 904 poor who received their ten kopecks charity probably constituted this workforce – enabled Novikov to turn his energies to agriculture and the improvement of his estate at the opportune moment when his lease of the University Press was about to expire. The labour intensive farming of his land from then to the date of his arrest reflected his serious attempts to experiment, 'to work the fields according to my own system', as he put it.[79] The available labour was supported by capital investment in implements: at Avdot'ino-Tikhvinskoye there were English ploughs and scythes, harrows with iron teeth, an English lathe, 'machines' for sowing, winnowing, churning and pulling hemp, three spinning-jennies and one loom in the estate's 'cloth factory' as well as a wide array of garden, wheelwright, smithy and carpenter's tools. The livestock was also of recognised breeds, and in his private library Novikov had about 100 volumes on estate and farm management.[80]

With the 'cloth factory' Novikov showed that he was ready to branch out from agriculture into manufacturing, and he also set in hand the exploitation of the one natural resource on his estate with the establishment of a brick works.[81] A visit to its kiln at night by Novikov's midsummer guests caused the writer of the Tikhvinskoye Festivities to record the one jarring line in the generally idyllic picture of his summer holiday: at midnight after one convivial supper the guests set off in boats along the Severka to view 'the famous blazing furnace which was established on a stony hill by the river. In the nocturnal gloom it appeared like splendid multicoloured fireworks. Observing the power of the flames and the heavy labour with which the workers serviced it gave our friends the opportunity for serious reflections. After a sufficient examination of this *dreadful* sight, we returned home at two in the morning.'[82]

The welfare of his own peasants was not, however, neglected by Novikov and they too benefited from their master's concentration of his affluence on his estate. Still standing at Avdot'ino as memorials to their squire's concern, and still inhabited by the collective farmers of today are the *izby* or traditional peasant cottages which, since they were constructed in stone, are the sole survivors of their type from the eighteenth century. Built in a row with plenty of space between them, they formed in the depths of the countryside a 'street' which surprised Longinov on his visit of 1858 and which would have been the envy of many a small provincial town of their period.[83] Although the construction of these stone cottages was interrupted by Novikov's arrest, presumably the work continued under his brother Aleksey's management, for eventually each peasant family on the estate had a separate cottage of its own.[84]

12

Martyrdom and meditation (1791–1818)

Forgive me this my virtue
For in the fatness of these pursy times
Virtue itself of vice must pardon beg,
Yea, curb and woo for leave to do him good . . .

quoted by Aleksey Kutuzov

Arrest and imprisonment

In the November number of *Moscow Journal*, in 1791, Novikov's protégé Karamzin noted that his periodical would have had fewer failings 'if the year 1791 for me had not been so gloomy'. Apart from the unexpected coolness of his masonic brothers to his literary enterprise,[1] there would have been other reasons for his personal despondency. One must have been the disintegration of the Typographical Company, the commercial *alter ego* of the Moscow freemasons, to whom Karamzin owed so much: in the November in which the latter noted his gloom, the company was formally wound up. Earlier in the year the brotherhood was affected by personal sorrow: Alexandra Yegorovna, the Trubetskoys' niece and Novikov's wife, lay dying of consumption, and Novikov was widowed in April.[2] Personal grief, the possible distraction from business affairs, the growing interference from the Moscow authorities might all have contributed to the failure of the Typographical Company. Also, as we have seen, Novikov's energy was already committed in another direction. Once more he had translated the ideas of enlightenment promulgated in his publications into practice: this time into practical philanthropy on a large scale at his estate.

If previously the pietistic act of publishing devotional works was supported in Moscow by the businessman's self-interest in Novikov, that pattern was now repeated at Avdot'ino-Tikhvinskoye: the urge to create a charitable famine relief centre and experiment in farming methods was intertwined with the seigneurial instincts to create a rich estate. Envious onlookers – and some no doubt resentful of their indebtedness to Novikov – saw his philanthropy in a distorting mirror which reflected only the self-advancement of freemasons through their hypocritical exploitation of the misfortune of others. This general mistrust of Novikov's intentions was distilled in clear terms in a decree sent by Catherine to Prince Prozorovsky, governor-general of Moscow, on May Day 1792 after the latter had begun an investigation of Novikov:

> You know that Novikov and his companions instituted a hospital, an apothecary's, a school and a book printing establishment, giving all this a plausible air, as if all these institutions were fashioned out of love for humanity; but there has long been a rumour abroad, that this Novikov and his companions embarked on this institutional venture not out of philanthropy, but for their own covetousness, enticing by their thrustfulness and false piety weakminded people and that they made money by robbing their estates, for which he may be exposed by incontrovertible proof.[3]

This curious accusation of mercenariness based on hearsay was one which the empress wished Novikov to defend in an ordinary law court; the other questions to be investigated were the publishing and sale by Novikov of banned books and the means by which he had made his fortune.

This May Day ukase was one stage in a muddled series of measures taken with regard to Novikov which were finally resolved into one definite act – his imprisonment in the Schlüsselburg Fortress for fifteen years. More and more in the received chronicle of Novikov's life, this sentence has been depicted as the spiteful reckoning by Catherine for Novikov's political stands against her personally, beginning with the *Drone–All Sorts* controversy over twenty years previously. Yet if Catherine had wished to silence a political opponent, the fumbling, ambiguous way in which proceedings against Novikov were pursued in 1792 was hardly the way of a determinedly vengeful autocrat.

It is indisputable that Catherine held no brief for the Moscow masons, or 'martinists', as they were pejoratively called as alleged followers of Saint-Martin.[4] Temperamentally she was deaf to the attractions of pious mysticism, politically she was wary of secret gatherings and had demonstrated her displeasure at masonry publicly in her series of anti-masonic plays.[5] Yet there are indications – even within the comedies – that her antipathy was tempered by an amused tolerance. Accepting the dedication to her of A. M. Kutuzov's translation of Klopstock's *Messias* in 1785, she remarked to Princess Dashkova that she could not understand the work but hoped that it would please the Moscow martinists.[6] Khrapovitsky, Catherine's secretary, once noted in his diary that he had been told by Derzhavin that the empress, having occasion to refer to Novikov as an 'intelligent and dangerous man', in the same breath had called Khrapovitsky, her own personal assistant, a martinist.[7] Martinist, a term used loosely and casually in the 1780s, had by the 1790s, in the uneasy aftermath of the French revolution, taken on a more precise and sinister connotation, and Bazhenov, an architect who had often acted as an emissary between the Moscow masons and the Grand Duke Paul who was sympathetic to them, was evidently taken aback by Paul's brusque change of attitude during a visit in the winter of 1791/92 when the grand duke warned him not to broach the subject of the Moscow masons, stressing that he received Bazhenov 'as an artist, not as a martinist'.[8]

For all its dramatic interest, it is an oversimplification to explain the events of 1792 in terms of a final reckoning in a gladiatorial combat between Novikov and Catherine, between the populist and the autocrat. By that year, against a background of worsening diplomatic relations with Prussia, there was a need for the imperial administrative authorities to deal with a scapegoat for all the evils, real and imagined, which were mounting abroad and at home. No better scapegoats were available than the secretive, subversive brotherhood of masons with their Prussian connections, their attempt – abortive though it had proved – to draw Grand Duke Paul into their Berlin-based Rosicrucian Order, and their flaunting of private charity as superior to state ventures; furthermore, the mocking of lethargy, obstructionism and plain corruption of the administration by Novikov in his magazines had not been forgotten by the *chinovniki* (functionaries). From the correspondence of the masons, it is clear that they realised their danger from the authorities, for in their letters – which they knew would be opened and recorded by the postal administration – they strove to demonstrate that their brand of masonry had nothing in common with the spectre of 'martinism' and loudly proclaimed their loyalty to Catherine, a loyalty which they stressed was nurtured by their masonry.[9] These appeals had to fail: not only was Catherine unsympathetic to the masonic ethos, but she must have been – as are all governors of men in troubled times – to a certain extent a hostage of her own police authorities.[10] It was a recognition of this that led Potemkin to warn her of the possible consequences of the appointment of Prozorovsky, a zealous upholder of military discipline and guardian of public order, as governor-general of Moscow in February 1790: 'Your Majesty has brought out of your arsenal a very old cannon which will undoubtedly fire at your target since it has not one of its own. But beware that it does not in the future stain with blood the name of your majesty.'[11] In the next two years an atmosphere of paranoiac hysteria gathered and security stiffened around the ageing empress who, with little emotional support on her isolated throne, was shaken by the fate of her fellow monarchs – the fall of Louis XVI, the assassination of Gustav III of Sweden and the sudden death of the Emperor Leopold II. She herself was beset by death threats. From the time of his appointment Prozorovsky, held the masons, one of Catherine's best-known targets of derision and suspicion, in his sights. He was eventually allowed to fire in the spring of 1792.

The imperial ukase sent to Prozorovsky on 13 April 1792 did not presage the ensuing events. A book had come to the notice of the authorities containing 'collected articles from schismatic chronicles' printed illegally in church characters by an unknown press. As had happened before in 1787 it was the discovery of a popular Old Believer text that initiated enquiries and Prozorovsky was instructed to search Novikov's properties 'for such a book, or others similar to it, or at least for church characters'. If the search proved positive, then Novikov was to be arrested and interrogated.[12]

Prozorovsky did much more than the letter of the decree demanded by searching the premises not only of Novikov but of all other Moscow booksellers associated with him. The searches did not discover the illegal work or any church type characters at Novikov's: essentially the searches proved negative. But, given Prozorovsky's cast of mind, inevitably a number of books deemed to be 'similar to it' came to light. These were copies of the condemned books of 1785 which – largely because of the easygoing surveillance of that time – had not been confiscated, and works printed privately for the masons' own use. Now considering that he had sufficient grounds to move against him, Prozorovsky, without waiting for further instructions from St Petersburg, arrested Novikov. The arrest itself was invested with a drama which displayed Prozorovsky's view of its great import: to Avdot'ino on 21 April 1792, the empress' birthday, a whole squadron of a dozen hussars under a Georgian Hussar, Major Prince Zhevakhov, was despatched to escort a sick and distressed Novikov back to Moscow where his interrogation began on 25 April in company with his manager Kolchugin and chief compositor Il'insky.[13]

On hearing of Novikov's arrest and receiving Prozorovsky's first reports of his interrogation, the decree directed specifically against Novikov was signed by Catherine on 1 May; it approved the governor-general's initiative, but at the same time instructed him to have Novikov tried by a court of law. This might have been an attempt by Catherine to restore some semblance of the rule of law, and respond to the indirect appeals to her enlightenment of the past which men like Lopukhin had attempted. A more direct appeal was made to the empress in a courageous poem 'To Mercy' by Karamzin, printed in the May number of his *Moscow Journal*, where the virtues of intellectual freedom were sung, and Catherine identified with mercy.[14] However, the sequel to this decree bears out the picture of administrative caprice and wilfulness which Lopukhin lamented, and suggests the extent to which Catherine was now hostage to her underlings:[15] Prozorovsky's response was that it would be unwise to try Novikov in a court of law. And since Catherine's view of the affair was now dependent on papers forwarded to her from her governor-general,[16] his decision was approved by an imperial decree of 10 May which ordered Novikov to be sent to St Petersburg – not, however, by direct route, but by the roundabout and quieter road via Vladimir, Yaroslavl, Tikhvin and Schlüsselburg. Was the reason for the choice of this route to avoid any chance of Novikov gaining the ear of influential men and, through them, that of the empress herself? For Prozorovsky, it certainly was not interpreted as a furtive move to mask the importance of the affair: once more a squadron of twelve under Prince Zhevakhov were ordered to convoy the captive – as an important prisoner of state – to the Schlüsselburg Fortress where he was to face interrogation by S. I. Sheshkovsky, a notorious inquisitor who had been recommended by Prozorovsky as someone able to deal with a man whom he had confessed to be too intelligent and wily for him.[17] In his notes later Lopukhin was to describe the details of the transference of Novikov and remarked, 'I describe these details in order to show how they acted; it may be said bluntly that they were fighting with their own shadow.'[18] Yet that shadow had by this time been projected into a frightening reality, and it was the magnified reality of a subversive trouble-maker created by police fears – 'Fright has big eyes', Lopukhin laconically quoted a Russian proverb – with which Catherine had to deal. At this stage, it would have seemed impossible for her to have dealt with Novikov other than as the dangerous anti-social plotter who had been presented to her by her vigilant security police.

Catherine now directly influenced the affair by writing a note in her own hand to Sheshkovsky suggesting the lines on which the interrogation might proceed.[19] This note might well reflect Catherine's real fear of masonic intrigue which was vented on Novikov, known as the most energetic and purposeful member of that brotherhood. But in this muddled affair, any motive cannot be ascribed with certainty to the astute empress. Her personal interest might well have been occasioned by a desire to see that the affair was not bungled, and to ensure that if Novikov was to be convicted – as he must – then that there should be good reasons for his conviction. Her posthumous reputation was not to be unnecessarily spattered with blood as a result of Prozorovsky's sweeping salvos. She noted twelve points in all: the first four dealt with the involvement in masonry itself which, she stressed, was 'injurious to the state and prohibited by the government'; the next five dealt with the masonic links with foreign courts, particularly with the now hostile Berlin; points ten and eleven dealt with the masonic links with the Grand Duke Paul, Repnin, Pleshcheyev and Kurakin; the final point – almost an afterthought it seems – dealt with Novikov's ignoring of the ban on a number of his publications to which he had already confessed.

The questions put to Novikov for his written answers followed Catherine's guidelines. When Novikov's replies veered away from the preconceived image of him conveyed in the empress's notes, then Sheshkovsky supplied a corrective in his own written comments or 'objections'. For the most part Novikov's depositions are written forcibly and coherently; his aim was to defend himself against the charges by a frank and reasoned explanation of his past conduct and interest in masonry. And it is this transparent frankness which makes the record of his examination so rich a mine for biographical information about Novikov's masonic activities. The level tone of the writing is even maintained when Novikov, with an air of weary resignation, throws himself on the mercy of Catherine, as he admits his guilt in publishing illegal works.[20] But the almost jauntily confident tone of Novikov's replies gave way to an abject and uncharacteristic grovelling when he was asked to explain his relationships in masonry with the Grand Duke Paul. At this point, he was faced with a document in the hand of Bazhenov who had acted as a go-between with Paul for the Moscow masons; unfortunately the document is lost. Nevertheless, the abjectness of Novikov's reply makes it plain that for him, his crime was the political blunder of attempting to lure Paul into a brotherhood with foreign connections:

In conclusion of this point I throw myself at the feet of Her Imperial Majesty with my sincere heartfelt remorse for this deed worthy of the severest punishment, no mercy do I even dare to expect from my so justly angered merciful monarch; let her will be done with me, but I, shedding tears of remorse and grief, dare beseech from her one drop of mercy for three poor infants, my children, and for my brother who through love of me entered into masonry and the Typographical Company and had no involvement in these affairs. Let Her Imperial Majesty's will be done with me! I have deserved my punishment by this deed and am worthy of it. Lord, thou seest my tears shed, soften the anger of the monarch angered by me, let one drop of her mercy fall on my poor children and brother!

The abject plea continued, and Sheshkovsky was able with satisfaction to note in his 'objection' that 'he himself acknowledges himself a transgressor'.[21]

That phrase reappeared – in the past tense – in Catherine's decree to Prozorovsky, dated 1 August 1792, which gave notice of her sentences.[22] Novikov's admission of his culpability allowed Catherine, in her own eyes, to remain a non-tyrannical autocrat in her sentencing: and doubtless the stressing of his own confession was aimed at preserving her image in the eyes of others. Novikov, noted the decree, had admitted his guilt in attempting to win over the heir to masonry and in publishing banned books. But even under these two points, it was not Novikov alone who was condemned, but also his fellow masons. The decree did not deal with Novikov in the singular but with the plural 'they': 'they' had set up secret gatherings and exercised dubious rites, 'they' had submitted to the authority of the Duke of Brunswick, 'they' had corresponded with the Prince of Hesse-Kassel and Wöllner. And during his interrogation Sheshkovsky had noted that the correspondence with Berlin was carried on principally by Trubetskoy, Turgenev and Lopukhin.[23] Yet the masonic collaborators were not given equal punishment: there is an incomprehensible difference in the punishment meted out. Whereas Trubetskoy, Turgenev and Lopukhin were given the lenient, if inconvenient, exile on their own estates – and Lopukhin, on the grounds that his aged father would suffer, was excused even this punishment on appeal[24] – Novikov was sentenced to fifteen years' incarceration in the Schlüsselburg Fortress. Even Prozorovsky confessed at the time his puzzlement – not at the sentence on Novikov, but at the leniency accorded his collaborators who were equally guilty.

Why should Novikov have been singled out for such severity? His special treatment is the main reason for the entrenched view that it was a demonstration of personal pique, the venting of the smouldering resentment which Catherine had harboured since the days of the 'polemics' between her *All Sorts* and Novikov's *Drone.* Yet personal animosity does not provide a plausible explanation, for there is no real evidence for any literary jealousy, and if Catherine wished to avenge herself on Novikov, then it seems unnecessary for her to have dealt with a rival in such a clumsy, halting fashion. It is possible, of course, that Catherine dealt with Novikov severely since he was without doubt the managing genius among the Moscow masons who was responsible for their independent social initiatives, and the one who had attracted public resentment by his apparent personal enrichment as a result of their charitable ventures. Lopukhin put forward this as one of his explanations of the affair, and the suggestion was developed by Pypin, who saw it as the deliberate smothering by the autocrat of an early attempt at independent social action in Russia. Yet, in that case, one would still share Prozorovsky's surprise at the leniency with which Catherine dealt with the socially influential Trubetskoy and Lopukhin. From a review of the events from Novikov's arrest, it must at least be considered that Novikov's punishment was a political tribute exacted from the intuitively astute politician who occupied the Russian throne by her over-zealous police authorities. While Catherine recognised that some tribute had to be paid when Novikov was delivered to her as an undoubted danger to the state, it has already been seen that she then sought to guide her authorities in finding reasonable cause for the inevitable punishment.

And it does not appear that Catherine was eager to pay her tribute at the earliest possible moment. Although the sentence was signed on 1 August, Khrapovitsky tells us that it was ready by mid-July: for two weeks the empress seems to have hesitated, a hesitation which has ironically been called the last sacrifice to her liberal image.[25] Yet it can be argued that the 'liberal' empress struggled to re-emerge in that document and in her subsequent, firmer dealings with Prozorovsky in the 'martinist' affair.

One silent rebuff to her Moscow governor-general was the leniency accorded Trubetskoy, Turgenev and Lopukhin whose sentences were handed down before their examination had ended. As early as 7 June, Prozorovsky had advised Catherine to summon Trubetskoy and Turgenev to Petersburg, then arrest them and interrogate them while still shocked by their arrest; but no action was taken, and her lenient sentence took the wind out of the sails of Prozorovsky, who continued meanwhile in Moscow to hope that he would discover a martinist plot in his hectoring interrogation of the other three leading masons. The sentences he was enjoined to read out to Trubetskoy, Turgenev and Lopukhin were clearly not those for which he had hoped. There was a further silent rebuff for Prozorovsky at the end of August, when a private letter from him reminding Sheshkovsky that there were other masons still to be dealt with received no reply. On one other occasion following Novikov's sentence, Prozorovsky's initiative was turned aside by Catherine. In a decree of 18 August, she ordered Prozorovsky to bring to lawful trial the fifteen booksellers whose premises, searched at the same time as Novikov's, had been found to harbour banned books. Again Prozorovsky suggested that this would be inconvenient, but this time Catherine insisted on a trial by law in a second decree of 31 August, but in the event Catherine did not enforce the sentences on the ten who were found guilty, and amnestied them on the birth of her grandson Nikolay in a decree of 2 July 1796 to a new governor-general of Moscow, M. M. Izmaylov. Prozorovsky received his final silent rebuke early in 1793 when, unbidden and unannounced, he presented himself to Catherine in St Petersburg. In his diary Khrapovitsky noted on 26 January that Catherine remarked ironically that her governor-general had come 'for his reward for destroying the martinists'; but Prozorovsky received no reward.[26] What is more, prominent declared masons who had been closely associated with Novikov were subsequently favoured: Kheraskov remained curator of Moscow University and was promoted, and Professor Chebotarev received a financial reward for his services.

Meanwhile Novikov began his imprisonment in the Schlusselburg Fortress, sharing it with his doctor Bagryansky and his serf manservant. There was to be no amnesty for him, although the commandant of the fortress was instructed by Catherine, through Sheshkovsky, to take particular concern over his health.[27] There was no more mercy. It was only after her death in four years' time and the accession of Paul that Novikov was pardoned and released.

Cultivating his garden

When he emerged from the prison gates of the Schlusselburg Fortress, Novikov did not find himself an outcast in a hostile world. Those friends and protégés from the Moscow days, many of whom had seen their talents nurtured under the assiduous encouragement of Novikov's circle, now hastened to greet him and help him find his feet in society. G. M. Pokhodyashin, who had put riches at the disposal of masonic charity, Ivan Vigant, professor of history at Moscow University from 1784–93, S. I. Pleshcheyev, a favourite of Paul who had drawn the latter into masonry and helped to obtain Novikov's pardon, D. G. Levitsky, Russia's most important painter who had painted Novikov's portrait, were among the many thanked profusely for their aid in St Petersburg in a letter which Novikov sent from his estate to A. F. Labzin whom he jokingly addressed in his letters – not without reason – as his 'nephew'.[28] Labzin was another mason who had flourished despite the inconclusive campaign against the 'martinists' in 1792: he had been a member of Schwarz's 'seminar', a collaborator of *Evening Twilight*, a member of the Friendly Society and was close to the Typographical Company. After service in the Moscow governor's office and in Moscow University Labzin transferred to the Post Office in St Petersburg in 1789 and by the time of Novikov's release was a state servant of high repute and an influential mason. His masonic influence increased with his standing in public life – a functionary of the College of Foreign Affairs (1799–1804), Director of the Department of the Minister of Naval Affairs (1804–5) and Permanent Member of the State Admiralty (1805–22) and simultaneously Conference Secretary to the Imperial Academy of Arts (1799–1818) of which he became vice-president on 12 January 1818. His public career ended in official disgrace which he deliberately courted on a matter of principle in 1822, when he facetiously suggested that Alexander I's coachman Il'ya Baykov should be admitted as a member of the Academy of Arts on the grounds that he was as well qualified as the recently proposed favourites Counts Arakcheyev, Gur'yev and Kochubey. From his secure public position Labzin set in motion a masonic and literary movement which mirrored the enthusiasms of his student days in the Moscow of the 1780s under Novikov's wing: in 1800 he founded his own lodge The Dying Sphinx, and Novikov accepted the invitation to become one of its members, mystical books were translated and published under his patronage, and he founded an influential literary magazine *Herald of Zion*.

Neither was the emperor indifferent to Novikov. Paul, as well as pardoning him, ordered the confiscated assets of the Typographical Company to be released. Still enough of a shrewd businessman, however, Novikov realised that this would be of no advantage to him. It would mean being importuned by the company's many creditors. So he asked for the assets to be retained by the Moscow Board of Social Welfare (Prikaz Obshchestvennogo Prizreniya) for distribution to creditors. Novikov clearly hoped that the bankrupt company would be treated as one with limited liabilities, so that his own personal estate would remain inviolate. Paul readily agreed, but his decree was not fully implemented, and as late as 1811, Novikov had to petition I. V. Gudovich, governor-general of Moscow, to have the disabilities of a bankrupt removed from him.[29] Again, an obstructive administration had frustrated the evident sympathy of the monarch.

Through his influential friends and social patronage also, the channels to imperial favour were available to Novikov, and Labzin pressed him to petition for his full rehabilitation; but by the autumn of 1797, Novikov had decided to withdraw from society. His health, he felt, would not stand the rigours of city life, and he pleaded that he would prefer now to practise the prescriptions of his quietist philosophy; this plea was not without its tinge of bitterness, for while Novikov reminded Labzin of the general truth that it were better to abandon oneself to the will of God than that of man, the biblical tag which accompanied the generalisation underlined the real reason why Novikov preferred not to be completely rehabilitated and chose to spend the remainder of his life as one of the first 'unpersons' of the Russian intelligentsia. 'And it is written', he noted, 'put not your trust in princes, in a son of man, but have hope only in the Lord God!'[30] He had not lost his early journalist's skill of thrusting home a pointed oblique allusion when necessary; even when engaged in an exchange of devotional pleasantries with Labzin, he could display the flash of humour of the sardonic satirist: 'For all that has happened to you, dear friend, within and without, there is but one prescription: patience, humility, constancy, forbearance, the curbing of one's will etc. etc.; mix together and take one tablespoonful morning and night.'[31]

There was a positive reason for Novikov not to return to the uncertainties of public life. After the harvest failures and famine of the late 1780s, followed by the greyness of the fortress walls, Novikov returned to an estate whose greening fields the following spring did not deceive and produced a rare harvest which made the corn in Avdot'ino-Tikhvinskoye in Novikov's eyes grow like the corn on the steppes.[32] The management of the estate, however, was now well established in the hands of Aleksey Novikov who was 'too firm in his views' and so the elder brother wisely decided to resist the temptation of interfering. To pass the time, Nikolay decided – somewhat self-consciously – to turn himself into a gardener. And the single-minded enthusiasm of the publisher was now directed at horticulture. Mingled with the devotional exchanges which filled out his letters to Labzin were requests for seed catalogues, high-quality flower and vegetable seeds, fruit trees and cuttings; precise instructions were given for the treatment of cuttings and plants from the famous gardens around St Petersburg and from farther afield.[33] Eventually he was prepared to undertake the training of apprentice gardeners; and Novikov's strictness with his workmen had not slackened with age, judging from the advice to M. P. Ryabov, a distant relative, to be severe with a man who was returned on completing his two years' training in 1807.[34] This abiding delight in his garden may have led his godson Pavel Schwarz – Johann Schwarz's son who had been brought up by Novikov as one of his own children – to become subsequently a leading horticulturist in Russia and the writer of many works on gardening.[35]

Novikov, however, was not allowed to cultivate his garden in peace for long. In 1799 his brother Aleksey died, and the management of the estate was once more thrust on Novikov; again there was a series of poor harvests and the unpractised farm manager, now plagued by a constant toothache and failing eyesight, struggled to make ends meet. For his first three years in charge, Novikov not only failed to make any income from his estate but was obliged to buy corn in order to feed his household and serfs. By the beginning of 1803 he had neither food nor money for its purchase left, and he complained to Labzin that he felt like the proverbial 'fish thrashing against ice'.[36] To break through that ice, he appealed to Konstantin Vasil'yevich Bazhenov, son of the late Vasiliy Ivanovich Bazhenov, the famous architect who had attempted to draw Paul into a liaison with the Moscow masons, to repay a debt of 4,401 roubles incurred by his father during the famine years of the late 1780s when, as Novikov pointedly reminded Konstantin Bazhenov, his father had been rescued through Novikov's magnanimity from the same desperate straits as those in which Novikov now found himself.[37] But Novikov was not too broken by misfortune to rely on pathetic appeals alone. The business instincts of the former publisher were aroused by the failure of agriculture, and Novikov acknowledged this by writing to Labzin that 'your uncle has turned from a book-printer into a cloth manufacturer' – then ruefully quoting a Russian proverb, 'necessity teaches even how to eat cake'.[38] He hoped to develop the small cloth manufactory which had existed on his estate before his imprisonment, and Novikov used his social connections to find a market for his cloth through contracts with government departments in St Petersburg and Moscow.

In taking to manufacturing, Novikov did not abandon the land. From Labzin and St Petersburg, Novikov received instructions on distilling vodka from sugar-beet, and by early 1804 he had made some successful and profitable experiments in producing vodka which had been declared first-rate by connoisseurs. He begged Pokhodyashin to do him yet another favour by sending him one of the large containers used by the Typographical Company as a makeshift for the fifty-gallon English still which he would have liked, but could not afford.[39] The respect for things English had been a constant in Novikov's life; from the utilisation of English literary genres in the early years, the flirtation with English masonry to the purchase of the English tools and implements which were itemised in the inventory of his estate. Now an English still attracted the admiration of Novikov the distiller, as had English seeds that of Novikov the gardener, and soon he was able to show his interest in English agricultural methods. On hearing that a course in English agriculture was about to be launched by Count

Rostopchin on 1 March 1804, as an act of patriotic benevolence, Novikov asked Labzin to use his influence in enrolling one of Novikov's men as a pupil with Rostopchin, explaining his straitened circumstances and that his need was matched by his interest in agriculture.[40] This profession of an interest in agriculture was not assumed if one recalls his development of his estate with his own methods before 1792, his exploitation of the labour offered as repayment of debts, his use of English machinery and the large library of about 100 books on agriculture which he possessed.

The relationship between Rostopchin and Novikov from 1800 is intriguing in that it gives us a glimpse of the continuing authority of the latter's reputation, despite his fall from favour and his subsequent deliberate withdrawal from public life. When, at the beginning of the 1800s, Labzin sought to acquaint Rostopchin with Novikov, it was the gap between the illustrious state servant and the lowly private citizen which Novikov cited as an excuse for not entering into any liaison with Rostopchin. He had become 'too wild and incapable' for society life, he pleaded.[41]

Although out of society and, therefore, unable to partake in the formal meetings of freemasonry, Novikov nevertheless retained for a time an unchallenged authority among Russian freemasons. When the late Paul's favourite S. I. Pleshcheyev decided with his friend A. A. Lenivtsev to travel westwards in 1801 in search of true freemasonry, it was to Novikov that they turned for instruction. He duly supplied them not only with advice but with a letter of introduction to a leading Prussian Rosicrucian, Martin Heinrich Klaproth, Professor of Chemistry at Berlin University, and wished them well.[42] Having become a member of Labzin's Petersburg lodge of The Dying Sphinx established in 1800, he realised that Labzin's desire to introduce him to Rostopchin was in order to bring the count into masonic circles. In September 1802 Novikov showed in a letter of recommendation in which he proposed that the Theoretical Gradus be conferred on Alexander Grigor'yevich Cherevin, a member of The Dying Sphinx, that he still retained considerable powers of patronage within Russian masonry. A further mark of this authority was Cherevin's pilgrimage to Avdot'ino in the spring of 1804, where Novikov saw in him the reflection of his own self as a young man, 'but with greater gifts and advantages in upbringing, learning and knowledge of languages'.[43] However, Novikov's isolation on his estate eventually led to a loss of control over Russian masonry. His position as leader was slowly usurped by I. A. Pozdeyev, who worked energetically at reorganising the lodges at the beginning of the new century. Finally, the growing coolness between the two men ended in a formal break when a meeting between them failed to soothe Novikov's hurt feelings. To the end of his life Novikov sought to win masons back from Pozdeyev's lodges to his own system.[44]

With the continued interest in the philosophy of masonry went an undiminished interest in its literature and the sphere of books created by the movement. Within masonry, Novikov's position was now cautiously conservative. It was to previous generations of masonic writers that he looked for the foundations of the order, and it is noteworthy that his first request for a book to Labzin was for a copy of *Bryusov kalendar' stoletniy*, a centennial almanach dedicated to Peter the Great, which was reputedly the work of a certain Bruce, the grand master of a seventeenth-century Muscovite lodge, whose name added a suitable British provenance to the antiquity of Russian masonry. Novikov assiduously collected the translations of his past pupil Labzin and had them bound in matching bindings, a practice which led him to complain that he would have preferred Labzin's New Year gift for 1804 – one of his translations from Eckartshausen – to have come unbound.[45] But his interest was not merely that of a bibliophile. He retained a critical attitude to mystical literature and did not fully share Labzin's enthusiasm for Eckartshausen,[46] distrusting the 'strange contradictions' in his work and warning Labzin against the convincingness of novel and possibly false prophets: 'Why abandon the spring from which we have long drunk', he asked, 'for the possibility of finding another good one? We seem to be entering upon a time when hundreds of Eckartshausens will appear but we must be careful! Matt. chapt. 24 verses 23–24. Mark chapt. 13 verses 21–23.'[47] Mark writes almost the same as Matthew: 'Then if anyone says to you, "Look here is the Messiah", or, "There he is", do not believe it. Impostors will come claiming to be messiahs or prophets and they will produce great signs and wonders to mislead even God's chosen, if such a thing were possible.' By quoting this particular chapter and verse, Novikov might well have been reminding Labzin gently of the authority which he had gathered by his own persecution, since both the gospel chapters warn of the official repression which Christians might expect. However, Novikov's guarded attitude sprang more from wariness of Eckartshausen's personal qualifications as a true prophet of freemasonry, for Novikov in turn continually pressed on Labzin as an 'excellent, necessary and useful book' a work of the previous generation, published in Marburg in 1775, Friedrich-Joseph-Wilhelm Schröder's *Geschichte der ältesten Philosophie und Chemie oder sogenannten hermetischen Philosophie der Aegypter.*[48] Novikov had an incomplete translation of this work in manuscript, and it is clear that the reading material which interested him was as likely to appear in the guise of manuscript as printed book. Sometimes, indeed, it was accepted that a work of masonic appeal could not be printed: 'not for the press' was Novikov's note on one German mystical work, *Fiktul'dov probirnyy kamen'*, which he suggested to Labzin as worthy of being translated anew.[49] On his birthday and saint's day Novikov regularly received a gift of a work in manuscript from his friend Gamaleya, a tradition which he suggested Labzin might follow, and he himself worked at translations of devotional and mystical essays which were sent to Labzin for correction.[50] The extent of the manuscript libraries held by the freemasons may be judged from Novikov's request to Pokhodyashin in January 1804 to send him, along with a copy of the *Life of John Bunyan*, a catalogue of all the manuscripts in his possession, so that his library could be supplemented by works in manuscript which had survived Novikov's disgrace.[51] That request may have been prompted by Novikov's discovery, as he turned sixty, that trembling hands were making writing extremely difficult for him: soon his daughter Vera had to act as her father's secretary. His reaction was to become an organiser of copyists: on 19 May, for example, three books and seventy-five packets of writing paper were dispatched to N. L. Safonov, an old freemason friend who had once offered to copy works for him, together with a homily on the need to work diligently.[52] These masonic addresses, often carefully reproduced by hand in a number of copies – Safonov had to make a copy for his own use as well as one for Novikov – could be considered the original Russian contribution to masonic literature, the only attempt to put them between covers being the short-lived *Free-Masonic Magazine* issued by Lopukhin's press in 1784.[53]

The loss of his position of supremacy in Russian freemasonry, his failing faculties, the succession of poor harvests, the crumbling of his business ventures, his own and his children's illnesses did not allow Novikov a contented old age. But so distressed was he by news received in January 1809 that for three days he was unable to put pen to paper. Six years earlier he had mortgaged his estate for 7,500 roubles with the Moscow Board of Social Welfare and the debt remained unpaid. The Board now proposed to sell Avdot'ino-Tikhvinskoye. 'Never yet in all my born days had such a painful and bitter cross befallen me as this last one', wrote Novikov to F. P. Klyucharev, begging him to be a Good Samaritan.[54] Other freemasons rallied to their master in his hour of need, in particular D. P. Runich, assistant to the Moscow Director of Posts. But although the sale of the estate was avoided, Novikov remained in fear of being driven from his birth-place. A further mortgage in 1814 proved impossible to service owing to inflation and failing harvests, and Novikov was obliged to make repeated appeals to the Empress Mariya Fedorovna, Alexander I's mother, and to others in order to avoid being put 'with my family on the street'.[55]

In constant distress, he lived through to Napoleon's invasion and the burning of Moscow when the enemy forces fanned out through the Moscow region as far as Avdot'ino. Then Novikov was given another opportunity to exercise his charity: French prisoners handed over to him as one of the few landowners who had remained on their estates were given a rouble each and had their wounds and illnesses treated at Avdot'ino before being delivered to the authorities after the French withdrawal. Once more, the charitable act roused the suspicion of his neighbours, and it is ironic, in view of his appreciation earlier in the century of Novikov's contribution to social life, that it was none other than Count Rostopchin, now governor-general of Moscow, who instructed his local agent Davydov on 12 October 1812 to examine Novikov's alleged associations with Napoleon's army. This time, however, the suspicions and rumours did not harden into official prosecution: the charges were declared to be unfounded.[56]

It was not only Novikov who was under suspicion of collaboration, but also his guest at that time, and old family friend Professor Kh. A. Chebotarev who was now librarian of Moscow University. The Chebotarev family remained close to the Novikovs, and Chebotarev's assistant as librarian, N. Ye. Cherepanov, Professor of Universal History, Statistics and Geography, willingly ran errands for Novikov – including obtaining the all-important snuff for which Novikov had an admitted weakness, and supplies of which were running out early in 1813. In return for this city luxury, the Novikovs' Moscow friends who had suffered grievously in the burning of Moscow received essential food from the country – a calf, two turkeys, five poods of best flour and thirty fresh eggs.[57] The friendship with the Chebotarevs and the Cherepanovs kept Novikov in touch with the world of books which he had done so much to help build in Moscow University: Novikov's private library of over 5,000 volumes had been taken over by the University Library on his arrest. That collection had now been destroyed in the fire of Moscow, and Novikov, restless in his enforced inactivity, wished Chebotarev well in his new labours of attempting to gather together the remnants of the ruined library and also looked forward to the new catalogue which Chebotarev had promised him.[58]

But Novikov could never engage fully in Moscow's literary world again. The new Russia which arose from the ashes of 1812 had no need of an old man who belonged to another century, who was racked with ill-health, beset by creditors and saddened at the thought that he would leave his children – with whom his noble line was to end – in penury. Death, which the Moscow freemasons had trained themselves to love, was overlong in coming to release their master from his earthly cares. The half-life which survived the disgrace of 1792 dragged on till 1818 when, soon after midsummer with its memories of the festivities a full thirty years before and only a symbolic cloud in the bright sky over Avdot'ino – on 3 July, Novikov aged 74 suffered a mortal stroke. On the eve of the anniversary of the imperial signature which had sent him to his earlier civic death, on 31 July the friendly death, which had been loved, at last embraced the unconscious Novikov.

Afterword

Despite the distant friendship which Novikov still enjoyed after his release from the Schlüsselburg Fortress, the solicitude of his past collaborators and the warm regard of his protégés, in comparison with his position at the centre of the intelligent, enlightened society of Moscow, it was as a not fully rehabilitated 'unperson' that Novikov lived out his days in the backwater of Avdot'ino in the early years of the new century. Despite the pardon from Paul, the fact of his public disgrace ensured that he was to remain distrusted and shunned by his suspicious, unenlightened peers. There were occasional attempts to rescue his memory: Karamzin wrote an eloquent plea on behalf of Novikov's bereaved family to Alexander I in 1818, and even if it had little practical effect, it kept the memory of Novikov flickering alive.[1] Kireyevsky's review of Russian literature in 1829, the year which ironically saw yet another edition of Novikov's anonymous *Painter*, reflected that:

> Were it not for Karamzin's mention of him, then perhaps many reading this article would be hearing for the first time of the work of Novikov and his companions and would doubt the credibility of events so close to us. The memory of him has almost perished; the participants of his labours have scattered and become immersed in the dark cares of private activity; many are no more; but the work completed by him has remained: it lives on, it bears fruit and awaits the gratitude of posterity.[2]

Kireyevsky's recollection of Novikov's contribution to Russian cultural life (which was noted by Pushkin in his review of the almanach *Dennitsa* in which Kireyevsky's piece had appeared[3]) was partial in that it referred mainly to Novikov's publishing and bookselling, yet even this work had to wait long for the gratitude of posterity. The civic opprobrium continued to stifle any appreciation of Novikov, and even when the time came to celebrate the centenary of Moscow University to which Novikov had been so loyally devoted and served so well, great difficulty was encountered in publishing any references to Novikov in the commemoration volumes.[4] Even when his work found a spirited response, as *Morning Light* did in Leo Tolstoy, the originator of that magazine remained unknown: Tolstoy believed in 1853 that *Morning Light* had been edited by Karamzin.[5] The gates of the Schlüsselburg Fortress were closed on Novikov's public reputation for some seventy years: it was only in the second half of the nineteenth century, when the Russian intelligentsia was more sure of itself after the death of Nicholas I, that material about him began to be sedulously collected, and posterity found that it had cause to be grateful.

Although for the young Tolstoy Novikov's name was eclipsed, yet the latter's passionate concern for moral and religious questions lived on in Russian writers. In the eighteenth-century journal Tolstoy was able to discover that the moral impulse which stiffened the robust framework of his mature work was part of the Russian literary tradition, and so he noted in his diary:

> Reading Karamzin's [*sic*] philosophical introduction to the periodical *Morning Light*, which he published in 1777 and in which he says that the aim of the periodical lies in philosophy, the development of man's mind, will and emotion by directing them towards virtue, I was amazed that we could to such an extent have lost the idea of literature's only aim – its moral aim – and that if you now begin to talk about the necessity of moralising in literature, nobody will understand you.[6]

Novikov as a journalist can be seen to have left an influence which was as much literary as historical. If Addison and Steele show themselves, in the animated social scenes and the gallery of entertaining persons who populate their pages, to be the precursors of the English domestic–social novelists, then Novikov, in the more engaged tone of his journalism with his orator's voice, foreshadows the engaged tone of much of Russian literature, exemplified by the earnestness of Dostoyevsky's narrator in *Brothers Karamazov*, which has been called an example of a philosophical–publicist genre.[7] A direct link has also been suggested between Novikov and the masons and the Dostoyevsky of *Brothers Karamazov* in the tradition of Russian Utopian thought.[8] Unlike the sweet reasonableness of Addison and Steele, the spiritual concern found in Novikov is distinctly combative. Faith was a clear-cut matter: 'Man cannot live without faith', he wrote to Chebotarev in 1813, 'and every man believes in something: if he does not believe in the truth, i.e. miracles, then he believes in the false, i.e. his fantasies.' And

Novikov goes on to attack theologians on the lines along which Dostoyevsky's Grand Inquisitor is attacked: 'They say that there were miracles, but there have been enough of them for our salvation and after that time, miracles stopped because they were no longer necessary. Miserable, miserable blindness!'[9]

For Ivan Karamazov, these convictions, implanted and nurtured in his fellow countrymen by Novikov, had become a characteristic of Russianness. So he pointed out that the 'Russian lads' in the tavern where he told his tale of the Grand Inquisitor talked about 'universal questions, and nothing else: does God exist, is there immortality? And those who don't believe in God, well, they talk about socialism and anarchism, about the refashioning of the whole of mankind according to a new order, but look, the same devil will out, they are all the same problems only from the other end. And many, many of the most original Russian lads talk only about these eternal questions in our time. Is not this so?'[10] Back to Novikov can be traced the passionate concern for religious questions which was to set the great Russian novels apart from their Western counterparts and which was to be carried over, even if 'from the other end', into the twentieth century.

Another way in which Tolstoy showed his awareness of the legacy of the unmentioned and unacknowledged Novikov was in his lengthy description in *War and Peace* of Pierre's induction into a masonic lodge:[11] the importance of the lodges in the civic education of young Russians in the first decade of the nineteenth century was demonstrated within the historical novel. Within Moscow University and the Friendly Learned Society Novikov was able, by his energetic personal example, to implant and nurture in impressionable young men the desire to engage in public life and contribute to the enlightenment of their society. His influence on pupils such as A. A. Petrov, Karamzin and Labzin was fully acknowledge by them, and even men of a younger generation were inspired by his reputation, judging from the recollections of the architect Vitberg who, dreaming of a plan to erect a Church of the Saviour as a memorial to Napoleon's defeat in Russia, gladly welcomed Mudrov's suggestions that he accompany him on one of his visits to Novikov in the country. Vitberg recalled:

> I accepted the suggestion with enthusiasm; I expected much from this man. Novikov who had laid the foundation of a new era of civilisation in Russia, who had begun the true movement of literature, an untiring worker, a man

of genius who had conveyed the light of Europe and shed it deep into the bosom of Russia. What could I not expect from the opinion on a temple erected by Russia of a great man who had spent his whole life erecting in her another, colossal and great temple.[12]

In his architectural metaphors – curiously Vitberg's project did not appeal to the austere Gamaleya who pointed out to him the moral danger of being seduced by fine art! – Vitberg showed the appreciation that one professional artisan had for another. For had all else been forgotten during the years of disregard, the memory of Novikov, publisher and bookseller, who had filled the bookshelves of the reading public with books in Russian, books which continued to pass from hand to hand even in the distant provinces of Russia in which he had established a network of booksellers, was continuously brought to mind by his imprint on the title pages of these books. The most eloquent tribute to Novikov, the publisher who created a book trade and fashioned a readership in Russia for Russian books, was given by Klyuchevsky, the eminent historian. The warmth of his tribute came from a personal awareness of the debt owed by many Russians to the exertions of Novikov in the 'Novikov decade' of the 1780s and of his followers in the 1790s.[13] Even at the beginning of the twentieth century, Klyuchevsky could recall a youth when, for men like him, a secular book was still a rarity in provincial Russia: among the first read by him were two of Novikov's publications – Bitaubé's *Josèphe* and Milton's *Paradise Lost*.[14]

One sign of the vitality of Novikov's continued presence in Russian life is the sharply different reactions of the Russian intelligentsia to him. For Makogonenko it was a paradoxical phenomenon that the 'sum of facts adduced to prove one or the other thesis is always identical and unchanged, but the conclusions of all scholars on the nature of Novikov's activity are different'.[15] The attitude to Novikov is often a key to understanding the outlook of his biographer and the time in which the latter wrote. Even Nezelenov in 1875 considered that there were five contrasting views on the significance of Novikov's work.[16] There was a Westernist view, represented by Pypin, who saw Novikov as a representative of a society striving for independence and autonomy of action against the residue of the old Muscovite centralisation. The Westernist impulse is seen as expressed in masonry, although Pypin dealt harshly with what he considered to be the uncritical acceptance of the ridiculous, non-rationalist side of masonry. An opposing view, although less well developed, was that Novikov was representative of the latent populist yearnings of society which were to lead to nineteenth-century Slavophilism. This guarded appraisal by critics such as Bessonov, Yeshevsky and Tikhonravov contrasted sharply with the dismissal of Novikov by the radical nihilist Dobrolyubov: for him, since there was no true education in eighteenth-century Russia, there was no independence of thought and so Novikov's journals also, perforce, lacked any independence and had no influence. His masonic activities were considered to be even less significant than the early journalistic ventures. Other nineteenth-century critics, without being nihilistically dismissive, did not allow Novikov any large independent role in the formation of the cast of mind of the Russian intelligentsia. By Longinov, he was seen above all as an instrument of the enlightenment: a practical printer, an educator, publisher and founder of schools, a philanthropist – but Longinov did not ask what were the convictions that put such a fine edge on the instrument. For others, such as Afanas'yev and Galakhov, Novikov was mainly a passive carrier and transmitter of the humanist views of eighteenth-century Europe: only in his freemasonry did he struggle against the libertine thought of the *philosophes*.

A century later, our longer view makes it clearer why Pypin did not find an element of Slavophilism in Novikov's journals nor indeed search for it, why Bessonov, Yeshevsky and Tikhonravov found an early populist Slavophile in him, why Dobrolyubov did not find a radical and why Longinov, the censor, preferred not to look for any convictions which might have animated Novikov's work. Yet the wide spectrum of views which seemed to disturb Nezelenov and Makogonenko is a sign of the vitality of Novikov's work which cannot be reduced to a simple formula. The warrings still continue to this day, with Makogonenko's attempts to deny Novikov any deep masonic convictions criticised by those who would prefer him portrayed in his historical complexity, religious warts and all.[17]

Despite the conflicting evaluations of Novikov's literary and social legacy, all his portrayers are united in recognising his energy which was fired by noble impulses. The dark shadow of disgrace and imprisonment, which overcast his later life and obscured his memory for immediate posterity, in time helped to magnify the light which Novikov sought to hold high in Russia. As more and more writers in the nineteenth century were called to play their sacrificial part and submit to the power of a state which seemed to hold them in excessively high regard, Novikov's imprisonment seemed more and more to have been an early rehearsal of a recurring drama. When Plekhanov, in a letter written probably towards the close of 1888, suggested to Stepnyak-Kravchinsky that they should collaborate in writing a book in English to be entitled *The Government and Literature in Russia*, it was envisaged as a 'martyrology of Russian literature beginning with Novikov and Radishchev'.[18] Novikov was to be the first in a line of literary martyrs to the state which would continue with Radishchev, Pushkin, Lermontov, Turgenev, Griboyedov, Polezhayev, Kostomarov, Shevchenko, Dostoyevsky, Mikhaylov, Chernyshevsky, and lead on to Plekhanov's contemporary Russia where 'almost all the talented writers of the present day have been or still remain in exile'.[19] For a century, the Russian state had persisted in conferring the peculiar authority of martyrdom on those whom it wished to silence: far from being silenced, the martyrs' words rang out more clearly to attentive listeners. Already their predecessor, Nikolay Novikov, had demonstrated the futility of administrative measures in dealing with a conscious literary intelligentsia bent on animating society with its ideals, through social action allied with literature, both imaginative and didactic.

Notes

ABBREVIATIONS

IS	*N.I. Novikov: Izbrannyye sochineniya*, edited by G.P. Makogonenko (Moscow–Leningrad, 1951).
MI	*Moskovskoye yezhemesyachnoye izdaniye* (1781).
NSIS	*N.I. Novikov i yego sovremenniki : Izbrannyye sochineniya*, edited by I.V. Malyshev and L.B. Svetlov (Moscow, 1961).
PT	*Pokoyashchiysya trudolyubets* (1784–5).
S	*The Spectator*, edited by Donald F. Bond, 4 vols. (Oxford, 1965).
SK	*Svodnyy katalog russkoy knigi grazhdanskoy pechati XVIII veka*, 5 vols. (Moscow, 1963–7).
SPUV	*Sanktpeterburgskiye uchenyye vedomosti na 1777 god.*
SZh	*Satiricheskiye zhurnaly N.I. Novikova*, edited by P.N. Berkov (Moscow–Leningrad, 1951).
US	*Utrenniy svet* (1777–80).
VV	*Vsyakaya vsyachina* (1769–70).

FOREWORD

1 For the conflicting views on Novikov see the report in *Russkaya literatura* (1969), No. 2, 238–40, of a conference to mark the 150th anniversary of Novikov's death held in Leningrad and Tartu 16–18 December 1968.

2 A.S. Pushkin, *Polnoye sobraniye sochineniy*, 6 vols. (Moscow–Leningrad, 1936–8), III, 41.

3 *ibid.*, V, 174.

4 V.O. Klyuchevsky, *Sochineniya*, 8 vols. (Moscow, 1956–9), VIII, 249.

5 *IS* 604–70, and *NSIS*, 421–76.

6 Ya. L. Barskov, *Perepiska moskovskikh masonov XVIII veka* (Petrograd, 1915).

1. NOBLE BEGINNINGS (1774–69)

1 See B.O. Unbegaun, *Russian Surnames* (Oxford, 1972), pp. 412–13.

2 'Nòvikov ili Novikòv?' in *SZh*, 519–21.

3 V.N. Storozhev, 'Materialy dlya istorii russkogo dvoryanstva',

Chteniya v obshchestve istorii i drevnostey rossiyskikh, 3, pt 1, (1909), 197.

4 Raymond T. McNally, *The Major Works of Peter Chaadaev: a Translation and Commentary* (Notre Dame, 1969), p. 35.

5 Marc Raeff, *Origins of the Russian Intelligentsia: The Eighteenth Century Nobility* (New York, 1966), p. 47.

6 V. P. Gur'yanov, 'Kogda rodilsya N. I. Novikov?', *Russkaya literatura*, 4 (1967), 219–20. To Gur'yanov's evidence to support the case for revising the well-entrenched view of 1744 as Novikov's year of birth can be added the fact that a passport issued in 1753 gave Novikov's age as twenty. See V. N. Storozhev, p. 196. See also W. Gareth Jones, 'The Year of Novikov's Birth', *Study Group on Eighteenth-Century Newsletter*, 2 (1974), 30–2.

7 Paul Dukes, *Catherine the Great and the Russian Nobility* (Cambridge, 1967), pp. 146–50.

8 M. N. Longinov, 'Poseshcheniye sela Avdot'ina-Tikhvinskogo prinadlezhavshego N. I. Novikovu', *Russkiy vestnik*, 22 (1858), 175–82.

9 *IS*, 604.

10 Marc Raeff, 'Home, School and Service in the Life of the 18th-Century Russian Nobleman', *Slavonic and East European Review*, 40 (1962), 296–8.

11 *ibid.*, 299.

12 M. V. Lomonosov, *Sochineniya* (Moscow–Leningrad, 1961), p. 515.

13 G. P. Makogonenko, *Nikolay Novikov i russkoye prosveshcheniye XVIII veka* (Moscow–Leningrad, 1952), pp. 49–53.

14 S. Shevyrev, *Istoriya imp. Moskovskogo universiteta* (Moscow, 1855).

15 An epistle, 'On the benefit of sciences and the education of youth in them', by Popovsky and dedicated to Shuvalov on the establishment of Moscow University, filled the eighth issue of Novikov's weekly *Zhivopisets* (The Painter), *SZh*, 305–11.

16 Quoted by A. Zapadov, *Novikov* (Moscow, 1968), p. 15.

17 Denis Fonvizin, *Sobraniye sochineniy* (St Petersburg, 1866), p. 534.

18 Marc Raeff, 'Home, School and Service in the Life of the 18th-Century Russian Nobleman', 304–5.

19 Marc Raeff, *Origins of the Russian Intelligentsia*, p. 114.

20 Denis Fonvizin, *Sobraniye sochineniy*, p. 535.

21 G. P. Makogonenko, *Nikolay Novikov*, p. 57.

22 V. Semennikov, *Materialy dlya istorii russkoy literatury i dlya slovarya pisateley epokhi Yekateriny II* (St Petersburg, 1914).

23 This early translation from Fénelon presaged the general authority which Fénelon would enjoy in the closing decades of the century. See Emile Haumant, *La Culture française en Russie (1700–1900)* (Paris, 1913), p. 157.

24 Paul Dukes, *Catherine the Great and the Russian Nobility*, p. 54.

25 *ibid.*, 55.

26 William Coxe, *Travels into Poland, Russia, Sweden and Denmark*

Interspersed with Historical Relations and Political Enquiries, 2 vols. (London, 1784), II, 93.

27 *Ibid.*, 94.

28 G. P. Makogonenko, *Nikolay Novikov*, pp. 85–6.

29 A. I. Bibikov, *Zapiski o zhizni i sluzhbe A. I. Bibikova* (Moscow, 1817), p. 108.

30 Catherine had in mind the official journals which the House of Commons had decided to have printed as late as 1742, the task being supervised by Samuel Richardson, printer to the House. See J. C. Trewin and E. M. King, *Printer to the House: The Story of Hansard* (London, 1952), p. 12.

31 G. P. Makogonenko, *Nikolay Novikov*, pp. 104–5.

32 An English version by Mikhail Tatishchev, a member of the Russian embassy in London, appeared in 1768. *The Grand Instructions to the Commissioners Appointed to Frame a New Code of Laws* is reproduced in W. F. Reddaway, *Documents of Catherine the Great* (Cambridge, 1933), pp. 215–309.

33 Etienne Dumon, *Bentham's Theory of Legislation*, translated by Charles Milner Atkinson, 2 vols. (London, 1914), II, 298.

34 *IS*, 313.

35 See *Istoriya russkoy zhurnalistiki XVIII–XIX vekov*, edited by A. V. Zapadov, (Moscow, 1963), pp. 40–8. For a discussion of M. D. Chulkov's *I to i syo* (This and That) see John Garrard, *Mixail Čulkov: An Introduction to His Prose and Verse* (The Hague–Paris, 1970), pp. 61–85.

36 For example, Antiokh Kantemir, *Sobraniye stikhotvoreniy* (Leningrad, 1956), p. 59, Medor in Satire I complains that with so much paper expended on books there would be none left for him to curl his hair. The *World* (London, 1756), no. 183, reported a message from a lady desiring 'Mr Dodsley will send her no more *Worlds*, for that she has cut off her hair, and shall have no further occasion for them any longer'. A correspondent of the *Painter* reports that, '. . . her hair is dressed in the *Painter*!', *SZh*, 368–9.

37 *VV*, 136: 'It is easier to read a paper than a book. Taking up a book makes many yawn, but they run to meet a paper with a smile.'

38 G. P. Makogonenko, *Nikolay Novikov*, p. 153.

39 V. G. Berezina, 'Zhurnal A. P. Sumarokova *Trudolyubivaya pchela* (1759)', *Voprosy zhurnalistiki*, 2, bk 2 (1960), 3–37.

40 Yu. D. Levin, 'Angliyskaya prosvetitel'skaya zhurnalistika v russkoy literature XVIII veka' in *Epokha prosveshcheniya: Iz istorii mezhdunarodnykh svyazey russkoy literatury* (Leningrad, 1967), p. 20.

41 A. G. Cross, '*By the Banks of the Thames*': *Russians in Eighteenth Century Britain* (Newtonville, Mass., 1980), pp. 53–4.

42 V. F. Solntsev, '"Vsyakaya Vsyachina" i "Spektator" (K istorii russkoy satiricheskoy zhurnalistiki XVIII veka)', *Zhurnal Ministerstva Narodnogo Prosveshcheniya*, CCLXXIX, 1 (1892), 125–56.

43 *VV*, 53.
44 *Istoriya russkoy zhurnalistiki XVIII–XIX vekov*, p. 38.
45 I. Z. Serman, 'Novikov and *The Tatler*', *Study Group on Eighteenth-Century Russia Newsletter*, 5 (1977), 37–8.
46 *Istoriya russkoy zhurnalistiki XVIII–XIX vekov*, p. 35.

2. A FAMILY OF SATIRICAL WEEKLIES (1769–73)

1 André Monnier, *Un publiciste frondeur sous Catherine II : Nicolas Novikov* (Paris, 1981), pp. 79–85.
2 *ibid.*, 119–20. I. F. Martynov, *Knigoizdatel' Nikolay Novikov* (Moscow, 1981), p. 13.
3 See, for example, G. P. Makogonenko, *Nikolay Novikov*, p. 109.
4 The stress on the conflict between Novikov and Catherine was a cornerstone of the populist Nezelenov's biography of Novikov. The conflict has since become one of the 'well-known facts' of literary history with, however, tenuous roots in reality. See A. I. Nezelenov, *N. I. Novikov, izdatel' zhurnalov 1769–1785 godov* (St Petersburg, 1875).
5 See my 'Novikov's Naturalized *Spectator*' in *The Eighteenth Century in Russia*, edited by J. G. Garrard (Oxford, 1973), pp. 149–65.
6 *S*, I, 45.
7 The essay in the *Tatler* No. 242 has been seen as 'the standard eighteenth century essay on satire'. See P. K. Elkin, *The Augustan Defence of Satire* (Oxford, 1973) p. 4.
8 See P. Pekarsky, *Materialy dlya istorii zhurnal'noy i literaturnoy deyatel'nosti Yekateriny II* (St Petersburg, 1863).
9 See John Garrard, *Mixail Čulkov*, for a discussion of the polemics which sprang up between *All Sorts* and Chulkov's *This and That*, the first of its emulators.
10 Pamela Currie, 'Moral Weeklies and the Reading Public in Germany, 1711–1750', *Oxford German Studies* (1968), 70–3.
11 This passage contradicts I. Z. Serman's claim that Novikov had no need to spell out his irony to his readers. See I. Z. Serman, *Russkiy Klassitsizm: Poeziya, Drama, Satira* (Leningrad, 1973), p. 253.
12 *SZh*, 370.
13 *ibid.*
14 *SZh*, 100–3.
15 For a view of social attitudes already decayed by the mid-eighteenth century, see John Keep, 'The Muscovite Elite and the Approach to Pluralism', *Slavonic and East European Review*, 48 (1970), 201–31.
16 *S*, I, xxxiv–xxxv.
17 *SZh*, 172–7.
18 The term is Donald F. Bond's in *S*, I, xxiv.
19 *SZh*, 191.
20 A. Skaftymov, 'O stile "Puteshestviye iz Peterburga v Moskvu"

A. N. Radishcheva' in *Stat'i o russkoy literature* (Saratov, 1958), p. 88.
21 *IS*, 35.
22 James T. Boulton, *The Language of Politics in the Age of Wilkes and Burke* (London, 1963), pp. 36–7.
23 *SZh*, 58.
24 *SZh*, 58–9.
25 G. P. Makogonenko, *Nikolay Novikov*, p. 130, produces two partial quotations from Pravdulyubov's letter to suggest that Novikov had singled out the editor of *All Sorts*: 'All her fault consists in not being able to understand Russian literature . . . '; but the end of the sentence, '. . . and this fault is peculiar to many of our writers' omitted by him, makes it plain that Pravdulyubov is not striking at a particular person but rather at a general weakness of Russian society. The second quotation given by Makogonenko as proof of Pravdulyubov's clear revelation has been even more severely doctored. His quotation reads: 'From the words used by her in section 52 a Russian can conclude nothing', whereas the original in full reads: 'From the words used by her in section 52, a Russian can conclude nothing else but that Mr A is right and that Madam All Sorts has criticised him wrongly.' In the arguments for seeing this letter as an unmasking of Catherine, there is something, therefore, of a *tour de force*. See also André Monnier, *Nicolas Novikov*, pp. 292–303, for a criticism of Makogonenko's thesis.
26 G. P. Makogonenko, *Nikolay Novikov*, p. 129.
27 *SZh*, 68.
28 *SZh*, 237.
29 *SZh*, 68.
30 *SZh*, 74–5.
31 'English salt' was the name given by Russians to 'Epsom salts', used by them as an aperient.
32 *SZh*, 71.
33 *SZh*, 70.
34 *SZh*, 71.
35 It must not be ignored that *All Sorts* was not always prepared to pretend that 'vices' and 'sins' did not exist in Catherine's Russia. Towards the close of 1769 the periodical voiced criticism of bribery and corruption which was as bitter as any in the *Drone*, and was more threatening in its authoritative tone which befitted the semi-official periodical: 'You have been given a salary not in order that you may be satisfied and live in idleness, but you receive it in order that you may work and not make an auction out of sacred justice; and having sufficient and being satisfied with your condition you may not be avaricious for money; and that you may render justice not to him who gives you most but to him whose demands are just. If you, who receive a salary, take bribes in addition, then you, apart from ignoring the laws, also show great ingratitude to the higher authorities which have supported you generously with the wherewithal to live, and make damaging what has been established for

the common good.' This passage ended with a direct warning, 'Truly you are deserving of a triple punishment, and one thing follows inexorably from the other two; either you will be destroyed, or you will reform while there is yet time.' (*VV*, 308–9). *All Sorts* could obviously speak with a far more authoritative voice than the *Drone* when necessary.

36 André Monnier, *Nicolas Novikov*, pp. 303–9, argues that Novikov's real target in the polemic was G. V. Kozitsky.

37 *S*, IV, 86.

38 Quoted by Ronald Paulson, *The Fictions of Satire* (Baltimore, 1967), pp. 8–9.

39 *VV*, No. 108.

3. THE *DRONE* (1769–70)

1 For example *IS*, 34–64. *Russkaya literatura XVIII veka*, edited by G. P. Makogonenko, (Leningrad, 1970), pp. 254–68. *The Literature of Eighteenth-Century Russia*, edited by Harold B. Segel, 2 vols. (New York, 1967), I, 260–300.

2 *SZh*, 48–9.

3 *SZh*, 51–2.

4 *SZh*, 91.

5 John Garrard, *Mixail Čulkov*, p. 66.

6 *SZh*, 108.

7 *SZh*, 129–36.

8 *SZh*, 225.

9 *SZh*, 226–7.

10 *SZh*, 237.

11 *SZh*, 97.

12 *SZh*, 531.

13 *Khrestomatiya po russkoy literature XVIII veka*, compiled by A. V. Kokorev (Moscow, 1965), p. 273.

14 *SZh*, 96.

15 *SZh*, 140–2, 155–8.

16 *SZh*, 135–6.

17 *SZh*, 544, where Berkov quotes a report to A. A. Bekleshov from the 'economic peasant' Ivan Govorukhin and others published in *Russkiy Arkhiv*, VII (1891), 299–300. It is interesting that the *Drone* had published a poem from Vasiliy Maykov addressed to Bekleshov on the death of his brother at the Battle of Khotin in its issue of 22 September; *SZh*, 126.

18 *SZh*, 109.

19 *SZh*, 113, 537–8. Petrov's over-embroidered ode *On the Carousel* (1766) had been parodied by Sumarokov in his *Dithyramb to Pegasus*.

20 *SZh*, 104.

21 William Coxe, *Travels*, p. 126.

22 *SZh*, 241–2.
23 *SK*, IV, 201.
24 *SZh*, 236.
25 V. P. Semennikov, *Russkiye satiricheskiye zhurnaly 1769–1774 gg.* (St Petersburg, 1914), pp. 82–3.
26 *SZh*, 239.
27 *SZh*, 246.
28 See my 'The Closure of Novikov's *Truten'*', *Slavonic and East European Review*, 50 (1972), 107–11.
29 *Sanktpeterburgskiye vedomosti*, 6 July 1770.
30 *SK*, IV, 176.
31 *SZh*, 253.
32 Chulkov's *Parnasskiy shchepetil'nik* (Haberdasher of Parnassus) (May 1770–December 1770) was the only publication with which Novikov could now cross swords. It was the successor to Chulkov's *This and That* which had ended after a year's run in 1769.
33 *SZh*, 265.
34 'The pen which wrote this', commented Novikov, 'is well enough known to learned Russian society and all lovers of literary science.' *SZh*, 277. Although the *Epistle* bore no author's name, there would have been no doubt among readers of his identity, for Fonvizin had published the poem the previous year as a supplement to his translation of Arnaud's *Sidney et Silli*.
35 *SZh*, 266.
36 *SZh*, 251.
37 *SK*, IV, 81–6.
38 Andrey Bolotov, *Zhizn' i priklyucheniya Andreya Bolotova opisannyye samim im dlya svoikh potomkov*, 3 vols. (Moscow–Leningrad, 1931), II, 227.
39 G. V. Plekhanov, *Literatura i estetika*, 2 vols. (Moscow, 1950), II, 7.
40 Schillerian echoes are sensed here, but an awareness of an eighteenth-century Russian tradition suggests how Dostoyevsky would have been prepared to be receptive to Schiller's idea of the beautiful man.
41 See Richard Peace, *Dostoyevsky: An Examination of the Major Novels* (Cambridge, 1971), p. 28.
42 A. Solzhenitsyn, *The First Circle*, chap. 24.

4. IMPERIAL PATRONAGE (1770–3)

1 *SK*, I, 184.
2 G. Makogonenko, *Ot Fonvizina do Pushkina: iz istorii russkogo realizma* (Moscow, 1969), pp. 287–8.
3 G. N. Moiseyeva, 'Literaturnyye i istoricheskiye pamyatniki Drevney Rusi v izdaniyakh N. I. Novikova', *Trudy Otdela Drevne-russkoy literatury Instituta Russkoy Literatury AN SSSR*, vol. 25, 284.
4 There quickly followed a partial English translation by 'a Lady dedi-

cated to the Czarina of Russia'; *The Antidote: or an Enquiry into the Merits of a Book entitled A Journey into Siberia* (London, 1772).

5 G. N. Moiseyeva, 'Literaturnyye i istoricheskiye pamyatniki Drevney Rusi v izdaniyakh N. I. Novikova', 285.

6 L. A. Derbov, 'N. I. Novikov i russkaya istoriya (k izdaniyu "Drevney Rossiyskoy Vivliofiki")', *Istoriograficheskiy sbornik 3* (Saratov), 10.

7 I. F. Martynov, '"Opyt istoricheskogo slovarya o rossiyskikh pisatelyakh" N. I. Novikova i literaturnaya polemika 60–70-kh godov XVIII veka', *Russkaya literatura*, 3 (1968), 184–91, suggests that it is an oversimplification to see Novikov as reacting only to the Leipzig articles. These were an early attempt to refute Chappe d'Auteroche, to be followed in 1770 by Catherine's anonymous *Antidote*. Novikov's *Essay* supported these two earlier attempts at refuting the libel on Russia.

8 The work has been reprinted in *IS*, 277–370.

9 *IS*, 277–8.

10 *SK*, I, 184.

11 *SK*, IV, 89.

12 *Sochineniya Imperatritsy Yekateriny II*, edited by A. N. Pypin, 12 vols. (St Petersburg, 1901), I, 10–11.

13 *Ibid.*, x. The close links between the satirical journals and Catherine's plays are indicated by Pypin.

14 *SZh*, 283–4.

15 *SZh*, 284.

16 *SZh*, 301–2.

17 K. Waliszewski, *Le Roman d'une impératrice: Catherine II de Russie* (Paris, 1894), p. 470.

18 *SZh*, 380.

19 G. P. Makogonenko, *Nikolay Novikov*, pp. 221–2.

20 Denis Diderot, *Correspondance*, edited by Georges Roth, 16 vols. (Paris, 1955–70), XIII, 81.

21 *SZh*, 324–6.

22 *SZh*, 568.

23 *Ibid.* André Monnier, *Nicolas Novikov*, p. 328.

24 *SZh*, 459–63.

25 In a letter to his daughter dated 23 October 1773 Diderot wrote with enthusiasm of Catherine: 'You are young enough to see my prediction come true; she will change the face of this country; the Russian nation will become one of the most honest, one of the wisest and one of the most redoubtable countries in Europe and the world.' The main justification for this enthusiasm was Catherine's patronage of the Smol'nyy Institute. Denis Diderot, *Correspondance*, XIII, 76. Particularly appealing to Diderot was the Smol'nyy Institute's play acting: *Ibid.*, XIII, 126. Diderot even attempted to influence the education of the girls: *Ibid.*, XIV, 44–64.

26 There is a detailed account of the Smol'nyy Institute in William Coxe,

Travels, pp. 156–8. He too was particularly attracted by the theatrical performances put on for his benefit.

27 For example G. P. Makogonenko, *Nikolay Novikov*, p. 183, and André Monnier, *Nicolas Novikov*, pp. 322–30.

28 G. P. Makogonenko, *Nikolay Novikov*, pp. 184–7, and André Monnier, *Nicolas Novikov*, pp. 128–30.

29 Rejected were 'writers of neither tragedy nor comedy' such as I. A. Dmitrevsky, who yearned merely for novelty in their revolt against over 2,000 years of well-founded tradition. This is further evidence for treating with circumspection Makogonenko's claims for Novikov as a perspicacious theatrical progressive. See G. Makogonenko, *Ot Fonvizina do Pushkina*, pp. 279–90.

30 John Nichols and George Steevens, *The Genuine Works of William Hogarth*, 2 vols. (London, 1808–10), II, 7.

31 *SZh*, 296.

32 *SZh*, 327.

33 *SZh*, 298.

34 See my 'The Eighteenth Century View of English Moral Satire: Palliative or Purgative?', in *Great Britain and Russia in the Eighteenth Century: Contacts and Comparisons*, edited by A. G. Cross (Newtonville, Mass., 1979), pp. 75–83.

35 *SZh*, 301.

36 *SZh*, 328–9.

37 See Yu. D. Levin, 'Angliyskaya prosvetitel'skaya zhurnalistika v russkoy literature XVIII veka', p. 55, on the two aspects of interest in things English: the search for a counterweight to French classicism by the pioneers of sentimentalism, and the 'official' approval of the English quest for tolerance and social harmony as Catherine's trust in the French *philosophes* fell away. The reasons are clearly not limited to these two.

38 *SZh*, 246–7.

39 A. N. Pypin, *Istoriya russkoy literatury*, 4 vols. (St Petersburg, 1902–3), IV, 212–13.

40 *Perepiska Karamzina s Lafaterom* (St Petersburg, 1893), p. 4.

41 A. I. Nezelenov, *N. I. Novikov*.

42 V. P. Semennikov, *Radishchev: Ocherki i issledovaniya* (Moscow–Petrograd, 1923), pp. 327–8.

43 *SZh*, 560–4; Berkov argues the case for Radishchev's authorship. G. Makogonenko, *Ot Fonvizina do Pushkina*, pp. 301–22, makes an exhaustive case for supporting Novikov's. His view was first advanced in *Nikolay Novikov*, pp. 239–54.

44 *SZh*, 569–70. G. P. Makogonenko, *Nikolay Novikov*, pp. 253–4, believes that the author was Novikov himself.

45 *SZh*, 336.

46 This is probably a reference to the experimental agricultural settlements of Orlov. See V.I. Semevsky, *Krest'yanskiy vopros v Rossii v XVIII i pervoy polovine XIX veka*, 2 vols. (St Petersburg, 1888), I, 37.

47 *SZh*, 571.

48 M. T. Belyavsky, 'Satiricheskiye zhurnaly N. I. Novikova kak istoricheskiy istochnik', *Vestnik Moskovoskogo Universiteta*, 3 (1963), quotes the documents of V. I. Suvorov's Vetluga estate (*Trudy vladimirskoy uchenoy arkhivnoy komissii*, VI (1904), 1–95) to show how Suvorov continually impressed one or more serfs who had been taken by him to St Petersburg, and then demanded an additional *obrok* of 360 roubles for each recruit.

49 *SZh*, 392–5.

50 *SK*, IV, 153.

51 *SZh*, 412.

52 M. I. Gillel'son, *P.A. Vyazemsky: Zhizn' i tvorchestvo* (Leningrad, 1969), p. 277.

5. IN SEARCH OF THE RUSSIAN READER (1773–5)

1 Denis Diderot, *Correspondance*, XII, 49.

2 *Ibid.*, VII, 85–96.

3 *Ibid.*, VII, 88–9.

4 *SZh*, 439–41.

5 *SZh*, 442.

6 G. P. Makogonenko, *Nikolay Novikov*, p. 219, attempts to show that the two societies were opposed to each other; Catherine's presenting an insincere 'official enlightenment' and Novikov's a 'true enlightenment'. This is an idiosyncratic reading of Paper 18 determined by a desire to maintain the schematic Catherine–Novikov controversy. Again it is a quotation torn from its context that supports Makogonenko's schema: 'Our enlightenment, or, so to say, the blind attachment to French books.' This charge of Gallomania is clearly levelled at the average nobleman in the capital cities and not at the empress personally.

7 *SZh*, 442–3.

8 I. M. Polonskaya, 'Novyye materialy o izdatel'skoy deyatel'nosti N. I. Novikova', *Zapiski otdela rukopisey Gosudarstvennoy biblioteki SSSR im. V. I. Lenina*, 38 (1977), 217.

9 *Ibid.*, 221.

10 Paul Dukes, *Catherine the Great and the Russian Nobility*, p. 167.

11 *Ibid.*, p. 66.

12 Denis Diderot, *Œuvres complètes*, edited by J. Assézat and Maurice Tourneux, 20 vols. (Paris, 1857–77), XVIII, 65.

13 *SZh*, 446–7.

14 See Diderot's résumé of the history of French publishing in Denis Diderot, *Œuvres complètes*, XVIII, 63.

15 I. M. Polonskaya, 'Novyye materialy o izdatel'skoy deyatel'nosti N. I. Novikova', 215–19.

16 V. P. Semennikov, 'Ranneye izdatel'skoye obshchestvo N. I. Novikova', *Russkiy bibliofil* (1912), No. 5, 39.

17 *Ibid.*, 39. Semennikov is mistaken in claiming that Müller handled the subscriptions of all Novikov's journals.
18 I. M. Polonskaya, 'Novyye materialy o izdatel'skoy deyatel'nosti N. I. Novikova', 221
19 V. P. Semennikov, 'Ranneye izdatel'skoye obshchestvo N. I. Novikova', 39.
20 A. A. Sidorov, *Istoriya oformleniya russkoy knigi* (Moscow–Leningrad, 1946), p. 182.
21 V. P. Semennikov, 'Ranneye izdatel'skoye obshchestvo N. I. Novikova', 41.
22 *Ibid.*
23 *Ibid.*
24 N. Tikhonravov, *Letopisi russkoy literatury i drevnosti* (Moscow, 1862), IV, sect. III, 45–6.
25 There are in existence copies of the first two volumes of Bell's work and copies of Suetonius' *Lives* with the original title pages of 1774 which bear the motto of the Printing Society; see *SK*, I, 86, 95.
26 N. Tikhonravov, *Letopisi russkoy literatury i drevnosti*, 45–6.
27 Advertisements appeared in official gazettes with lists of books from which intending translators could choose; see A. Startsev, *Radishchev v godakh 'Puteshestviya iz Peterburga v Moskvu'*, Moscow, 1960, pp. 20–2.
28 *SK*, I, 56–9.

6. DISILLUSIONS AND DOUBTS (1774)

1 Thomas Jefferson, *Memoirs, Correspondence and Miscellanies*, 4 vols. (London, 1829–30), IV, 487.
2 Thomas Carlyle, *Life of Frederick the Great*, bk VI, chap. vii.
3 *SZh*, 477.
4 Denis Diderot, *Œuvres complètes*, XIII, 227.
5 A. N. Pypin, *Istoriya russkoy literatury*, IV, 141.
6 L. N. Tolstoy, *War and Peace*, bk III, part 2, chap. XVII.
7 A. Zapadov, *Novikov* (Moscow, 1968), p. 97.
8 *SZh*, 479.
9 *SZh*, 505.
10 *SZh*, 505–6.
11 *SZh*, 482.
12 *SZh*, 486–7.
13 *SZh*, 488.
14 Yu. M. Lotman, 'Russo i russkaya kul'tura XVIII veka', in *Epokha Prosveshcheniya*, p. 215.
15 Jean-Jacques Rousseau, *Discours sur les sciences et les arts*, edited by George R. Havens (New York–London, 1946), pp. 103–4.
16 Marcel Bouchard, *L'Académie de Dijon et le Premier Discours de Rousseau* (Paris, 1950), p. 51.

17 Jean-Jacques Rousseau, *Discours sur les sciences et les arts*, pp. 100–1.
18 *Ibid.*, 101.
19 *Ibid.*, 106–7.
20 The humour is there in the introduction to his essay where Rousseau speaks with the voice of a *philosophe* to fellow philosophers and not with the voice of the honest Geneva burgher which is heard in the preface. Attention has been rightly drawn to the presence of different voices in the essay; see Roger D. Masters, *The Political Philosophy of Rousseau* (Princeton, 1968), pp. 211 and 215–6.
21 *SZh*, 289.
22 See Yu. M. Lotman, 'Russo i russkaya kul'tura XVIII veka', p. 226, on Sumarokov's bewilderment at the paradox of a *philosophe* attacking learning.
23 Jean-Jacques Rousseau, *Discours sur les sciences et les arts*, p. 10.
24 *SZh*, 289.
25 Jean-Jacques Rousseau, *Du Contrat social*, bk II, chap. 8.

7. THE HISTORIAN (1773–91)

1 *SZh*, 488.
2 *SZh*, 489.
3 P.N. Berkov, *Istoriya russkoy zhurnalistiki XVIII veka* (Moscow–Leningrad, 1952), pp. 302–3, indicates an apparent gap in the journal. Although it runs from 1 to 9 numbers, the pagination shows that the seventh number ends on page 112 and the eighth begins on page 129. It would appear that a whole issue of sixteen pages was dropped and Berkov suggests that this would have contained the twice-promised editorial reply to the 'correspondent' presumably banned by the censorship. However, this suggestion is not wholly convincing since the *Popular Play* runs on uninterruped from the seventh to the eighth number.
4 *SZh*, 489.
5 *SZh*, 490.
6 *SZh*, 492.
7 *Ibid.*
8 The formula here of 'slanderers of Russia' anticipates the title of Pushkin's poem *Klevetnikam Rossii* (To the Slanderers of Russia).
9 *SZh*, 494.
10 L. A. Derbov, 'N. I. Novikov i russkaya istoriya (K izdaniyu "Drevney Rossiyskoy Vivliofiki")', is an excellent study of the history and significance of this publication. See also L. A. Derbov, 'Istoricheskiye publikatsii i trudy N. I. Novikova', *Istoriograficheskiy sbornik* (Saratov, 1965), 3–44.
11 *NSIS*, 325–6.

12 *The Letters of Philip Dormer Stanhope, Earl of Chesterfield with the Characters*, edited by John Bradshaw, 3 vols. (London, 1905), II, 511.
13 *SZh*, 241–2.
14 N. Tikhonravov, *Letopisi russkoy literatury i drevnosti*, 43.
15 Lindsey Hughes, 'Prince V. V. Golitsyn: Biography of a Seventeenth-Century Statesman', *Study Group on Eighteenth-Century Russia Newsletter*, 10 (1982), 6–8.
16 N. Tikhonravov, *Letopisi russkoy literatury i drevnosti*, 42.
17 *Drevnyaya Rossiyskaya Vivliofika*, 20 vols. (Moscow, 1788–91), I. p. VIII.
18 *NSIS*, 326–7.
19 *SPUV*, 28. Novikov was consciously more rigorous than his predecessor Tatishchev. See the review of V. N. Tatishchev, *Istoriya Rossiyskaya*, vols. I–VII (Moscow–Leningrad, 1962–8), by Ye. M. Dobrushkin and Ya. S. Lur'ye, 'Istorik-pisatel' ili izdatel' istochnikov?', *Russkaya literatura*, 2 (1970), 219–24.
20 William Coxe, *Travels*, pp. 193–4.
21 *SK*, IV, 128.
22 I. M. Polonskaya, 'Novyye materialy o izdatel'skoy deyatel'nosti N. I. Novikova', 219.
23 *Ibid.*, 221–2.
24 N. Tikhonravov, *Letopisi russkoy literatury i drevnosti*, 42–3.
25 *Ibid.*, 44.
26 *Ibid.*, 43–4.
27 *Ibid.*, 44.
28 *Ibid.*, 45–6.
29 *Ibid.*, 46.
30 Until the recent discovery of a single copy of *Sokrovishche rossiyskikh drevnostey* in the Scientific Library of Central State Archives, it was supposed that the journal had never appeared. See S. R. Dolgova, '"Prodolzhat' pechataniyem zapreshcheno...": Neosushchestvlennoye izdaniye N. I. Novikova', *Literaturnaya gazeta*, 28 February 1973, p. 7.
31 *NSIS*, 333.

8. THE FREEMASON (1775–80)

1 A.N. Pypin, *Istoriya russkoy literatury*, IV, 264.
2 *NSIS*, 423.
3 Paul Hazard, *La Pensée européenne au XVIIIème siècle, de Montesquieu à Lessing*, 3 vols. (Paris, 1946), I, 367.
4 G. V. Vernadsky, *Russkoye masonstvo v tsarstvovaniye Yekateriny II* (Petrograd, 1917), p. 17. For the English connections of 'Perfect Union' see A. G. Cross, 'British Freemasons in Russia during the Reign of Catherine the Great', *Oxford Slavonic Papers* (1971), 49–58.

5 G. V. Vernadsky, *Russkoye masonstvo*, p. 13.
6 Robert Freke Gould, *The History of Freemasonry, its Antiquities, Symbols, Constitutions, Customs, etc.*, 6 vols. (London, 1884–7), III, 216. G. V. Vernadsky, *Russkoye masonstvo*, p. 125.
7 René Pomeau, *La Religion de Voltaire* (Paris, 1956), p. 429.
8 *NSIS*, 423.
9 G. V. Vernadsky, *Russkoye masonstvo*, pp. 21–2.
10 *Ibid.*, 25.
11 *Ibid.*, 201.
12 *NSIS*, 424.
13 G. V. Vernadsky, *Russkoye masonstvo*, p. 33.
14 *NSIS*, 424.
15 *Ibid.*
16 G. V. Vernadsky, *Russkoye masonstvo*, p. 39.
17 *Ibid.*, p. 40.
18 *NSIS*, 424. Novikov refused to embrace the Swedish system because of Reichel's warning that any freemasonry with political aspects was false.
19 A. N. Pypin, *Istoriya russkoy literatury*, IV, 179–80, recognised that 'the religio-humanist or philanthropic point of view' of Novikov, the mystic, was present in the early journals.
20 G. V. Vernadsky, *Russkoye masonstvo*, p. 109.
21 *NSIS*, 425.
22 G. V. Vernadsky, *Russkoye masonstvo*, p. 176.
23 *NSIS*, 334.
24 *Pis'ma russkikh pisateley XVIII veka*, edited by G. P. Makogonenko (Leningrad, 1980), letters from M. N. Murav'yev to his father and sister, pp. 259–354.
25 *Ibid.*, p. 310.
26 *Ibid.*, p. 270.
27 *Ibid.*, p. 297.
28 *NSIS*, 334.
29 *Ibid.*
30 *SPUV*, 10.
31 *SPUV*, 84–5.
32 Ralph Straus, *Robert Dodsley: Poet, Publisher and Playwright* (London, 1910), pp. 180–1.
33 *SK*, III, 428–9.
34 *SK*, II, 36–7, 42; III, 428–9.
35 *SPUV*, 170.
36 *NSIS*, 198.
37 James H. Billington, *The Icon and the Axe: An Interpretive History of Russian Culture* (London, 1966), pp. 242–59.
38 Lester G. Crocker, *The Age of Enlightenment* (London, 1969), p. 24.
39 *US*, IX, 208.
40 *NSIS*, 178.

41 This is another fictional characteristic that has been foisted on Novikov himself; see *NSIS*, 497.
42 *US*, IX, 26.
43 G. P. Makogonenko, *Nikolay Novikov*, p. 310.
44 For a discussion of the importance of Bacon's *De sapienta veterum* in his work, and an elucidation of the nature of the appeal it would have had for the Russian freemasons, see Paolo Rossi, *Francis Bacon: From Magic to Science* (London, 1968), pp. 80–134.
45 *NSIS*, 496.
46 *Pis'ma russkikh pisateley XVIII veka*, p. 311. Murav'yev refers to a St Petersburg rumour that Ivan Shuvalov was the 'anonymous' donor of 100 roubles.
47 See my article, 'The *Morning Light* Charity Schools, 1777–80', *Slavonic and East European Review*, 56 (1978), 49–51.
48 For a typical view see N. A. Trushin, 'Obshchestvenno-pedagogicheskaya deyatel'nost' N. I. Novikova', *Sovetskaya pedagogika*, No. 6 (June 1956), 74. 'Catherine II . . . responded with clear hostility to his latest "seditious" enterprise in organising popular schools on voluntary subscriptions. She saw in it . . . another manifestation of the enlightener's oppositionist attitude to the government.'
49 Isabel de Madariaga, *Russia in the Age of Catherine the Great* (London, 1981), pp. 567–8.
50 W. Gareth Jones, 'The *Morning Light* Charity Schools, 1777–80', 63.
51 *Ibid.*, 61.
52 *US*, ix, 250.
53 The experience was sometimes hard. Early copies of *Morning Light* dispatched to Tver' went astray: see *Pis'ma russkikh pisateley XVIII veka*, pp. 333–4. Novikov eventually hoped to regularise distribution problems by transferring the work from amateur agents to the Moscow Post Office; see *US*, vi, 395–6.
54 I. I. Dmitriyev, *Vzglyad na moyu zhizn'* (Moscow, 1866), p. 45.

9. A MOVE TO MOSCOW (1779–83)

1 *NSIS*, 450–1.
2 N. Tikhonravov, *Letopisi russkoy literatury i drevnosti*, pp. 45–6.
3 *The Correspondence of Jeremy Bentham*, edited by Timothy L. S. Sprigge *et al*. (London, 1968–), II (1971), p. 126.
4 *NSIS*, 451.
5 N. Tikhonravov, *Letopisi russkoy literatury i drevnosti*, p. 31.
6 *SZh*, 239.
7 *SK*, IV, 15.
8 *Moskovskiye vedomosti*, 1972, No. 39.
9 N. M. Karamzin, *Izbrannyye sochineniya*, 2 vols. (Moscow–Leningrad, 1964), II, 177.
10 Andrey Bolotov, *Zhizn'*, III, 280.

11 *Ibid.*, 254.
12 *Ibid.*, 276.
13 N. Tikhonravov, *Letopisi russkoy literatury i drevnosti*, p. 44.
14 A. N. Pypin, *Russkoye masonstvo: XVIII i pervaya chetvert' XIX v* (Petrograd, 1916), pp. 273–4.
15 Vyazemsky records an anecdote which illustrated Novikov's severity. According to D. P. Buturlin, a young serf secretary who was honoured with the privilege of dining at his master's table was missing during one summer visit by the Buturlins. Novikov explained that the secretary had become spoilt and so had been sent into the army. P. Vyazemsky, *Staraya zapisnaya knizhka*, edited by L. Ginsburg, (Leningrad, 1929), p. 127.
16 Ye. I. Tarasov, 'Novyye danyye k istorii Novikovskogo kruzhka (iz neizdannykh dokumentov)', *Izvestiya otdeleniya russkogo yazyka i slovesnosti*, XIII (1908), 453.
17 *NSIS*, 426.
18 *NSIS*, 427.
19 *NSIS*, 428.
20 *NSIS*, 428–9.
21 *NSIS*, 422.
22 *NSIS*, 429.
23 G. V. Vernadsky, *Russkoye masonstvo*, p. 53.
24 *NSIS*, 430.
25 *NSIS*, 430–1.
26 See G. V. Vernadsky, *Russkoye masonstvo*, p. 38. Wöllner had been a member of the Privy Committee in Germany to which the first St Petersburg strict observance lodges of the 1760s were subordinated.
27 *NSIS*, 432.
28 *NSIS*, 433.
29 *Ibid.*
30 Ya. L. Barskov, p. 257.
31 *Ibid.*, p. 259.
32 G. V. Vernadsky, *Russkoye masonstvo*, p. 66.
33 *NSIS*, 434.

10. THE RUSSIAN READER DISCOVERED (1779–82)

1 V. P. Semennikov, *Knigoizdatel'skaya deyatel'nost' N. I. Novikova i Tipograficheskoy Kompanii* (Petrograd, 1921), pp. 28, 31.
2 N. Gogol', *Revizor*, Act I, Scene iii.
3 G. V. Vernadsky, *Russkoye masonstvo*, p. 207.
4 *Biograficheskiy slovar' professorov i prepodavateley imp. Moskovskogo universiteta*, 2 vols. (Moscow, 1855), II, 576.
5 G. V. Vernadsky, *Russkoye masonstvo*, p. 598.
6 *Biograficheskiy slovar' professorov i prepodavateley imp. Moskovskogo universiteta*, p. 598.

7 M. N. Longinov, *Novikov i Shvarts* (Moscow, 1857), p. 10.
8 *Ibid.*, pp. 11–12.
9 G. V. Vernadsky, *Russkoye masonstvo*, p. 209.
10 *Ibid.*, p. 209.
11 *NSIS*, 204.
12 See A. I. Nezelenov, *N. I. Novikov*, pp. 274–5, where the preface is viewed incorrectly as a total refutation of the ideas of the *encyclopédistes*.
13 Another skein in Novikov's awareness of 'Englishness' was the sense of gratitude to the English divines who had bridged the gulf between theology and philosophy by showing that Reason, man's guide, was a divine gift; *MI*, March, 221–2.
14 Herbert Dieckmann, *Le Philosophe: texts and interpretation* (St Louis, 1948), argues persuasively that the *Encyclopédie* article was a revision of an article by Dumarais.
15 *Ibid.*, p. 90.
16 There is no paradox in Novikov's true Christian philosopher enjoying the comforts and pleasures of society, if he upholds a virtuous society by his propriety and decorum. The definition of the *philosophe* is naturally related to affluence: see Herbert Dieckmann, *Le Philosophe*, p. 89.
17 *MI* April, 286.
18 *MI* April, 287.
19 *MI* June, 139; May, 42.
20 *MI* August, 293.
21 *MI* November, 180.
22 *MI* December, 290.
23 *SK*, IV, 123.
24 *NSIS*, 216.

11. THE TYPOGRAPHICAL COMPANY (1784–91)

1 A. N. Pypin, *Russkoye masonstvo*, pp. 343–4.
2 *Ibid.*, p. 343. Alekseyev has been confused with Novikov's brother, Aleksey, by In-Ho L. Ryu, 'Moscow Freemasons and the Rosicrucian Order: A Study in Organisation and Control', in *The Eighteenth Century in Russia*, edited by J. G. Garrard (Oxford, 1973), p. 228.
3 Compare In-Ho L. Ryu, 'Moscow Freemasons', pp. 226–8.
4 A. N. Pypin, *Russkoye masonstvo*, p. 345.
5 See M. G. Jones, *The Charity School Movement: A Study of Eighteenth Century Puritanism in Action* (Cambridge, 1938), pp. 12–13.
6 A. N. Pypin, *Russkoye masonstvo*, pp. 346–7.
7 *Ibid.*, pp. 342–3; Novikov's report to Schroeder.
8 V. P. Semennikov, *Knigoizdatel'skaya deyatel'nost' N.I. Novikova i Tipograficheskoy Kompanii*, pp. 60–72.
9 See A. P. Vlasto, 'A noble failure – Kheraskov's *Vladimir Voz-*

rozhdyonny', in *Gorski Vijenac: A Garland of Essays offered to Professor Elizabeth Mary Hill* (Cambridge, 1970), pp. 276–89.

10 *NSIS*, 435.
11 A. N. Pypin, *Russkoye masonstvo*, p. 351.
12 *NSIS*, 436.
13 G. V. Vernadsky, *Russkoye masonstvo*, pp. 74–5.
14 *NSIS*, 434–5.
15 *SZh*, 436.
16 G. P. Makogonenko, *Nikolay Novikov*, pp. 446–61, argues at length for viewing Novikov as a reluctant mason.
17 M. N. Longinov, *Novikov i Shvarts*, pp. 18–19.
18 *SK*, III, 459.
19 M. N. Longinov, *Novikov i Shvarts*, p. 20.
20 *IS*, 577.
21 L. N. Tolstoy, *War and Peace*, bk III, part 3, chap. VI.
22 *IS*, 577.
23 *Sbornik imp. Russkogo istoricheskogo obshchestva*, XXIII, 22.
24 V. Bogolyubov, *N.I. Novikov i yego vremya* (Moscow, 1916).
25 M. N. Longinov, *Novikov i Shvarts*, p. 22.
26 *IS*, 577–8.
27 M. N. Longinov, *Sochineniya* (Moscow, 1915), p. 358.
28 *Ibid.*, p. 362.
29 *IS*, 579.
30 For an account of Plato as a churchman, see A. V. Kartashev, *Ocherki po istorii russkoy tserkvi*, 2 vols. (Paris, 1959), II, 491–7.
31 William Coxe, *Travels*, p. 298.
32 *Voltaire's Correspondence*, edited by Theodore Besterman (Geneva, 1962–5), LXXIX, pp. 70, 74. That Voltaire's boast was not mere flattery meant for Catherine's eyes alone may be judged from his letter to Antoine Léonard Thomas, *ibid.*, p. 121, 'un archimandrite nommé Platon, aussi éloquent que celui d'Athènes, remercia Pierre le Grand . . .'
33 *IS*, 579.
34 *Moskvityanin* (1842), 3, p. 129.
35 *IS*, 582.
36 *Ibid.*
37 *IS*, 579–80.
38 *SK*, III, 388.
39 *IS*, 585–7.
40 *IS*, 587.
41 Alan Ross in a paper read to the Study Group on Eighteenth-Century Russia at the University of East Anglia, 7 July 1972.
42 M. N. Longinov, *Novikov i Shvarts*.
43 M. N. Longinov, *Novikov i moskovskiye martinisty* (Moscow, 1867), p. 037.
44 *IS*, 588.

45 Mystical societies also contributed to the institutionalising of intellectual movements in England. See Serge Huten, *Les Disciples anglais de Jacob Boehme* (Paris, 1960), p. 77.
46 S. P. Timofeyev, 'Studencheskiy zhurnal proshlogo veka', *Russkaya mysl'* (1889), No. 12, 109–24, stresses the student participation in *PT*. Novikov's preceding journals could also, of course, be seen as 'student journals'.
47 Collaborators are listed in *NSIS*, 504, and *SK*, IV, 162–3.
48 *NSIS*, 242.
49 *PT*, II, 225.
50 *PT*, III, 68–9.
51 *PT*, IV, 70–1.
52 *PT*, IV, 48–53.
53 *PT*, IV, 72.
54 *PT*, I, 93.
55 *PT*, IV, 197–204.
56 A. I. Nezelenov, *N. I. Novikov*, p. 417.
57 Ya. L. Barskov, *Perepiska moskovskikh masonov XVIII veka*
58 *PT*, II, 230–4.
59 *PT*, IV, 160.
60 *PT*, I, 224–43.
61 *PT*, II, 125–34.
62 Ya. L. Barskov, *Perepiska moskovskikh masonov XVIII veka*, p. xli.
63 A. G. Cross, *N.M. Karamzin: A Study of His Literary Career (1783–1803)* (Carbondale and Edwardsville, 1971), p. 33.
64 *Ibid.*, p. 25.
65 The revival of publishing might have owed something to the posting of Bryus to St Petersburg as governor-general and his replacement by Yeropkin. The latter's retirement, and the appointment in his place of Prozorovsky, accompanied another change in Novikov's fortunes.
66 A. G. Cross, *N. M. Karamzin*, pp. 15–19.
67 Ye. I. Tarasov, 'Novyye dannyye k istorii Novikovskogo kruzhka (iz neizdannykh dokumentov)', pp. 438–55.
68 *Ibid.*, 450.
69 *Ibid.*, 438.
70 G. V. Vernadsky, *Russkoye masonstvo*, pp. 70–1.
71 Ye. I. Tarasov, 'Novyye dannyye k istorii Novikovskogo kruzhka (iz neizdannykh dokumentov)', 450.
72 *Russkiy arkhiv* (1866), p. 1756.
73 Ye. I. Tarasov, 'Novyye dannyye k istorii Novikovskogo kruzhka (iz neizdannykh dokumentov)', 451.
74 M. T. Belyavsky, 'Novikovskoye Avdot'ino v 1792 g', *Problemy istorii obshchestvennogo dvizheniya i istoriografii* (Moscow, 1971), 51.
75 *NSIS*, 472.
76 The inventory was discovered by V. P. Gur'yanov in one of the

Moscow archives, and forms the basis of M. T. Belyavsky's article, 'Novikovskoye Avdot'ino v 1792 g'.

77 M. T. Belyavsky, 'Novikovskoye Avdot'ino v 1792 g', 51–2.
78 *IS*, 665–6.
79 *IS*, 666.
80 M. T. Belyavsky, 'Novikovskoye Avdot'ino v 1792 g', 55.
81 *Ibid.*, 56.
82 Ye. I. Tarasov, 'Novyye dannyye k istorii Novikovskogo kruzhka (iz neizdannykh dokumentov)', 454.
83 M. T. Belyavsky, 'Novikovskoye Avdot'ino 1792 g', 56.
84 *Ibid.*, 58.

12. MARTYRDOM AND MEDITATION (1791–1818)

1 Ya. L. Barskov, *Perepiska moskovskikh masonov XVIII veka*, pp. 49, 55, 58, 70, 86–7, 89, 94–5, 99–100, 106.
2 M. N. Longinov, *Novikov i Shvarts*, p. 32.
3 *IS*, 600.
4 Novikov's masonic group did not see themselves as 'martinists' and feigned complete ignorance of the significance of the label. See *Perepiska moskovskikh masonov XVIII veka*, pp. 85, 96–8, 111.
5 Catherine composed three comedies which mocked masonic ritual and intrigue in 1785–6: *Obmanshchik* (The Deceiver) aimed at Cagliostro who had recently toured Russia; *Obol'shchennyy* (The Deluded) and *Shaman Sibirskiy* (Siberian Shaman). See also her satirical anti-masonic tract composed in French in 1780 and translated by her secretary Khrapovitsky, *Tayna protivo-nelepogo obshchestva (Anti-absurde) otkrytaya ne prichastnym onomu.*
6 *Mémoires de la princesse Daschkoff*, 4 vols. (Paris, 1859), III, 184.
7 Quoted by G. P. Makogonenko, *Nikolay Novikov*, p. 516.
8 *NSIS*, 456.
9 Ya. L. Barskov, *Perepiska moskovskikh masonov XVIII veka*. The letters of the Moscow freemasons, so valuable for an appreciation of their awareness of their predicament, have paradoxically survived thanks to the zeal of Prozorovsky who received one of the two copies made of each letter by I. B. Pestel, the Moscow Director of Posts, and father of the future Decembrist revolutionary. The second copy was for A. A. Bezborodko who would pass on the most interesting letters to Catherine.
10 *Ibid.*, pp. 32, 46. This is suggested in letters between A. M. Kutuzov and I. V. Lopukhin which they knew would be intercepted and the contents possibly transmitted to Catherine.
11 *Ibid.*, p. xiii.
12 *IS*, 590.
13 D. N. Bantysh-Kamensky, *Slovar' dostopamyatnykh lyudey russkoy zemli* (Moscow, 1836), IV, 28–9, *IS*, 593.

14 N. M. Karamzin, *Izbrannyye sochineniya*, II, 30–1.
15 I. V. Lopukhin, 'Zapiski', *Russkiy arkhiv* (1884) 1, pp. 51, 56–7.
16 A. I. Nezelenov, *Literaturnyye napravleniya v Yekaterinskuyu epokhu.* (St Petersburg, 1889), p. 380.
17 *IS*, 601.
18 I. V. Lopukhin, 'Zapiski'.
19 A. I. Nezelenov, *Literaturnyye napravleniya v Yekaterinskuyu epokhu.* pp. 361–2.
20 *NSIS*, 447–8.
21 *NSIS*, 454–9.
22 *NSIS*, 477.
23 M. N. Longinov, *Sochineniya*, p. 408.
24 *Sbornik imp. Russkogo istoricheskogo obshchestva*, II, 106.
25 V. Bogolyubov, *Nikolay Novikov*, pp. 436–7.
26 Ya. L. Barskov, *Perepiska moskovskikh masonov XVIII veka*, p. xiii.
27 A. I. Nezelenov, *Literaturnyye napravleniya v Yekaterinskuyu epokhu*, p. 380.
28 B. Modzalevsky, *K biografii Novikova. Pis'ma yego k Labzinu, Chebotarevu i dr. 1797–1815* (St Petersburg, 1913), pp. 101–1.
29 Ye. I. Katsprzhak and A. P. Tolstyakov, 'Iz neizdannykh pisem Nikolaya Ivanovicha Novikova', *Kniga: Issledovaniya i materialy*, vol. 22, 185–6.
30 B. Modzalevsky, *K biografii Novikova*, p. 12. The quotation is from Psalm 146.
31 *Ibid.*, p. 14.
32 *Ibid.*, p. 12.
33 *Ibid.*, pp. 13, 17.
34 Ye. I. Katsprzhak and A. P. Tolstyakov, 'Iz neizdannykh pisem', p. 173.
35 See *Russkiy Biograficheskiy Slovar'*, 25 vols. (St Petersburg – Moscow – Petrograd, 1896–1918), *III*, 631–2. Also Novikov's letter of recommendation to D.P. Runich in 1814 in *Russkiy arkhiv* (1871), p. 1053.
36 B. Modzalevsky, *K biografii Novikova*, p. 27.
37 *Ibid.*, pp. 29–31.
38 *Ibid.*, 25.
39 *Ibid.*, p. 45.
40 *Ibid.*, p. 44.
41 *Ibid.*, p. 19.
42 Ye. I. Katsprzhak and A. P. Tolstyakov, 'Iz neizdannykh pisem', pp. 167–8.
43 B. Modzalevsky, *K biografii Novikova*, pp. 22–3, 47.
44 Ye. I. Katsprzhak and A. P. Tolstyakov, 'Iz neizdannykh pisem', pp. 171–2.
45 B. Modzalevsky, *K biografii Novikova*, p. 38.
46 See James H. Billington, *The Icon and the Axe* (London, 1966), pp. 279–80.

47 B. Modzalevsky, *K biografii Novikova*, pp. 33–4, 36.
48 *Ibid.*, pp. 38, 42, 44.
49 *Ibid.*, p. 38.
50 *Ibid.*, p. 50.
51 *Ibid.*, p. 43.
52 Ye. I. Katsprzhak and A. P. Tolstyakov, 'Iz neizdannykh pisem', pp. 169–70.
53 B. Modzalevsky, *K biografii Novikova*, pp. 66–75 for examples of these mystical compositions.
54 Ye. I Katsprzhak and A. P. Tolstyakov, 'Iz neizdannykh pisem', p. 176.
55 *Ibid.*, pp. 190–1.
56 B. Modzalevsky, *K biografii Novikova*, pp. 51–2.
57 *Ibid.*, pp. 53–4.
58 *Ibid.*, pp. 52–3.

AFTERWORD

1 N.M. Karamzin, *Izbrannyye sochineniya*, II, 231–3.
2 *Polnoye sobraniye sochineniy I. V. Kireyevskogo*, edited by M. O. Gershenzon, 2 vols. (Moscow, 1911), II, 15. See also Abbott Gleason, *European and Muscovite: Ivan Kireevsky and the Origins of Slavophilism* (Cambridge, Mass., 1972), pp. 58–9.
3 A. S. Pushkin, *Polnoye sobraniye sochineniy*, V, 38–9.
4 M. N. Longinov, *Novikov i moskovskiye martinisty*, p. 3.
5 L. N. Tolstoy, *Polnoye sobraniye sochineniy*, 90 vols. (Moscow, 1928–58), vol. 46, 213–4.
6 *Ibid.*
7 V. Ye. Vetlovskaya, 'Nekotoryye osobennosti povestovatel'noy manery v "Brat'yakh Karamazovykh"', *Russkaya Literatura* (1967), No. 4, p. 67.
8 Yu. M. Lotman, 'Russo i russkaya kul'tura XVIII veka', p. 247.
9 B. Modzalevsky, *K biografii Novikova*, p. 57.
10 F. M. Dostoyevsky, *The Brothers Karamazov*, bk V, chap. III.
11 L. N. Tolstoy, *War and Peace*, bk II, part 2, chaps. III–IV.
12 'Zapiski akademika Vitberga', *Russkaya starina* (1872), No. 4, p. 560.
13 V. O. Klyuchevsky, *Sochineniya*, 8 vols. (Moscow, 1956–9), VIII, 249.
14 *Ibid.*, VIII, 248.
15 G. P. Makogonenko, *Nikolay Novikov*, p. 16.
16 A. I. Nezelenov, *N. I. Novikov, izdatel' zhurnalov 1769–1785 godov*.
17 V. N. Mikhaylov, 'Ob odnoy nevernoy otsenke mirovozreniya N. I. Novikova', *Voprosy filosofii* (1956), No. 6, pp. 218–20.
18 G. V. Plekhanov, *Literatura i estetika*, 2 vols. (Moscow, 1958), II, 7–8.
19 Novikov has also been recently mentioned, as a precursor, by Alexander Solzhenitsyn, *Arkhipelag Gulag* (Paris, 1973), p. 287.

Bibliography

A listing of Novikov's works, published correspondence, bibliographical material and critical literature is to be found in V. P. Stepanov's and Yu. V. Stennik's *Istoriya russkoy literatury XVIII veka: Bibliograficheskiy ukazatel'* (History of 18th Century Russian Literature: A Bibliographical Index) (Leningrad, 1968), items 5986–6168. The general part of the *Bibliograficheskiy ukazatel'*, particularly its sections on 'Masonry' and 'Periodical Press', is also useful. Most of the works listed in the *Bibliograficheskiy ukazatel'* were consulted but will not appear in this bibliography unless they have been cited in the text or notes. Some books and articles which did not appear in the *Bibliograficheskiy ukazatel'* are included.

Extensive bibliographical information on Novikov's publications is available in *Svodnyy katalog russkoy knigi grazhdanskoy pechati XVIII veka, 1725–1800* (Union Catalogue of 18th Century Books in Secular Type, 1725–1800), 5 vols. (Moscow, 1963–7) with a Supplement (Moscow, 1975).

The first section of the bibliography, 'Editions of Novikov's Works', includes not only works of which he was the main author, but also those periodicals which he brought into being, but for which he subsequently acted mainly as publisher. It is not possible to estimate in any one case the extent of Novikov's separate contribution as author, editor and publisher. This section also includes the modern anthologies of Novikov's works which I have used. Sources in Russian are listed in the second section, and the third section contains works cited in languages other than Russian.

EDITIONS OF NOVIKOV'S WORKS

Truten' [The Drone], *yezhenedel'noye izdaniye na 1769 god*, St Petersburg 1769–70.

Truten' N. I. Novikova (1769–1770), ed. P.A. Yefremov, St Petersburg 1865.

Truten', yezhenedel'nyy zhurnal N. I. Novikova, ed. A. S. Suvorin, St Petersburg 1902.

Pustomelya [The Tattler], *yezhemesyachnoye sochineniye 1770 god*, St Petersburg 1870.

Pustomelya, satiricheskiy zhurnal 1770, ed. A. N. Afanas'yev, Moscow 1858.

Zhivopisets [The Painter], *yezhenedel'noye na 1772 god sochineniye*, St Petersburg 1772–3.

Zhivopisets, yezhenedel'noye satiricheskoye sochineniye: Izdaniye 3-e vnov' peresmotrennoye, ispravlennoye i umnozhennoye, St Petersburg 1775. (This 'third edition' was an anthology including satirical pieces from *Truten'* as well as from *Zhivopisets*.)

Zhivopisets N. I. Novikova (1772–1773), ed. P. A. Yefremov, St Petersburg 1864.

Zhivopisets, yezhenedel'niy zhurnal N. I. Novikova, ed. A. S. Suvorin, St Petersburg 1900.

Koshelek [The Bag], *yezhenedel'noye sochineniye 1774 goda*, St Petersburg 1774.

Koshelek, satiricheskiy zhurnal N. I. Novikova 1774, ed. A. N. Afanas'yev, Moscow 1858.

Koshelek, yezhenedel'niy zhurnal N. I. Novikova, ed. A. S. Suvorin, St Petersburg 1900.

Satiricheskiye zhurnaly N. I. Novikova: Truten' 1769–1770: Pustomelya 1770: Zhivopisets 1772–1773: Koshelek 1774, ed. P. N. Berkov, Moscow–Leningrad 1951.

Opyt istoricheskogo slovarya o rossiyskikh pisatelyakh [An Essay at an Historical Dictionary of Russian Writers], St Petersburg 1772.

Drevnyaya rossiyskaya vivliofika [The Ancient Russian Library], *ili Sobraniye raznykh drevnykh sochineniy, yako to: rossiyskie posol'stva v drugiye gosudarstva, redkiye gramoty, opisaniya svadebnykh obryadov i drugikh istoricheskikh i geograficheskikh dostopamyatnostey, i mnogiye sochineniya drevnykh rossiyskikh stikhotvortsev; izdavayemaya pomesyachno Nikolayem Novikovym* [or a Collection of various ancient compositions, such as: Russian embassies to other states, rare documents, descriptions of marriage ceremonies and other historical and geographical memorabilia, and many compositions of ancient Russian versifiers; published monthly by Nikolay Novikov], St Petersburg 1773–5.

Drevnyaya rossiyskaya vivliofika... Moscow 1782.

Drevnyaya rossiyskaya vivliofika, soderzhashchaya v sebe: sobraniye drevnostey rossiyskikh, do istorii, geografii i genealogii rossiyskoy kasayushchikhsya; izdannaya Nikolayem Novikovym, chlenom Vol'nogo Rossiyskogo sobraniya pri Imp. Moskovskom universitete; izdaniye vtoroye, vnov' ispravlennoye, umnozhennoye i v poryadok khronologicheskoy po vozmozhnosti privedennoye [The Ancient Russian Library, including: a collection of Russian antiquities pertaining to Russian history, geography and genealogy; published by Nikolay Novikov, member of the Free Russian Society at the Imperial University of Moscow; second edition, newly corrected, augmented and arranged where possible in chronological order], Moscow 1788–91.

Sankpeterburgskiye uchenyye vedomosti na 1777 god [St Petersburg Academic News for 1777], St Petersburg 1777.

Utrenniy svet [Morning Light], *ezhemesyachnoye izdaniye*, St Petersburg 1777–80.

Modnoye ezhemesyachnoye izdaniye, ili Biblioteka, dlya damskogo tualeta [The Fashionable Monthly, or Library for Ladies' Toilette], St Petersburg 1779.

Ekonomicheskiy magazin [The Economic Magazine] *ili Sobraniye vsyakikh ekonomicheskikh izvestiy, opytov, otkrytiy, primechaniy, nastavleniy, zapisok i sovetov, otnosyashchikhsya do zemledeliya, skotovodstva, do sadov i ogorodov, do lugov, lesov, prudov, raznykh produktov, do derevenskikh stroyeniy, domashnikh lekarstv, vrachebnykh trav i do drugikh vsyakikh nuzhnykh i nebezpoleznykh gorodskim i derevenskim zhitelyam veshchey, v pol'zu rossiyskikh domostroiteley i drugikh lyubopytnykh lyudey obrazom zhurnala izdavayemoy* [or a Collection of all kinds of economic news, trials, discoveries, observations, precepts, notes and advice, pertaining to agriculture, cattle-raising, orchards and gardens, meadows, woods, ponds, various produce, rural buildings, home medicines, herbs and all other kinds of things necessary and of some use to town- and country-dwellers, published for the use of Russian householders and other curious persons in the form of a journal], Moscow 1780–9.

Moskovskoye ezhemesyachnoye izdaniye [The Moscow Monthly]. *V pol'zu zavedennykh v Sanktpeterburge Yekaterininskogo i Aleksandrovskogo uchilishch, zaklyuchayushcheye v sebe sobraniye raznykh luchshikh statey, kasayushchikhsya do nravoucheniya, politicheskoy i uchenoy istorii, do filosoficheskikh i slovesnykh nauk i drugikh poleznykh znaniy, sluzhashcheye prodolzheniyem Utrennego sveta* [For the benefit of the Catherine and Alexander schools in St Petersburg, containing a collection of various best articles, pertaining to moral teaching, political and academic history, philosophical and literary science and other useful knowledge, being a continuation of *Morning Light*], Moscow 1781.

Vechernyaya zarya [Evening Light] *yezhemesyachnoye izdanie, v pol'zu zavedennykh v Sanktpeterburge Yekaterininskogo i Aleksandrovskogo uchilishch, zaklyuchayushcheye v sebe luchshiye mesta iz drevnykh i noveyshikh pisateley, otkryvayushchiye cheloveku put' k poznaniyu boga, samogo sebya i svoikh dolzhnostey, kotoryye predstavleny kak v nravoucheniyakh, tak i v primerakh onykh, to yest', ne bol'shikh istoriyakh, povestyakh, anekdotakh i drugikh sochineniyakh stikhami i prozoy: sluzhashcheye prodolzheniyem Utrennego sveta* [a monthly for the benefit of the St Petersburg Catherine and Alexander schools, containing the best passages from ancient and modern writings, opening up for man the path to knowledge of God, himself and his duties which are presented not only in moral teachings but in examples of them, that is, in short stories, tales, anecdotes and other compositions in verse and prose; being a continuation of Morning Light], Moscow 1782.

Gorodskaya i derevenskaya biblioteka [The Town and Country Library], *ili Zabavy i udovol'stviye razuma i serdtsa v prazdnoye vremya, soderzhashchiye v sebe: kak istorii i povesti nravouchitel'niye i zabavniye, tak i priklyucheniya veselyye, pechal'nyye, smeshnyye i udivitel'nyye* [or, Amusements and delight for mind and heart in leisure time, containing: not only moral and amusing stories and tales but also gay, melancholy, comic and amazing adventures], Moscow 1782–6.

Pribavleniye k Moskovskim vedomostyam [Supplement to Moscow News], *1783–1784 goda*, Moscow 1783–4.

Pokoyashchiysya trudolyubets [The Diligent at Repose], *periodicheskoye izdaniye, sluzhashcheye prodolzheniyem Vecherney zari. Zaklyuchayushcheye v sebe bogoslovskiye, nravouchitel'nyye, istoricheskiye, i vsyakogo roda kak vazhnyye tak i zabavnyye materii, k pol'ze i udovol'stviyu lyubopytnykh chitateley, sostoyashchiye iz podlinnykh sochineniy na rossiyskom yazyke i perevodov s luchshikh inostrannykh pisateley v stikhakh i proze* [a periodical being a continuation of Evening Light. Containing theological, moral, historical and all kinds of important and amusing material, for the benefit and delight of curious readers, consisting of original compositions in Russian and translations from the best foreign writers in verse and prose.] Moscow 1784–5.

Detskoye chteniye dlya serdtsa i razuma [Children's Reading for Heart and Mind], Moscow 1785–9.

N. I. Novikov i yego sovremenniki: Izbrannyye sochineniya, ed. I. V. Malyshev and L. B. Svetlov, Moscow 1961.

SOURCES IN RUSSIAN

Bantysh-Kamensky, D.N., *Slovar' dostopamyatnykh lyudey russkoy zemli*, Moscow 1836.

Barskov, Ya. L., *Perepiska moskovskikh masonov XVIII veka*, Petrograd 1915.

Belyavsky, M.T., 'Satiricheskiye zhurnaly N.I. Novikova kak istoricheskiy istochnik', *Vestnik Moskovskogo Universiteta*, 1963.

Belyavsky, M.T., 'Novikovskoye Avdot'ino v 1792 g.', *Problemy istorii obshchestvennogo dvizheniya i istoriografii*, Moscow 1971.

Berezina, V.G., 'Zhurnal A.P. Sumarokova *Trudolyubivaya pchela* 1759', *Voprosy zhurnalistiki*, 1960.

Berkov, P.N., *Istoriya russkoy zhurnalistiki XVIII veka*. Moscow–Leningrad 1952.

Bibikov, A.I., *Zapiski o zhizni i sluzhbe A.I. Bibikova*, Moscow 1817.

Bilinkis, B., 'Zametki o N.I. Novikove', *Quinquagenario: Sbornik statey molodykh filologov k 50-letiyu prof. Yu. M. Lotmana*, Tartu 1972.

Biograficheskiy slovar' professorov i prepodavateley imp. Moskovskogo universiteta, Moscow 1855.

Bogolyubov, V, *N.I. Novikov i yego vremya*, Moscow 1916.

Bolotov, Andrey, *Zhizn' i priklyucheniya Andreya Bolotova opisannyye samim im dlya svoikh potomkov*, Moscow–Leningrad 1931.

Derbov, L.A., 'Istoricheskiye publikatsii i trudy N.I. Novikova', *Istoriograficheskiy sbornik*, Saratov 1965.

Derbov, L.A., 'N.I. Novikov i russkaya istoriya (k izdaniyu "Drevney Rossiyskoy Vivliofiki")', *Iz istorii obshchestvennogo dvizheniya i obshchestvennoy mysli v Rossii*, Saratov 1968.

Derbov, L.A., 'Voprosy russkoy istoriografii v literaturnom nasledstve N.I. Novikova', *Istoriograficheskiy sbornik*, Saratov 1973.

Derbov, L.A., *Obshchestvenno-politicheskiye i istoricheskiye vzglyady N.I. Novikova*, Saratov 1974.

Dmitriyev, I.I., *Vzglyad na moyu zhizn'*, Moscow 1866.

Dolgova, S.R., 'Prodolzhat' pechataniyem zapreshcheno . . . : Neosushchestvlennoye izdaniye N.I. Novikova', *Literaturnaya gazeta*, 28 February 1973.

Dolgova, S.R., '"Sokrovishche rossiyskikh drevnostey" N.I. Novikova', *Kniga: Issledovaniya i materialy*, 1975.

Fonvizin, Denis, *Sobraniye sochineniy*, St Petersburg 1866.

Gillel'son, M.I., *P.A. Vyazemsky: Zhizn' i tvorchestvo*, Leningrad 1969.

Gur'yanov, V.P., 'Kogda rodilsya N.I. Novikov?', *Russkaya literatura*, 1967.

Kantemir, Antiokh, *Sobraniye stikhotvoreniy*, Leningrad 1956.

Karamzin, N.M., *Izbrannyye sochineniya*, Moscow–Leningrad 1964.

Kartashev, A.V., *Ocherki po istorii russkoy tserkvi*, Paris 1959.

Katsprzhak, Ye. I. and Tolstyakov, A.P., 'Iz neizdannykh pisem Nikolaya Ivanovicha Novikova', *Kniga: Issledovaniya i materialy*, 1970.

Kireyevsky, I.V., *Polnoye sobraniye sochineniy I.V. Kireyevskogo*, ed. M.O. Gershenzon, Moscow 1911.

Klyuchevsky, V.O., *Sochineniya*, Moscow 1959.

Kokorev, A.V., *Khrestomatiya po russkoy literature XVIII veka*, Moscow 1965.

Levin, Yu. D., 'Angliyskaya prosvetitel'skaya zhurnalistika v russkoy literature XVIII veka', *Epokha prosveshcheniya: Iz istorii mezhdunarodnykh svyazey russkoy literatury*, Leningrad 1967.

Literaturnoye nasledstvo, 1933, vol. 9–10.

Longinov, M.N., *Novikov i Shvarts: Materialy dlya istorii russkoy literatury v kontse XVIII veka*, Moscow 1857.

Longinov, M.N., 'Poseshcheniye sela Avdot'ina-Tikhvinskogo prinadlezhavshego N.I. Novikovu', *Russkiy vestnik* 1858.

Longinov, M.N., *Novikov i moskovskiye martinisty*, Moscow 1867.

Lopukhin, I.V., 'Zapiski', *Russkiy arkhiv*, 1884.

Lotman, Yu. D., 'Russo i russkaya kul'tura XVIII veka', *Epokha prosveshcheniya*, Leningrad 1967.

Lukin, V.I., *Sochineniya i perevody Vladimira Lukina*, St Petersburg 1765.

Makogonenko, G.P., *Nikolay Novikov i russkoye prosveshcheniye XVIII veka*, Moscow–Leningrad 1952.

Makogonenko, G., *Ot Fonvizina do Pushkina: Iz istorii russkogo realizma,* Moscow 1969.

Makogonenko, G.P. (ed.), *Pis'ma russkikh pisateley XVIII veka*, Leningrad 1980.

Martynov, I.F., 'Opyt istoricheskogo slovarya o rossiyskykh pisatelyakh N.I. Novikova i literaturnaya polemika 60–70 godov XVIII veka', *Russkaya literatura*, 1968.

Martynov, I.F., *Knigoizdatel' Nikolay Novikov*, Moscow 1981.

Mikhaylov, V.N., 'Ob odnoy nevernoy otsenki mirovozzreniya N.I. Novikova', *Voprosy filosofii*, 1956.

Modzalevsky, B., *K biografii Novikova: Pis'ma yego k Labzinu, Chebotarevu i dr. 1797–1815*, St Petersburg 1913.

Moiseyeva, G.N., 'Literaturnyye i istoricheskiye pamyatniki Drevney Rusi v izdaniyakh N.I. Novikova', *Trudy Otdela Drevne-russkoy literatury Instituta Russkoy Literatury AN SSSR*, 1970.

Moiseyeva, G.N., 'Dopolnitel'nyye dannyye k obstoyatel'stvam presledovaniya N.I. Novikova', *XVIII vek, No. 11*, Leningrad 1976.

Murav'yev, M.N., 'Pis'ma otsu i sestre 1777–1778 godov', *Pis'ma russkikh pisateley XVIII veka*, ed. G.P. Makogonenko, q.v.

Nezelenov, A.I., *N.I. Novikov, izdatel' zhurnalov 1769–1785 godov*, St Petersburg 1875.

Nezelenov, A.I., *Literaturnyye napravleniya v Yekaterinskuyu epokhu*, St Petersburg 1889.

Pekarsky, P., 'Materialy dlya istorii zhurnal'noy i literaturnoy deyatel'nosti Yekateriny II', *Zapiski imperatorskoy akademii nauk*, vol. 3, 1863, supplements 1–90.

Perepiska Karamzina s Lafaterom, St Petersburg 1893.

Plekhanov, G.V., *Literatura i estetika*, Moscow 1950.

Polonskaya, I.M., 'Novyye materialy o izdatel'skoy deyatel'nosti N.I. Novikova', *Zapiski otdela rukopisey Gos. b-ki SSSR im. V.I. Lenina*, 1977.

Pushkin, A.S., *Polnoye sobraniye sochineniy*, Moscow–Leningrad 1936–8.

Pypin, A.N. (ed.), *Sochineniya Imperatritsy Yekateriny II*, St Petersburg 1901.

Pypin, A.N., *Istoriya russkoy literatury*, St Petersburg 1902–3.

Pypin, A.N., *Russkoye masonstvo: XVIII i pervaya chetvert' XIX v*, Petrograd 1916.

Rozenberg, V.A., *N.I. Novikov: podvizhnik russkoy knigi*, Berlin 1923.

Russkiy biograficheskiy slovar', St Petersburg–Moscow–Petrograd 1896–1918.

Semennikov, V.P., 'Ranneye izdatel'skoye obshchestvo N.I. Novikova', *Russkiy bibliofil*, 1912.

Semennikov, V.P., *Materialy dlya istorii russkoy literatury i dlya slovarya pisateley epokhi Yekateriny II*, St Petersburg 1914.

Semennikov, V.P., *Russkiye satiricheskiye zhurnaly 1796–1774 gg*, St Petersburg 1914.

Semennikov, V.P., *Knigoizdatel'skaya deyatel'nost' N.I. Novikova i Tipograficheskoy Kompanii*, Petrograd 1921.

Semennikov, V.P., *Radishchev: Ocherki i issledovaniya*, Moscow–Petrograd 1923.

Semevsky, V.I., *Krestyanskiy vopros v Rossii v XVIII i pervoy polovine XIX veka*, St Petersburg 1888.

Serman, I.Z., *Russkiy Klassitsizm. Poeziya, Drama, Satira*, Leningrad 1973.

Serman, I.Z., 'Novikov and *The Tatler*', *Study Group on Eighteenth-Century Russia Newsletter*, 1977.

Sidorov, A.A., *Istoriya oformleniya russkoy knigi*, Moscow–Leningrad 1946.

Skaftymov, A., 'O stile "Puteshestviye iz Peterburga v Moskvu" A.N. Radishcheva', *Stat'i o russkoy literature*, Saratov 1958.

Solntsev, V.F., '"Vsyakaya Vsyachina" i "Spektator" (K istorii russkoy satiricheskoy zhurnalistiki XVIII veka)', *Zhurnal Ministerstva Narodnogo Prosveshcheniya*, 1892.

Startsev, A., *Radishchev v godakh 'Puteshestviya iz Peterburga v Moskvu'*, Moscow 1960.

Storozhev, V.N., 'Materialy dlya istorii russkogo dvoryanstva', *Chteniya v obshchestve istorii i drevnostey rossiyskikh*, 1909.

Tarasov, Ye. I., 'Novyye dannyye k istorii Novikovskogo kruzhka (iz neizdannykh dokumentov)', *Izvestiya otdeleniya russkogo yazyka i slovesnosti*, 1908.

Tikhonravov, N., *Letopisi russkoy literatury i drevnosti*, IV, Moscow 1862.

Timofeyev, S.P., 'Studencheskiy zhurnal proshlogo veka', *Russkaya mysl'*, 1889.

Trushin, N.A., 'Obshchestvenno-pedagogicheskaya deyatel'nost' N.I. Novikova', *Sovetskaya pedagogika*, No 6. (June 1956).

Vernadsky, G.V., *Russkoye masonstvo v tsarstvovaniye Yekateriny II*, Petrograd 1917.

Vitberg, A.L., 'Zapiski akademika Vitberga', *Russkaya starina*, 1872.

Vyazemsky, P., *Staraya zapisnaya knizhka*, ed. L. Ginsburg, Leningrad 1929.

XVIII vek, No. 11, *N.I. Novikov i obshchestvenno-literaturnoye dvizheniye yego vremeni*, Leningrad 1976.

Yefremov, P.A. (ed.), *Sochineniya i perevody V.I. Lukina i B. Ye. Yel'chaninova*, St Petersburg 1868.

Zapadov, A.V., 'Zhurnal Chulkova "I to i syo"', *XVIII vek, No.2*, Moscow–Leningrad 1940.

Zapadov, A.V., *Istoriya russkoy zhurnalistiki XVIII–XIX vekov*, Moscow 1963.

Zapadov, A.V., *Novikov*, Moscow 1968.
Zapadov, V.A., 'K istorii pravitel'stvennykh presledovaniy N.I. Novikova', *XVIII vek, No. 11*, q.v.

SOURCES IN LANGUAGES OTHER THAN RUSSIAN

The Antidote: Or an Enquiry into the Merits of a Book Entitled A Journey into Siberia, London 1772.
Becker, Carl L., *The Heavenly City of the Eighteenth-Century Philosophers*, New Haven 1932.
Bentham, Jeremy, *The Correspondence of Jeremy Bentham*, London 1968.
Betzky, I. *Les Plans et les status des différents établissements ordonnés par SMI Catherine II pour l'éducation de la jeunesse et l'utilité générale de son empire*, Amsterdam 1775.
Billington, James H., *The Icon and the Axe: An Interpretive History of Russian Culture*, London 1966.
Boileau-Despréaux, *Satires*, ed. Albert Cahen, Paris 1932.
Bouchard, Marcel, *L'Académie de Dijon et le Premier Discours de Rousseau*, Paris 1950.
Boulton, James T., *The Language of Politics in the Age of Wilkes and Burke*, London 1963.
Coxe, William, *Travels into Poland, Russia, Sweden and Denmark Interspersed with Historical Relations and Political Inquiries*, London 1784.
Crocker, Lester G., *The Age of Enlightenment*, London 1969.
Cross, A.G., *N.M. Karamzin: A Study of His Literary Career (1783–1803)*, Carbondale and Edwardsville 1971.
Cross, A.G., 'British Freemasons in Russia during the Reign of Catherine the Great', *Oxford Slavonic Papers*, 1971.
Cross, A.G., *'By the Banks of the Thames': Russians in Eighteenth Century Britain*, Newtonville, Mass. 1980.
Currie, Pamela, 'Moral Weeklies and the Reading Public in Germany, 1711–1750', *Oxford German Studies*, 1968.
Dashkova, Ye. R., *Mémoires de la princesse Daschkoff*, Paris 1859.
Diderot, Denis, *Correspondence*, ed. Georges Roth, Paris 1955–70.
Diderot, Denis, *Œuvres complètes*, ed. J. Assézat and Maurice Tourneux, Paris 1857–77.
Dieckmann, Herbert, *Le Philosophe: Texts and Interpretation*, St Louis 1948.
Dukes, Paul, *Catherine the Great and the Russian Nobility*, Cambridge 1967.
Dumon, Étienne, *Bentham's Theory of Legislation*, tr. Charles Milner Atkinson, London 1914.
Elkin, P.K., *The Augustan Defence of Satire*, Oxford 1973.

Garrard, John, *Mixail Čulkov: An Introduction to His Prose and Verse*, The Hague–Paris, 1970.
Garrard, John (ed), *The Eighteenth Century in Russia*, Oxford 1973.
Gleason, Abbot, *European and Muscovite: Ivan Kireevsky and the Origins of Slavophilism*, Cambridge, Mass. 1972.
Gould, Robert Freke, *The History of Freemasonry, its Antiquities, Symbols, Constitutions, Customs etc.*, London 1884–7.
Haumant, Émile, *La Culture Française en Russie (1700–1900)*, Paris 1913.
Hazard, Paul, *La Pensée européenne au XVIIIème siècle, de Montesquieu à Lessing*, Paris 1946.
Hughes, Lindsey, 'Prince V.V. Golitsyn: Biography of a Seventeenth-Century Statesman', *Study Group on Eighteenth Century Russia Newsletter*, 1982.
Huten, Serge, *Les Disciples anglais de Jacob Boehme*, Paris 1960.
Jefferson, Thomas, *Memoirs, correspondence and miscellanies*, London 1829–30.
Jones, M.G., *The Charity School Movement: A Study of Eighteenth Century Puritanism in Action*, Cambridge 1938.
Jones, W. Gareth, 'The Closure of Novikov's "Truten'"', *Slavonic and East European Review*, 1972.
Jones, W. Gareth, 'Novikov's Naturalized *Spectator*' in *The Eighteenth Century in Russia*, ed. J.G. Garrard, q.v.
Jones, W. Gareth, 'The *Morning Light* Charity Schools, 1777–80', *Slavonic and East European Review*, 1978.
Jones, W. Gareth, 'The Eighteenth Century View of English Moral Satire: Palliative or Purgative?' in *Great Britain and Russia in the Eighteenth Century: Contacts and Comparisons*, ed. A.G. Cross, Newtonville, Mass. 1979.
Jones, W. Gareth, 'The Polemics of the 1769 Journals: A Reappraisal', *Canadian–American Slavic Studies*, 1982.
Keep, John, 'The Muscovite Elite and the Approach to Pluralism', *Slavonic and East European Review*, 1970.
Krasinski, Valerian, *Sketch of the Religious History of the Slavonic Nations*, Edinburgh 1849.
Macarthur, G.H. 'Catherine II and the Masonic Circle of N.I. Novikov', *Canadian Slavic Studies*, 1970.
McNally, Raymond T., *The Major Works of Peter Chaadaev: A Translation and Commentary*, Notre Dame 1969.
Madariaga, Isabel de, *Russia in the Age of Catherine the Great*, London 1981.
Marker, G.J., 'Novikov's Readers', *The Modern Language Review*, 1982.
Masters, Roger D., *The Political Philosophy of Rousseau*, Princeton 1968.
Monnier, André, *Un publiciste frondeur sous Catherine II: Nicolas Novikov*, Paris 1981.
Nichols, J. and Steevens, G., *The Genuine Works of William Hogarth*, London 1808–10.

Papmehl, K., *Freedom of Expression in Eighteenth Century Russia*, The Hague 1971.

Paulson, Ronald, *The Fictions of Satire*, Baltimore 1967.

Peace, Richard, *Dostoyevsky: An Examination of the Major Novels*, Cambridge 1971.

Pomeau, René, *La Religion de Voltaire*, Paris 1956.

Raeff, Marc, 'Home, School and Service in the Life of the 18th-Century Russian Nobleman', *The Slavonic and East European Review*, 1962.

Raeff, Marc, *Origins of the Russian Intelligentsia: The Eighteenth-Century Nobility*, New York 1966.

Raeff, Marc (ed.), *Russian Intellectual History: An Anthology*, New York 1966.

Reddaway, W.F., *Documents of Catherine the Great*, Cambridge 1933.

Rossi, Paolo, *Francis Bacon: From Magic to Science*, tr. Sacha Rabinovitch, London 1968.

Rousseau, Jean-Jacques, *Discours sur les sciences et les arts*, ed. George R. Havens, New York–London 1946.

Ryu, In-Ho L., 'Moscow Freemasons and the Rosicrucian Order: A Study in Organisation and Control', *The Eighteenth Century in Russia*, ed. J.G. Garrard, q.v.

Segel, Harold B. (ed. and tr.), *The Literature of Eighteenth Century Russia*, New York 1967.

The Spectator, ed. Donald F. Bond, Oxford 1965.

Straus, Ralph, *Robert Dodsley: Poet, Publisher and Playwright*, London 1910.

Trewin, J.C. and King, E.M., *Printer to the House: The Story of Hansard*, London 1952.

Unbegaun, B.O., *Russian Surnames*, Oxford 1972.

Van Tieghem, P., *Revue de synthèse historique*, 1930.

Vlasto, A.P., 'A noble failure – Kheraskov's *Vladimir Vozrozhdyonny*' in *Gorski Vijenac: A Garland of Essays offered to Professor Elizabeth Mary Hill*, Cambridge 1970.

Voltaire, *Voltaire's Correspondence*, ed. Theodore Besterman, Geneva 1962–5.

Von Herzen, Michael, 'Catherine II – Editor of *Vsiakaia Vsiachina*? A Reappraisal', *Russian Review*, 1979.

Walicki, Andrzej, *A History of Russian Thought from the Enlightenment to Marxism*, tr. Hilda Andrews-Rusiecka, Oxford 1980

Waliszewski, K., *Le Roman d'une impératrice: Catherine II de Russie*, Paris 1894.

Index

For EU product safety concerns, contact us at Calle de José Abascal, 56–1°, 28003 Madrid, Spain or eugpsr@cambridge.org.

www.ingramcontent.com/pod-product-compliance
Ingram Content Group UK Ltd.
Pitfield, Milton Keynes, MK11 3LW, UK
UKHW010345140625
459647UK00010B/837

* 9 7 8 0 5 2 1 1 1 1 4 4 7 *